For my mother, Violet Zeffert

Poor Penelope

Lady Penelope Rich
An Elizabethan Woman

Sylvia Freedman

THE
KENSAL
PRESS

British Library Cataloguing in Publication Data.

Freedman, Sylvia
    Poor Penelope: Lady Penelope Rich an Elizabethan Woman.
    1. Rich, *Lady* Penelope
    I. Title
    942.05'5'0924   DA358.R/

    ISBN 0-946041-20-2

Published by The Kensal Press
Kensal House, Abbotsbrook, Bourne End, Bucks.

Printed and bound in Great Britain by
Butler & Tanner Ltd., Frome & London.

Preface

Penelope Rich, the most celebrated beauty of the Elizabethan age, was mistress of Sir Philip Sidney and inspiration for his best poetry; daughter of Lettice Knollys who defied the anger of Queen Elizabeth to marry her favourite Robert Dudley, Earl of Leicester; married at eighteen against her will, protesting at the ceremony itself; mother of eleven children, six of them illegitimate; mistress and later wife of Charles Blount, Lord Mountjoy, England's successful leader against the Irish; fellow-intriguer with her brother Robert the Earl of Essex in his rebellion saving her head by her cool conduct though her brother lost his; a key woman at the courts of Elizabeth and James.

The facts indicate an eventful life and she cannot be dismissed as merely being famous for her connections rather than in her own right. Her life was immensely fascinating and she had a direct influence on some of the leading figures in Elizabethan history. She lived at a time of crucial change in the place of women in society and her life illuminates this period of progress.

Apart from a Victorian-style biography published seventy years ago, (where she is referred to in such terms as 'For me she walks ever in a rose-garlanded pleasaunce at noon'), there has been no biography of Penelope Rich. When she does appear in the biographies of others, there are at best tantalising glimpses, at worst she is dismissed in derogatory terms. No serious, comprehensive, and balanced portrait has been attempted.

Fragmentary glimpses of Penelope Rich in the lives of others convinced me that her own story would be worth the telling. Today, she is remembered, if at all, as the original model for Philip Sidney's Stella. As I began to piece together the events of her life it became apparent that she was very much more. The stories of her forced marriage, her two famous lovers, each so different from her own husband, her contrasting roles as star of the court and wife of a puritan Justice of the Peace, her two families of children, her eventual divorce and illegal remarriage, were all full of immediate interest.

No claim has been made for her to take even a modest place in Elizabethan politics and yet she played a central role in an event that could have turned the course of English history, the Essex Rebellion. Her part in the rebellion intrigued me. She was very close to the two most important military leaders of the time, her brother the Earl of Essex and her lover Lord Mountjoy. She participated in the events of the rebellion and was denounced by her brother as the person who had urged him on. She was herself charged with involvement in the plot to march on the queen, and of all those actively involved she alone succeeded in obtaining her release. Was this because she was able to establish her complete innocence, or did the queen recognise the possibility that Mountjoy, at the head of the army in Ireland, might return to protect or avenge his mistress?

Unravelling the web of her story has been complicated by a paucity of ascertainable facts for parts of her life while for other events there is a plethora of conflicting evidence. A number of myths have evolved and become perpetuated by constant repetition. The first of these concerns the suspected poisoning of Penelope's father, the first Earl of Essex, by the man who later became her stepfather, Robert Dudley, Earl of Leicester. Connected with it and arising from the same source is the alleged adultery of her mother and Leicester during her father's lifetime. Another myth suggests that Penelope had been secretly engaged to Charles Blount before he became Lord Mountjoy and long before both her marriage to Lord Rich and her affair with Philip Sidney. Her sister Dorothy also is the subject of misunderstanding, with suggestions that her first marriage was annulled and that she remarried in her first husband's lifetime, just as her sister did. Finally there is a story of Penelope's conversion to Catholicism on her death-bed.

By tracing all these stories back to their original source it has been possible to see just how and why they arose in the first place and so try to put the record straight.

I have found new facts about Penelope's life that have never previously been brought to light and have examined in detail material that has never been fully explored. For example, I have re-dated the birth of her's and Mountjoy's first child to show that there was no overlap between her two families of children, as previously believed. This misunderstanding was based on a gravestone and so taken as fact, until the record of baptism, now unearthed, revealed the true dating. Once the correct date is established the reason why this daughter, also named Penelope, claimed to be two years older than she really was, is quickly established. I have also found the baptism record of a child previously not recorded elsewhere, a son called Scipio.

The story of the repeated attempts to overturn Lord Mountjoy's will so as to prevent Penelope and her children from inheriting his fortune has never previously been told. The will and other documents were attacked in no less that six separate court actions in as many different courts, including bringing criminal charges against Penelope and the lawyers who drew them up, and till now these have never been investigated. In these criminal proceedings Penelope was branded a harlot and a whore and painted as a mercenary adventuress, only intent on gaining Mountjoy's estate and using every form of deceit, forgery and corruption to obtain it.

Penelope Rich's burial place has never been established till now. She, once so famous and linked to such powerful families, had apparently disappeared without trace. Solving the mystery enabled me to appreciate the full extent of her rejection by society.

In spite of some misfortunes, her story is basically a very happy one, telling of a life fully and energetically lived and enjoyed on many levels. What finally emerges is a picture of an irrepressible woman of immense vitality, able to live her life in defiance of convention and exert a considerable influence over some of the most powerful figures of her day.

Contents

Illustrations

Acknowledgements

I should like to thank the staffs of the following for their assistance: the British Library; the Guildhall Library; the Public Record Office; Westminster City Council Archives; Greater London Council Record Office; Chiswick Reference Library; Lambeth Palace Library; the Historical Manuscripts Commission.

I am grateful to the following for answering queries: Professor J. P. Kenyon; Sir Roy Strong; M. W. Farr, County Archivist at Warwickshire County Record Office; Victor Gray and his staff at Essex Record Office; R. H. Harcourt Williams, Librarian and Archivist to the Marquess of Salisbury; Jane Fowles, Archivist to the Marquess of Bath; Mary L. Robertson, Curator of Manuscripts at the Huntington Library; and particularly to Sylvia England for her help with the most difficult transcriptions.

I am obliged to His Grace the Duke of Northumberland for opening up Syon House out of season to enable me to photograph a portrait, to His Grace the Archbishop of Canterbury for a similar courtesy and indeed to the owners of all the photographs included, for permission to reproduce them.

Finally, I acknowledge with gratitude the following debts: to Robert Gittings, for his receptive response and generous enthusiasm; to Beryl Gray, for reading my first draft and giving helpful advice and encouragement; to my sister, Yvonne Zeffert, for translations from Latin texts; and especially to my husband Conrad, for his constructive criticism, advice, unfailing interest and support.

NOTE

Spelling has been modernised in the quotations. Dating is New Style.

Table of Events

1600	Essex's arrest
1601	Essex rebellion; his trial and execution
1603	Queen Elizabeth dies; James I accedes to throne
1603	Lord Mountjoy created Earl of Devonshire
1605	Lord Rich divorces his wife
1605	Penelope Rich marries Earl of Devonshire
1606	Earl of Devonshire dies
1607	Penelope Rich dies
1619	Dorothy, Countess of Northumberland dies
1634	Lettice Knollys dies

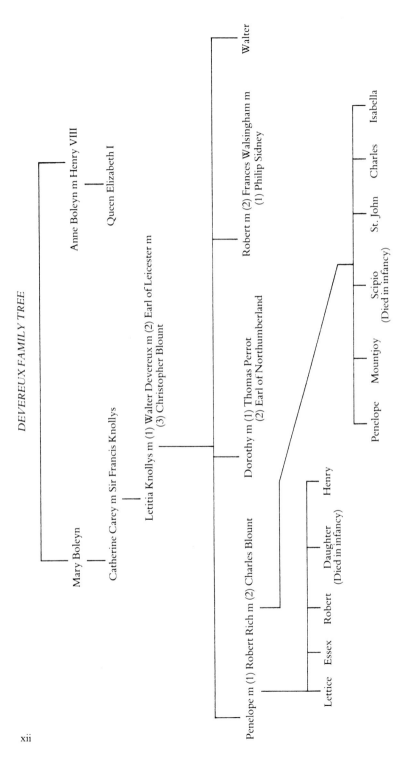

DEVEREUX FAMILY TREE

Poor Penelope. Penelope Rich

James Joyce's *Ulysses*

CHAPTER ONE

The Wedding

It was the lst of November 1581, the wedding day of Lady Penelope Devereux and Robert, third Lord Rich. She was eighteen years old, beautiful, intelligent, accomplished, with the particularly striking colouring of golden hair and black eyes. Her husband-to-be was an ugly little man, churlish and uncouth, but his very name spelled money. Her father had been dead since she was thirteen; her sister and brothers were all younger than she; her mother, banished from the court of Elizabeth after her remarriage to the queen's favourite, the powerful Earl of Leicester, had at the late age of forty-one recently born him a son. Penelope had been in the care of guardians and a marriage had been arranged for her, to this obnoxious but wealthy suitor.

Penelope had come to the court of Elizabeth that January, in the care of her guardian who in only a month had found her this rich husband. Her relatives felt they need look no further and Queen Elizabeth herself had given her blessing to the match. Penelope had on her arrival at court, quickly become one of the queen's maids of honour and Elizabeth took a deep interest in the marriage proposals for her ladies-in-waiting. The plans had been made without consulting the prospective bride and when the couple met she expressed her dislike of the man they had chosen to be her husband. But her relatives' say was final and the marriage arrangements went ahead as planned.

The occasion would have been not unlike a church wedding today, since the marriage service in the Church of England Book of Prayer had been in use throughout Elizabeth's reign. Now, at the solemn occasion of the ceremony itself, Penelope Devereux spoke out, protesting that she did not want to marry this man. Her relatives and friends who had played their parts in arranging this match and regarded it as most suitable, persuaded her that she had no choice but to go through with it and in these conditions the ceremony was performed. And so it came about that 'A lady of great birth and virtue, being in the power of her friends, was by them married against her will unto one against whom she did protest at the very solemnity and ever after'.[1]

The remarkable thing about the scene is not only that the marriage was allowed to take place in such circumstances but that Penelope Devereux had the courage openly and defiantly to speak out against it.

Before her arrival at court Penelope had led a strict and sheltered life in the household of her puritan guardians. The delights of the court of Elizabeth had opened up her horizons but almost immediately she had found herself involved in these unwelcome marriage plans. Her own wishes were ignored, since her relatives saw it as fulfilling their duty to find her a rich husband, as quickly as possible. They had secured the queen's all-important approval. In daring to object in public, Penelope was openly disobeying not only her family and friends, but her sovereign. With her personal happiness at stake she was prepared to take her stand, but without support and with no alternative open to her, eventually she was forced to capitulate and submit to the will of others.

To understand the full extent of Penelope's open defiance, it is necessary to appreciate the degree of influence which one's relatives were entitled to and did indeed exert at this point in the sixteenth century.

In arranging the marriage, her relations would look first at the needs of the family. As an orphan, the elder of two sisters both of marriageable age, with her mother remarried and starting a second family, financial considerations were paramount. The bulk of her father's estate passed on his death to his eldest son, the third child of the family. The future power and influence of the family depended upon the preservation of as large a part as possible for the heir. Penelope would have a dowry on her marriage. If by any chance she failed to marry she would receive the dowry herself at the age of twenty-one, under the terms of her father's will. It amounted to two thousand pounds, insufficient to support her for life as the daughter of an earl. Marriage was the only career open to her and without it she would be a drain on the family resources.

Had she been a wealthy heiress an alliance with one of the more powerful aristocratic families might have been preferred. But even then the family needs and considerations would have been uppermost.

This whole concept of marriage as a treaty between two families rather than a contract between two individuals was still fundamental to society in the latter part of the sixteenth century. It had been a very important element in medieval society where power was maintained and increased by alliances between great houses. Children were expected to obey their parent's wishes without question and to marry to suit the dictates of family needs. Indeed obedience to parents was considered a religious duty. However, with a strong monarchy and a centralised government the political power of these great families had declined, though the practice of arranged marriages continued.

The reason for its continuance was the financial benefit to be gained. Members of the property-owning classes were not free to marry where they pleased because their marriages represented lucrative feudal property rights. The early deaths of husbands and fathers, whether from violent or natural causes, perhaps fighting in Ireland like Penelope's father, or in the Netherlands, left behind widows and children who inherited on their deaths. The marriages of these beneficiaries were valuable assets, to be bargained for and sold.

Penelope's father, Walter Devereux Earl of Essex, had died poor, leaving his young son and heir Robert, the second Earl of Essex as 'the poorest Earl in England'.[2] (These are the words of Sir Francis Knollys, Robert's maternal grandfather). Walter had been a good father, and though desperately anxious to secure his children's futures, would not have been satisfied with a marriage for his eldest daughter that was purely mercenary. Had he lived Penelope's marriage to Lord Rich would not have taken place.

Penelope's guardians and relatives had the absolute right to choose her marriage for her. They chose to sell her off to the highest bidder. When she protested, they ignored her protests because in their eyes what they had done was right. She was not entitled to object to their choice. Indeed by her relatives' standards Penelope had not been unconsidered since they had chosen a man 'very fit in years' for her.[3] Her dislike was something to be brushed aside. After all, many women expected no less, hiding their dislike of their husbands over many years of marriage.

For Penelope to dare to put her own personal happiness first and risk upsetting an arrangement made for the good of her whole family would not be seen by Elizabethan standards as admirable. Her courage would merely seem foolhardy and potentially destructive.

When we begin to appreciate the contemporary social background her behaviour is all the more remarkable. It shows a strongly individualistic personality and a great deal of courage. These were qualities she was to evince time and again in her life.

Penelope's stand came at the beginning of a period of social change in the position of women. Up to about 1580 women had still been in the medieval era, treated as chattels to be married off as their families thought fit. Whereas obedience to parents was the duty of all children, girls were also expected to be docile and submissive to a degree that would have been inconsistent with the manly virtues encouraged in boys.

Girls had to stay at home all the time whilst their brothers might go away to school, to the universities and perhaps later to travel. Even the boys who did not do these things could get out of the house, hunting, fishing and generally leading an active outdoor life. Girls might walk and ride for a little light exercise, but their outings were much more curtailed and they spent a great deal of their time actually in the house. They were therefore under constant supervision and surveillance, and it is no wonder that this atmosphere encouraged the development of docility and submission.

The period from about 1580 to 1650 saw a progressive advancement in the status of women. They began to emerge out of medievalism and into a more modern role.

This can partly be attributed to the very fact of having a woman on the throne, who was proving to be so incomparable and popular a ruler, irrespective of sex. Elizabeth had learnt to use her sex to positive advantage in her role as leader. To take just one example, her famous speech to the camp at Tilbury before the arrival of the Spanish Armada won her immense love and admiration: 'I know I have the body but of a weak and feeble woman; but I have the heart and stomach of a king.'[4]

Having a woman on the throne also increased the role played by women at court. More and more girls and women came to court to attend on the queen and their influence began to be felt. Whilst Elizabeth's advisers were men like Lord Burghley and the Earl of Leicester, her lady attendants, in constant daily contact with their sovereign, could exert a degree of influence impossible if they were merely attending a queen consort. Direct and easy access to the queen gave them opportunities, for example, to favour their friends or bring matters to her notice. Elizabeth loved to gossip with her ladies and they formed one of her channels of communication.

Another reason for the gradual advancement of the status of women that has been traced to having started at about this time applies to a much wider section of society than to the queen and her court. With men frequently away at the wars, and with their early deaths, women needed to be able to manage their affairs in their absence. If they were of the richer property-owning families it became sensible to educate them so as to develop their practical skills and be competent to manage their houses and estates.

Penelope was to be one of the first of a new kind of woman. A woman of influence at court, a woman of wit and intelligence, a practical and successful woman. Her defiant attitude to her marriage was an early indication of a strong will. Her marriage was to be the start of an adult life that was to defy convention and help shape contemporary views on women.

Lady Penelope Rich, at Lambeth Palace. Labelled on the reverse 'A Countess of Devonshire'.

CHAPTER TWO

'The Fineness of her Wit'

Lady Penelope Devereux was the eldest child of Walter Devereux, Viscount Hereford and his wife Letitia (Lettice). Lettice Knollys was the first cousin once removed of Queen Elizabeth, since Lettice's grandmother was Mary Boleyn, sister to Anne Boleyn. Lettice's mother, Lady Catherine Knollys, was therefore Elizabeth's first cousin. Her father was Sir Francis Knollys, a Protestant who fled the country on the accession of Queen Mary. Elizabeth wrote a farewell letter to her cousin, calling their journey a 'pilgrimage' which was 'rather a proof of your friends than a leaving of your country', and promising them her help: 'when your need shall be most you shall find my friendship greatest'.[1] When Elizabeth became queen, Sir Francis Knollys returned to Court and was appointed Treasurer of the Royal Household. The women of the Knollys family became attendants on the queen and Lettice, seven years younger than her royal cousin, was one of Elizabeth's first maids of honour.

The Devereux were descendants of the Norman Evereux who had come to England with William the Conqueror and had settled in Herefordshire near the border of Wales, a connection that is commemorated in the title Walter's grandfather took of Viscount Hereford. They had been aristocracy since medieval times and Walter could claim royal descent from the Plantagenets. His family too had been Protestants for some time.

The couple had married in 1561, an advantageous match on both sides, though it was not to prove a happy one. As their children grew up much of their time was spent apart whilst Walter tried to win fame and fortune by his military campaigns in Ireland. In all they had five children: Penelope, the eldest, born in 1563, Dorothy (1565), Robert (1567) and Walter (1569); a fifth child, Francis, died in infancy.

Walter inherited from his grandfather the titles of Lord Ferrers of Chartley, Bourchier and Lovaine and Viscount Hereford and made his career as a soldier. In 1569 he had joined the army of the Earl of Warwick against the rebellion of the Northern Lords who supported Mary Queen of Scots. The uprising was suppressed and he became joint keeper with his cousin Lord Huntingdon of the Scottish queen. His success in this campaign earned him advancement and, in recognition of his services, he was in 1572 elevated to an earldom, becoming the first Earl of Essex. It was an old family title last held by his great-grand uncle, restored in his honour.

The principal family home was at Chartley in Staffordshire, a few miles to the north-west of Stafford, with the Needwood Forest to the east stretching towards the borders of Derbyshire. There Penelope was born and spent most of her early childhood.[2] It was a moated house set in a park of nearly a thousand acres and built on a small island. The engraving of Chartley in Plot's *History of Staffordshire* shows a half-timbered manor house with gables, tall chimneys and many windows, built around a large courtyard. (The house was burnt down in 1781.) In the grounds were the ruins of the old Chartley Castle and these combined with the distinctive feature of the moat to make it especially fascinating for children. This was cattle country, famous for its beef, and the Chartley cattle were renowned as a unique breed with their long branching horns.

The family also owned an estate at Lamphey in Pembrokeshire, South Wales. This had been the bishop's palace before the Reformation, the rural retreat of the bishops of St David's. It had a deer park, fish ponds, mills and orchards. To this remote spot the Devereux family would come during the summer months. They took little part in the life of the court.

Until she was six years old Penelope saw as much of her father as any Elizabethan child did. Thereafter he was to devote more and more time to military exploits and less to his family. In consequence, during their childhood the children saw less and less of their father. His military career was not compatible with a domestic life. With their father away a great deal the children, in their early years, came under the influence of their mother. It was her dominant personality that was their shaping force. For her daughters she set a pattern of strong womanhood with which they could identify.

Their education began at Chartley, under their tutor called Holmes, who taught Penelope and Dorothy throughout their early childhood. Their mother took the education of her daughters seriously. When their tutor Holmes wanted to go up to London to plead to Lord Burghley for the continuance of his annuity of ten pounds she refused to let him go. She did not want her daughters to miss their lessons. The main difference between the education given to the two girls at this stage from that received by their brothers was that they did not learn Latin and Greek. There had been a brief period when a classical education for girls was regarded as an ideal to be encouraged. Queen Elizabeth had herself benefited from a classical education, as had Lady Jane Grey, Mary Sidney and other daughters of the nobility. The queen was able to speak fluently in Latin. So proud was she of this accomplishment that she maintained she was 'more afraid of making a fault in my Latin than of the Kings of Spain, France, Scotland, the whole House of Guise and all their confederates'.[3] The confidence such an education had given her enabled her to dismiss Philip of Spain in this acid manner: 'I am not afraid of a King of Spain who has been up to the age of twelve learning his alphabet'.[4] Philip Sidney's sister Mary knew Latin, Greek and Hebrew, taught to her by her tutors at home, whilst Philip went away to school and university.

The experiment of a classical training for the daughters of the elite was short-lived. With the publication in English in 1561 of Castiglione's *The Courtier* the emphasis on education for aristocratic young ladies moved back towards proficiency in the social arts. Castiglione's ideal young woman had a sprinkling of letters, but the prime qualities were the social graces: skill in music, painting, drawing, dancing, needlework. She must also represent the puritan ideal as a docile housewife and diligent upholder of matrimony.

As to what Penelope studied, we can make certain deductions about her education from subsequent descriptions of her.

She had an 'attentive ear and eye', so that her particular talents were for languages and music. She acquired a 'perfect knowledge' of French, Spanish was 'a language so well-known' to her and she also knew Italian, corresponding in all these languages.[5] Her intelligence and literary skills were to be admired by King James of Scotland who 'commended much the fineness of her wit, the invention and well-writing' of her letters.[6] Wit for the Elizabethan had the larger meaning of intelligence and understanding. Letter-writing was a form of expression in which the women of the period were to excel. The letters of Penelope and her sister Dorothy were stylishly written and clearly phrased, bold and confident in their expression. She was a skilled musician and was reckoned to play the lute 'divinely well'.[7] Her beautiful voice was frequently praised, being more than once likened to the nightingale's and it was this that was said to have captivated her lover, Lord Mountjoy. She was a graceful and spirited dancer.

The girls would not have taken part in the more active of the outdoor pursuits. Queen Elizabeth's tutor, Roger Ascham, listed the 'courtly exercises and gentleman-like pastimes' which 'young men should use and delight in' as 'to ride comely; to play at all weapons; to shoot fair in bow or surely in gun; to vault lustily; to run; to leap; to wrestle; to swim; to dance comely; to sing, and play of instrument cunningly; to hawk; to hunt; to play at tennis'; these were the pastimes for 'a courtly gentleman to use'.[8] Of these pastimes only singing, playing of musical instruments, and riding 'comely' would have been considered suitable for young ladies. Riding was an essential accomplishment for anyone who travelled as the Devereux did.

Education for girls began and ended in the home, whilst their brothers went away to school and university. Robert as the eldest son had his own tutors. For a time he was taught by Thomas Ashton, headmaster and virtual founder of Shrewsbury School, then by an ex-pupil of his, Robert Wright. Later he was to attend Lord Burghley's school and afterwards Trinity College Cambridge, whilst the younger boy Walter went up to Oxford. The education of the eldest son was a matter of particular importance. Unable to be at hand to supervise the education of his heir himself, the Earl of Essex, soon after his arrival in Ireland, had written to Lord Burghley, holder of the highest administrative offices at the court of Elizabeth, suggesting he take on this role. Robert was only six when his father suggested that Lord Burghley should have 'the direction, education and marriage of mine eldest son,' setting out the financial settlements he was prepared to make if the match went ahead.[9] It was never too early to arrange an advantageous marriage and Essex clearly saw the advantages of a marriage alliance with the Cecil family. Although nothing came of this proposal, the approach had been made for Robert's education to be undertaken by Lord Burghley when the time came 'to draw him from his mother's wing'.

Amongst his many administrative powers Lord Burghley held the post of Master of the Court of Wards. These wards were the heirs of landowners who were unable during their minority to hold land. Until the heir came of age, at twenty-one, he was not entitled to the benefits of the land under the old feudal rule that all land was held from the crown in return for services rendered to the crown. Since knight-service, as the military obligations were termed, could not be performed by a minor, he in turn could not hold land, and his land passed to the crown during the period of his minority. The lands came within the province of Lord Burghley's administration and he could either retain the rights for the benefit of the crown or sell them off with the proceeds passing to the exchequer. During their minority the heirs' marriages and education also came within the control of the Master of the Wards.

As his responsibility for the education of young boys grew, Lord Burghley established a school to educate them, not solely for the wards of court but other sons of the nobility whose fathers might be away on service. As well as his own two sons, the pupils included the Earls of Oxford, Essex and Southampton. The school, set up in his own house, Cecil House in the Strand, was of the highest repute and there was great competition for admission. By getting Robert accepted at Lord Burghley's school, Essex had secured the best possible beginning for his son's further advancement. Not only did it excel in its formal education but its pupils were placed in a favourable position for the future.

The preparation of the eldest son and heir for his future role was of particular concern in those families where the father was away from home and at risk. Equally concerned about the education of their eldest boy was the Sidney family. Their son Philip was not only his father's heir, but heir to two earls, his uncles the Earls of Warwick and of Leicester. The Devereux family was to become closely linked with the Sidney family by their involvement in Ireland and it is this political connection which was both to bring together the personal lives of Philip Sidney and Penelope Devereux and later to part them.

The Sidney family had certain similarities to the Devereux, both being noble and aristocratic, yet at the same time with insufficient resources to support them in their high positions and both sinking themselves further into debt over the Irish wars. Each time Sir Henry Sidney returned from holding the Lord Deputyship of Ireland he was three thousand pounds poorer than when he went. Sir Henry had been offered a barony by the queen but without any grant of lands and could not afford to maintain it. At the same time, he was most anxious not to offend the queen by refusing the honour. He debated the matter with his wife, Lady Mary Sidney, who found her husband 'greatly dismayed with his hard choice'.[10] In the end he turned it down, risking Elizabeth's disfavour. Lady Mary Sidney was treated even more shabbily by the queen, nursing Elizabeth through the smallpox without reward and catching the illness through her services. Sir Henry described in a letter how 'I left her a full fair lady, in mine eye at least the fairest, and when I returned I found her as foul a lady as the smallpox could make her; which she did take by continual attendance of Her Majesty's most precious person, sick of the same disease, the scars of which, to her resolute discomfort ever since, hath done and doth remain in her face, so as she liketh solitariness.'[11]

Their son Philip grew up very proud of his family connections, in particular on his mother's side, and that he was nephew to the great Leicester, who was his mother's brother. 'I am a Dudley in blood, that Duke's daughter's son and do acknowledge though in all truth I may justly affirm that I am by my father's side of ancient and always well-esteemed and well-matched gentry yet I do acknowledge I say that my chiefest honour is to be a Dudley.'[12]

Again, this family was strongly Protestant. In deference to Queen Mary, then on the throne, Philip had been named after the King of Spain, who was one of his godfathers, ironically enough since Philip of Spain was to be his great enemy as the Protestant oppressor.

Philip's education began with a private tutor at Penshurst in Kent, the family seat. At the age of nine he went to Shrewsbury School, enrolling on the same day as his life-long friend and biographer, Fulke Greville, and they were contemporaries of Robert Wright, later to be Robert Devereux' tutor. When he was eleven he visited Kenilworth, his uncle the Earl of Leicester's seat, and then on to Oxford on the occasion of the queen's visit. He set out from Shrewsbury School riding on the horse given to him by Penelope Devereux' father. Leicester, as Chancellor of the University, played official host to the queen and his illustrious uncle singled him out for special favour. Determined that his nephew should impress the queen, whom Philip was meeting probably for the first time, he ordered several sets of sumptuous clothes for him: a taffeta coat covered with lace, a crimson satin doublet with crimson velvet hose.

Later Philip himself went up to Oxford to continue his classical education at Christ Church. He left Oxford without taking a degree, not uncommon at the time and no reflection on his academic abilities. It may well have been because in 1571 the plague was spreading. After leaving Oxford he seems to have spent some time at Cambridge.

His formal academic education was over, and then began the final grooming. It was decided that he should continue his education by travel, the foreshadowing of the Grand Tour, which was becoming the customary mode of completing the education of a young courtier. Travel was more than merely seeing the sights; it informed the traveller of matters which might later be useful both to himself and the state, and included the observation of such matters as the power and resources of other nations.

It also encouraged insight into larger questions of 'religion, policies, laws, bringing up of their children, discipline both for war and peace' (the quotation is from a letter Philip himself was to write years later to his younger brother Robert on this theme).[13] Above all, it enabled one to meet others, great men whose influence would be educational.

At the age of seventeen-and-a-half (May 1572) Philip received the queen's permission to travel and he was to spend the next three years completing his education in this way. He left, according to his uncle Leicester, 'young and raw'[14] and was to return the most accomplished, cultured and idolised young man of his day.

His first port of call was France, where he travelled in the company of the Earl of Lincoln. Another in the party was Robert Lord Rich, father of the man whom Sidney was later to scorn as the despicable husband of Penelope. The party arrived in Paris in June 1572 and Sidney went to stay with the English ambassador, Sir Francis Walsingham (his father-in-law to be). It was from Walsingham's house that Philip witnessed the St Bartholomew's Day massacre which made a deep and lasting impression on him.

It was in his letter of introduction of the young Philip to Sir Francis that Leicester had apologetically described him as 'young and raw'. It may be that Leicester had been unobservant of the progress Philip had made, but used to seeing him as a child, may not have appreciated how remarkable he had become. To others meeting him from this time onwards he appeared a model of excellence in every way. He was noted to have 'ready and witty answers' and to astonish those who heard him 'speak the French language so well and aptly having been so short a while in the country'. He met for the first time in Paris his great friend and mentor Hubert Languet, who similarly complimented him on his French. 'I have watched you closely when you were speaking my own language, but I hardly ever detected you pronouncing a single syllable wrongly.'[15]

During the three years abroad, Sidney broadened his horizons reading and studying and learning, to become a highly educated young man, proficient in languages and accepted by much older men as a most worthy equal. Languet was able to report of him to the Elector of Saxony: 'He has an excellent mind, and almost more experience in affairs than his years can support.'[16]

By the time he returned at the end of May 1575, the world united in his praise, as a poem written in Latin to celebrate his return expressed it. It translates as:

> Thus Philip returned, praised by the whole world, the hope of so many peoples, the outstanding offspring of the Sidney family.[17]

This is how Sidney had appeared to foreigners abroad and even more so to his fellow countrymen on his return. Heady praise indeed for any young man, particularly one inclined to take himself very seriously. He reached England on the last day of May 1575, almost exactly three years after setting out and six months short of his twenty-first birthday. He was almost at once caught up with the preparations for the queen's progress to Kenilworth, his uncle Leicester's seat, where she spent nineteen days in July 1575, the most magnificent of all the progresses.

Penelope, twelve years old at that time, did not herself attend the Kenilworth festivities, but her mother did. At that impressionable age she could not fail to have listened spellbound to the fabulous tales about that spectacular visit. Leicester had spent vast amounts on turning Kenilworth into a luxurious palace fit to receive the queen and for her visit had planned fresh delights to entertain her each day. There were fireworks, banquets, music and dancing, bear-baiting, picnics, plays, tournaments, acrobatics and hunting, each diversion imaginatively conceived and lavishly presented, with the guests appearing in all their richest finery. Enough to capture the imagination of any young girl.

Then, even more exciting, came the news that for the next stage of her progress, the queen would honour the Devereux family with a visit to Chartley. Walter was away in Ireland and Lettice received her royal cousin in his absence. She could not attempt to compete with the splendid celebrations at Kenilworth but for the honour of the family was determined to offer her best hospitality. The queen was accompanied by the Earl of Leicester and his nephew Philip.

It is possible that Penelope was moved out of her home for the occasion, to make room for the royal party, as the queen's and Leicester's entourages were large. Even if she were, it is not likely that the children would have been moved far no further perhaps than their friendly neighbours the Bagot family at nearby Blithfield. The queen loved to meet children and Lettice would have been proud to show her family to their queen. There is a reference in his poetry, written much later, to Philip's meeting Penelope as a child but not appreciating her full potential. If indeed he met the twelve-year-old Penelope on this occasion, no wonder that the sophisticated young man of nearly twenty-one, much travelled, treated as an equal by the greatest men of his day, should not have noticed her.

Lettice Knollys, Countess of Leicester, attributed to George Gower.

CHAPTER THREE

'The Delights of the English Egypt'

In 1573, when Penelope was ten, her father disappeared out of her life virtually permanently. As the Earl of Essex he had undertaken a dangerous and formidable task, the suppression of the rebellion then raging in Ulster and the subsequent colonisation of the state. Ireland at that time was a wild and desolate country, where feudal chieftains waged constant war on each other. Part of it, the part within the English Pale, was ruled by England under a governor appointed by the queen, her Lord Deputy. The rest, beyond the Pale, was virtually ungovernable.

Ruling such a country presented heavy responsibilities and insuperable problems. As well as trying to administer and bring law and order into a state of near chaos, the governor also himself had to conduct military campaigns to subdue the warring rebels and bring them under control.

This unenviable task had fallen to Sir Henry Sidney, father of Philip. He had spent two terms (of three years each) in this post from 1566 to 1571, prior to the Earl of Essex's arrival, and was to return again during Essex's campaign for a third term of office.

Whilst the Lord Deputyship was the highest public office in Ireland, Essex's role was, surprisingly we may think, a private venture. He financed the expedition himself from his own resources, borrowing ten thousand pounds from the queen for the purpose at ten per cent interest, and mortgaging his lands to the queen as security for the loan.

The boundaries between public and private enterprise were not clearly demarcated and it was in the queen's interest to encourage private ventures. Money from the exchequer for campaigns was short and Essex was speculating on being able to recoup his losses and win himself not only honour but the more tangible rewards of lands and financial gains. Getting men to behave as Essex did was Elizabeth's method of conducting expensive campaigns with insufficient revenue.

It was an arduous undertaking and Essex approached it as a professional soldier making war on barbarians to whom the standards of civilised conduct did not apply. At one point, having invited the rebel leaders to a banquet to discuss terms for peace, he proceeded to massacre his guests. In this outlandish spot, civilised behaviour had broken down and only the will to survive remained.

Henry Sidney's successor as Lord Deputy was his brother-in-law Sir William Fitzwilliam, who held the post during the first two years of Essex's campaign. The success of Essex's venture depended upon the degree of assistance he was given by the Lord Deputy and his forces. Although the campaign was controlled by the queen from England she was far away and did not always fully appreciate, or want to know, the difficulties. At one point she actually wrote to Essex urging him 'not to fester reproachfully in the delights of the English Egypt, where many take greatest delight in holding their noses over the beef pots'.[1]

Shakespeare had not yet written his *Antony and Cleopatra* but the queen had read the story in Plutarch. Elizabeth's vision, conjured up in the comparison, of Essex basking in the delights of Ireland, that 'English Egypt' had perhaps been inspired by her own recent progress that summer to Kenilworth, where the Earl of Leicester had so lavishly and spectacularly entertained her. Whatever delights Essex had been able to find for himself in Ireland could hardly have borne comparison.

The queen, trying to control the campaign from a distance, did not assist by her lack of firm direction. She vacillated in her instructions, 'sometimes so, sometimes no, at all times uncertain.'[2]

She was reluctant to expend funds from the exchequer unless forced to do so. From the Lord Deputy's point of view, the queen would not thank him for spending her money fruitlessly and any co-operation he gave to Essex would only serve to advance the Earl's personal position. The two men were at loggerheads, unable and unwilling to co-operate.

Essex's career was at a low ebb when in March 1575 he wrote to the queen describing his future as he saw it. At the age of thirty-five he had resigned himself to spending what was left of his life in, at best, peaceful obscurity: 'being now altogether private, I do desire your Majesty's good licence so to live in a corner of Ulster which I hire for my money; where though I pass my time somewhat obscurely (a life, my case considered, fittest for me) yet shall it not be without some stay in these parts and comfort to such as hoped to be rid from the tyranny of rebels.'³

His spirits have reached the blackest depths, but even allowing for the mood of despair it is noteworthy that his plans for a humble future did not include his wife. Lady Mary Sidney had, in spite of bad health and with as large a family as the Devereux, managed to accompany her husband to Ireland, which Lettice never did. However, his careful plans for his children before his death and his death-bed concern for their futures showed him as a loving father.

Essex's expedition had failed. In May the queen wrote to him to confirm that the Ulster scheme was at an end and he was to return as soon as he could. However, two events at this point restored his position to some extent. The first was his siege of the island of Rathlin, where all the inhabitants were slaughtered. The second was the conclusion of a peace treaty with the rebel leader Turlough O'Neill (the forerunner of that other O'Neill rebel leader the Earl of Tyrone, who was to confront Essex's son Robert twenty-four years later).

The Lord Deputy Fitzwilliam had fallen seriously ill and Henry Sidney was called upon to return to Ireland. He had spent most of the intervening time in carrying out his duties as Lord President of Wales, a post he enjoyed and was to hold for twenty-six years, and for which he had to pay a Deputy when he was appointed to Ireland. Sidney was most reluctant to return, but was eventually persuaded by what looked like favourable terms. He was allowed the huge sum of twenty thousand pounds a year payable quarterly in advance in return for governing without further demands on the exchequer. However, none of these men was to get rich in Ireland. It broke their health and far from rescuing them from financial difficulties drove them still deeper into debt.

In August 1575 Sir Henry Sidney was re-appointed Lord Deputy for his third term of office. By now Essex, thoroughly disillusioned, wanted only to cut his losses, and achieve compensation and some recognition for his services. He had been appointed Earl Marshall but this was an empty title without significant financial benefits attached to it. He was convinced that the Lord Deputy was standing in his way. The two men were equally wary and suspicious of each other. Trouble was brewing between them, stirred up by 'tale bearers who make their profit by dissention'. Their respective roles, of governor and general, overlapped and they were in effect rivals, competing for the same rewards. Essex, unable to work with the previous Lord Deputy, now found his successor, if anything, worse. He wrote to the queen threatening resignation. He had come to Ireland, he told her, to win honour and if she did not consider his continuance an assistance to the Lord Deputy he would return.

In November 1575 he returned to England, spending Christmas in London at Durham House in the Strand. He needed to be near at hand to make his approaches to the queen and the Privy Council. Philip Sidney was at that time staying with his uncle at nearby Leicester House. In spite of the difference in their ages – Essex was then thirty-six, Philip twenty-one – the two became warm friends. The seeds of friendship had been sown long ago, in Philip's childhood, when Penelope's father had given him the horse on which he set off so proudly from Shrewsbury School on his first visit to Kenilworth. The name Philip means lover of horses and Philip delighted in puns on his name. The choice was, therefore, particularly felicitous and it was an exciting gift for any young boy. Such a present could not fail to endear the giver and make him remembered.

By March 1576 Essex had still not secured his future position. He had rejected the queen's first offers as insufficient. To help settle the matter, assistance was sought from other quarters.

Henry Sidney was asked to intervene and persuade Essex to return to Ireland by offering him a post there on terms he could not refuse. He used his son's friendship with the earl to advantage, getting Philip to deliver his letters in person. These tactics proved remarkably successful. Henry Sidney's letters were so modestly written and Philip delivered them with such expressions of goodwill from his father that the earl was completely won over. He 'uttered honourable speeches' of Sir Henry and offered in return 'mutual friendship'.[4] He was captivated by Philip, and began to speak of him as his son. It was at this point that the idea of marriage between Philip and his daughter Penelope first suggested itself. The goodwill now growing between the two families could be cemented in this way.

Essex was now prepared to return to Ireland, on terms acceptable to him. Henry Sidney, by extending the hand of friendship and convincing the earl of his good intentions, had persuaded Essex that he should return to Ireland and continue his campaign.

In fact, Sir Henry Sidney had never liked Essex. He was a plain man, not normally given to dissemblance, and he had to be persuaded to play the role he did, hiding his dislike and mistrust. Several people had played a part in urging Sir Henry to make these overtures to the earl. Firstly, the queen, who was finding Essex's demands for compensation too pressing. He had spent thirty-five thousand pounds on the expedition and had a good case for saying that this had largely been spent on matters of public defence for which he deserved recompense. He had singularly failed to make any private fortune against which the expenditure could be set off. If he could be sent back to Ireland this would solve the problem temporarily at least. Besides, he knew Ireland, she needed a general and army there, and there were few enough she could send to that land of misery.

The Earl of Leicester's part in the plan has frequently been distorted. Leicester was subsequently to marry Essex's widow and was later to be accused of having had an adulterous affair with Lettice Devereux during her husband's lifetime and even of poisoning Essex. That there was a carefully worked out plan to win over Essex's confidence and that Leicester played a part in it is clear from a letter written by Essex's secretary to Sir Henry Sidney, telling him of its success.

This secretary, Edward Waterhouse, was no double-dealer. He had previously given loyal service to Sir Henry Sidney in the same capacity. Devoted to his old master, at the same time he very much had his new master's interests at heart. He was trusted by both men. The letter he now wrote has been used as evidence, and indeed the only piece of historical evidence, that Leicester wanted Essex out of the country to serve his own ends. However, there is nothing in the letter to indicate that Leicester had any personal motive for wanting Essex to return to Ireland.

Leicester's first misgiving had been that his brother-in-law had not made it sufficiently clear to the queen and the Lords that he sincerely wanted Essex back in Ireland. Leicester had expected Sir Henry to offer a specific appointment to Essex or to his friends. The fact that the appointment could be offered to friends of Essex indicates that it was not necessarily personal to him but as an overture of friendship. As it turned out, Sir Henry's letters had been successful and Leicester had withdrawn his objections, well pleased with the results.

Leicester was both the person closest to the queen and Sir Henry's brother-in-law. His role was to persuade his brother-in-law to make friends with Essex and to do it convincingly so that the queen, Essex and everyone else would actually believe it. By standing in the way of the general wishes of the queen and council to reach agreement with Essex, Sir Henry was only harming his own position, and appearing too haughty and intractable. His brother-in-law's personal antagonism must be overcome or at least concealed.

We can be sure that Sir Henry would have listened to his powerful brother-in-law. By marrying Leicester's sister he had committed his allegiance to the Dudley family and carried the Dudley emblem, the bear and ragged staff, as his own. His son Philip was heir apparent to both his Dudley uncles, the Earls of Leicester and Warwick. Leicester was playing a part, just as Edward Waterhouse and Philip Sidney were, in bringing together the two rivals in a public show of goodwill.

After the professions of friendship and co-operation from the Lord Deputy, Essex resolved to return to Ireland. For the time being, and in public at least, the hatchet was buried between the two men. The post that he was now offered was that of Earl Marshall of Ireland for his lifetime. But the financial arrangements were still not satisfactory. The real prizes still eluded him.

That he was most seriously concerned about his financial position at this point is clear. He returned to Chartley to put his private affairs in order, using his brief visit home in June 1576 to arrange some land transactions and to make his will. He had a premonition he would die. This was to be the last time Penelope ever saw her father.

In July 1576 he returned to Ireland, travelling back with his 'son by adoption' Philip Sidney, going to join his own father. Here was a further chance to advance his cherished plan for a marriage between Philip and his daughter. Although Penelope was still only thirteen, everything had suddenly begun to close in on him, and there was indeed little time.

Only a few weeks after his return Essex fell ill. He described his sickness in a letter to his legal adviser Richard Broughton, the man who looked after his estate at Chartley. He had been taken ill on the last day of August, as had his page and a gentleman with whom he had been drinking. This made him suspicious of 'some evil' in his drink, for he had been troubled ever since, as he described it, with a 'flux', i.e. dysentery.[5] The page, although quite ill at first, had since recovered. At this time Essex himself had hopes of recovering. By his next letter to Richard Broughton, written five days later, on the 18th September, he had already given up hope. He asked his legal adviser to 'be loving to my children and not to grieve yourselves with the discontented news of my death'. He gave special instructions regarding his two daughters and his younger son. They were to go to his cousin Lord Huntingdon 'for maintenance' as he had already made provision for in his will. Now he gave directions for the payment to his cousin of yearly sums to cover their expenses.

He was to suffer a lingering death. Two days later he wrote to the queen, on his children's behalf, hoping that 'it will please your Majesty to be as a mother unto them, at the least by your gracious countenance and care of their education and matches'.

He reminded her that his eldest son Robert, upon whom the continuance of his house depended, was himself dependent upon her: 'for the smallness of his living, the greatness of my debt, and the dowries that go out of my lands, make the remainder little or nothing towards the reputation of an earl's estate'.[7] He specifically stated that he did not want his son to follow in his footsteps in the office of Earl Marshall of Ireland. He himself had suffered too much from its consequences. On the following day, the day before he died, he wrote to Lord Burghley to confirm his previous wish that Robert's education should be undertaken by him. An account of his death has been preserved. The only worldly matter he now cared about was for his children, to whom he frequently gave his love and blessing. He prayed for his daughters in particular, that they should be protected against 'the vile world', 'lamenting the time which is so vain and ungodly considering the frailness of women, least they should learn of the vile world, God defend them and bless them and make them to fear Thy name. The Lord give them grace to live a virtuous and godly life'.

He then went on to send a final message to Philip Sidney, hoping to see him before he died. 'Tell him I send him nothing but I wish him well and so well that if God do move both their hearts I wish he might match with my daughter. I call him son; he is so wise, so virtuous and godly; and if he go on in the course he hath begun, he will be as famous and worthy a gentleman as ever England bred.'[8]

Philip hurried to the dying man, but he arrived too late. On the 22nd September 1576 the Earl of Essex died.

The family did not travel to Carmarthen in Wales where the Earl's body had been brought for the funeral on the 26th November 1576. Robert wrote to his new guardian Lord Burghley to explain that he would have attended if 'my weak body could bear this journey' but it was bitterly cold weather to travel from Staffordshire to Wales.[9]

Amongst other tributes a sonorous elegy was written for the occasion in Welsh by the poet Huw Lleyn. In this poem the thirteen year old Penelope is described as:

> Penelope, countenance of grace,
> Truly splendid, great and deserving respect.[10]

It was an early beginning to what was to be a long line of tributes to her in poetry and the arts.

Penelope never forgot the death of her father in Ireland. When, many years later, she came to intercede with the queen on her brother's behalf, she compared their common fate, both brought down by fighting for their country in Ireland: 'so hard a destiny, two of them perishing by being employed in one country, where they would have done you loyal service to the shedding of their last blood'. With her father's death, the bonds of Devereux family life were broken and the happy, sheltered world of Penelope's childhood came to an end.

CHAPTER FOUR

'More Dishonour than can be Repaired'

The calamity of their father's death changed the lives of the Devereux children. As the eldest, Penelope had seen more of her father than the others and knew him best. At thirteen she was old enough to understand the nature of their loss to an extent that the younger children could not share. For Robert, not yet nine, it meant not only inheriting his father's title but the premature assumption, at an impossibly early age, of a role in the adult world where much was expected of him. Admonitions as to how he should conduct himself so as to be worthy to take his father's place were heaped upon him. Overnight he had to pass from childhood to head of the family.

For a time it seemed that the queen's heart had softened towards the Devereux children, as their father had pleaded on his death-bed. She promised to cancel the debt owed to her, although later she was to think better of this gesture of goodwill. For the time being, however, the young Devereux children were the object of much sympathy.

Edward Waterhouse, the late earl's secretary, took charge of the practical arrangements. Anxious to carry out his late master's wishes, he was particularly concerned about the marriage proposal between Penelope and Philip, reporting to Sir Henry Sidney in these terms:

All these Lords that wish well to the children and I suppose all the best sort of the English Lords besides, do expect what will become of the treaty between Mr. Philip and my Lady Penelope. Truly, my Lord, I must say to your Lordship as I have said to my Lord of Leicester and Mr. Philip, the breaking off from this match, if the default be on your parts, will turn to more dishonour than can be repaired with any other marriage in England. And I protest unto your Lordship, I do not think that there is at this day so strong a man in England of friends, as the little Earl of Essex, nor any man more lamented than his father since the death of King Edward.[1]

Waterhouse was doing his utmost to see that the marriage plan went ahead, pointing out the disgrace that would fall on the Sidney family if it were broken off. The new earl, though young, was as strong as any man in England, because he had powerful friends. By comparing the Earl of Essex's death to that of King Edward, Waterhouse was directly appealing to Sir Henry Sidney's own feelings, for the boy-king, whom he had dearly loved, had died in his arms.

In spite of the threat of dishonour, the marriage treaty did not proceed. One explanation of why it fell through is on financial grounds. The next step in the marriage negotiation procedures would have been for a written legal contract to be drawn up setting out the financial settlements. On Penelope's side this was clear-cut, since her father in his will had given her a dowry of two thousand pounds with an allowance of a hundred pounds a year. Though by no means small, and probably more than Essex could afford (there was to be a similar amount for Dorothy) it was not large enough to tempt the Sidney family. Philip's family was not in a position to make him a sufficiently generous settlement to enable him to marry and set up an establishment of his own, even if his father had wanted the marriage. Both the Sidneys and the Devereux were comparatively poor and an alliance between them would make no particular sense in financial terms.

The Sidney family no longer had a need to continue with the match. Essex had been an important ally in Ireland and a potential rival, so that the marriage would have cemented a political alliance. In spite of Edward Waterhouse's assurances, with a young boy as earl, the Devereux family no longer wielded the same political power, for the time being at least.

Over and above the political and financial aspects, Sir Henry Sidney's personal dislike of Essex no longer had to be suppressed. He had no further need to entertain for political reasons a marriage for his beloved son with the daughter of his old enemy. Philip as heir to his two childless uncles, the Earls of Leicester and Warwick, was placed with the highest prospects of influence and wealth. It was not to be wondered at if Sir Henry Sidney let the marriage treaty die with Essex.

Penelope was only thirteen. Although she was over the age of consent for marriage (twelve for a girl, fourteen for a boy) it was still young to marry, and fifteen was usually the earliest age for an Elizabethan girl actually to wed. It had not been intended that the proposed marriage should take place immediately, for arrangements were frequently made well in advance of the event. Her father had been prudently planning ahead.

Philip himself seems to have done nothing to encourage the continuance of the proposal. It was to be a matter of bitterest regret to him later. But at this stage he was not interested in marriage, perhaps partly because of the number of proposals that came his way, though none advanced so far as that with Penelope. He wanted to make his way in the world first before settling down to marriage. These were his feelings for at least the next two years, which he expressed in a letter, written when he was twenty-three, to his friend Hubert Languet who was urging him to marry:

I wonder what has come into your mind that, when I have not as yet done anything worthy of me, you would have me bound in the chains of matrimony, and yet without pointing out any individual lady, but rather seeming to extol the state itself, which, however, you have not yet sanctioned by your own example.[2]

In choosing Philip Sidney for his son-in-law, the Earl of Essex had initially been motivated by the desire to ally himself with a family whose co-operation he needed in his Irish campaign. In getting to know Philip he had come to recognise the wisdom of his choice, appreciating his personal merits. After his death the marriage plan was quietly allowed to lapse.

There were rumours that Essex had been poisoned and Sir Henry Sidney, as governor of Ireland, was called upon to investigate. He sent a lengthy report of his findings to the queen's secretary, Francis Walsingham. His report set out all the events surrounding the earl's death, so far as he had been able to establish them. It gave details of Essex's food and drink, who had handled it, whether the water he took with his wine had been properly boiled, as well as commenting on the status of his doctors and the treatment they had given. The Irish doctor who attended him did not think he had been poisoned. One of his two doctors was his chaplain, Knell, who also had a medical training. Knell's version was enclosed with the report. It asserted that Essex himself suspected poison but acquitted 'the yeoman of his cellar', and 'thought some other of Ireland had done it; but none of his own house'. Knell had then proceeded to administer to the patient, as a treatment for poison, doses of 'unicorn's horn'. Nevertheless Knell was not certain of the nature of Essex's complaint. His conclusion was: 'as I knew nothing certain, so I suggest no man else doth'.

Sir Henry Sidney's overall conclusion was that the earl had not been poisoned and that the suspicions were unfounded. Basically his report followed Essex's own account of the events, as told to his legal adviser Broughton, though it contained more factual details. It also went on to give some personal details omitted from the earl's own version of the fatal supper. In his account Essex had only mentioned his page and a gentleman with whom he had been drinking. Sir Henry Sidney's report refers also to 'two gentlewomen' with whom he had supped. The party had, it seems, consisted of the two men, the two gentlewomen, and Essex's page, to pour the wine.[3]

It is perhaps significant to recall that Essex on his death-bed grieved over his children but did not mention his wife although the 'frailness of women' was in his mind as he prayed for his daughters. Nevertheless he had in his will, made only three months before, bequeathed to his 'right wellbeloved wife' a share of his property.[4] After he fell ill he did nothing to alter his will, although he had ample time and opportunity to do so if he had wanted.

For Penelope's mother, this was a difficult time. After her husband's death she returned to her father's home in Oxfordshire, whilst his estate was being settled, taking her two daughters, Penelope and Dorothy, and her younger son Walter with her. The new earl, Robert, went to live in Lord Burghley's house in London, attending the school there.

The Countess's immediate problems were financial ones, and in the first few months, whilst the estate was being wound up, these were very pressing. Four months after his death she wrote in desperation to Lord Burghley as Lord Treasurer (another of his offices) and to the Lord Chamberlain, the Earl of Sussex, asking for their assistance. She was trying to 'provide a house of mine own for my abode', but found herself 'by no means able'. She begged their Lordships 'to let me have some small things of my late Lord's, as he hath left me to supply my wants therein: otherwise I must be unwillingly driven to seek my friends' houses from time to time, as presently I do, for that my position is scant able to find me and my company meat and drink, and therefore no surplus to pay my debts withall, much less to furnish myself with such things as necessity I must have towards my house.'[5] A sad tale, patently true, written as it was to the highest officers of state who would certainly know if it were not.

Her husband had left her in his will jewels, plate and properties, but there were large debts to be paid and the main estate must pass, as intact as possible, to his son and heir, Robert, the new earl. Lettice's first concern, whilst these matters were being sorted out, was with the basic necessities of life. Robert had become a Ward of Court on his father's death, because he was heir to lands owing knight-service to the Crown. Lettice, as the widow of such a landowner, also came within the province of that Court. Before she could have her 'portion' she had to apply to Court, and until this Court application was finalised she was to be extremely short of money.

Lettice seems to have been badly advised as to what she should claim. Her application to the Court for her widow's entitlement was described as 'a suit for dower by Lettice, Countess of Essex, [who] by some froward advice did utterly renounce and refuse the jointure to her assigned by her late husband'. She claimed one third of his lands but 'was adjudged to be content with the jointure, with £60 per annum by her demanded'.[6] (Dower was a widow's life interest in a third of her husband's estate. Jointure was a wife's share under a marriage settlement). It was not until the end of April, seven months after her husband's death, that she wrote to tell Lord Burghley the good news, that she had been granted her decree in the Court of Wards for her 'portion of living'.

At the same time Lettice was concerned about an equally vital matter, to try to secure the best possible inheritance for her son. She was anxious not to do anything 'prejudicial unto my son', and described herself at this difficult time as 'content to respect my children more than myself'.

Essex's debts, incurred during his Irish campaign, did not die with him and the estate would be severely impoverished by them. This financial burden could crush her son. She therefore wrote to the Lord

Treasurer and Lord Chamberlain seeking their advice in dealing with the debts:

> I am not unmindful of the great debts wherein my son is left, which I trust by your Lordships' good order will be well mitigated during his minority with the revenues of the lands and leases left for the discharging thereof; chiefly if Her Majesty vouchsafe to deal graciously with him touching the debt unto her (as I trust she will).[7]

Lettice was too optimistic and Elizabeth did not release or reduce the debt owed to her. This was the ten thousand pounds Walter had borrowed from the queen at ten per cent interest to equip himself for his Ulster campaign. Her only hope of extricating herself from her serious financial problems lay in finding a new husband. The alternatives were non-existent.

Robert had, as planned, gone to live with his guardian Lord Burghley. Her daughters and her younger son remained with her during this period, continuing to take their lessons from their tutor Holmes, before going to live with their guardians the Earl and Countess of Huntingdon. Essex had taken a great deal of care over his children's future, even if he had been unable to leave them financially well-off.

Though it had been an early plan for Robert to be educated away from home, their father's wish to place Penelope and the others in his cousins' care, instead of leaving them with their mother, was made only on his last visit to Chartley. As he was at home with his family at the time their mother may well have been consulted and agreed with the decision. Even if he thought they would be better off with the Earl of Huntingdon as their guardian, this is not necessarily an indication of distrust in her. The fact that they needed a strong male protector must have weighed heavily. The Earl of Huntingdon was Walter's most powerful relative ruling the North in the queen's name as her Lord President.

For Penelope, Dorothy and the young Walter the time had come to leave Chartley and go to live with their guardians. Penelope as the eldest had to take charge of the others after the parting from their mother, their home and all they knew, as they set off for an unfamiliar world. The earl and countess lived mainly at Ashby-de-la-Zouche in Leicestershire, moving to York when the earl's duties as Lord President of the North took him there. The household was a pious one and the children were strictly brought up whilst in their guardians' care. The Countess of Huntingdon was a Dudley, sister to the Earls of Leicester and Warwick, and Philip Sidney's aunt. A formidable woman and a strict disciplinarian, she took into her home a number of young girls and educated them there, in a similar, though less illustrious way to Lord Burghley with his school for young boys. The education of these girls was in a style to prepare them for their future lives where the sole vocation open to them was marriage.

There is no first-hand information about Penelope and Dorothy's stay in the Huntingdon household, which lasted in Penelope's case for about four years. However, some information can be gleaned from another pupil at the school. This pupil later wrote her diary and it is from this diary, although covering the writer's adult years, that impressions of the education given can be gathered. The writer Lady Margaret Hoby, born Margaret Dakins, had closer connections with the Devereux family, for she was to marry the youngest child, Walter Devereux.

Margaret does not appear to have known any foreign languages, so Penelope's fluency in languages clearly came from her education at her parents' home. She turned out to be an accomplished household manager, not only running her home efficiently but involving herself in the making of medicines and remedies, and even carrying out some surgery and midwifery. Above all she appears as a woman of strong religious convictions, studying the Bible daily, her life centred on prayers. There is very little indeed of the lighter side, and though she could sing and play the alpharion (a stringed instrument), these accomplishments were used for the singing and playing of hymns. Margaret was seven years younger than Penelope and went into the Huntingdon household at an earlier, and more formative, age than the Devereux girls.

The countess seems to have been complacent about her talents for educating young girls, complimenting herself in a letter in this way: 'Though myself do say it, I think there will be none make question but I know how to breed and govern young gentlewomen.'[8] Her husband shared her views. His ideal woman 'fears God, loves the Gospel and hates Popery'. Undoubtedly from this standpoint they had a success with Margaret Dakins. Their influence over the characters of Penelope and

Dorothy Devereux is more difficult to discern. Perhaps these two went too late into their pious care for the influence to be strong. At any rate neither Devereux girl was to show the puritan ideals for women of docility and submission. It is easy to imagine how the constraints must have seemed very tedious to two vivacious and lively girls.

Meanwhile, their mother, released by her husband's careful arrangements for the children from the responsibilities of a young family, was free to remarry. Two years after his death, in September 1578, she married Robert Dudley Earl of Leicester, the queen's favourite.

Robert Dudley's friendship with Elizabeth had begun long ago in their childhood, when they had shared the same tutor. Her girlhood had held very few certainties and he remained from that time a rock on which she had learnt it was safe to rely. 'I have known her better than any man alive since she was eight years old,' he claimed proudly. She trusted him as she did no one else. When there were murmurs about their over-familiarity and rumours that she might marry him she answered (as Hubert Languet explained to the Duke of Saxony in 1561):

> That she had never thought of contracting a marriage with my Lord Robert; but she was more attached to him than to any of the others because when she was deserted by everybody in the reign of her sister not only did he never lessen in any degree his kindness and humble attention to her, but he even sold his possessions that he might assist her with money, and therefore she thought it just that she should make some return for his good faith and constancy.[9]

She rewarded his constancy by remaining loyal to him in return.

Lettice Knollys was an ambitious woman. She had seen her cousin Elizabeth crowned Queen of England. As Elizabeth's nearest female relative she expected her own position to be an elevated one. To this end she encouraged her first husband in his Irish enterprise, in the hopes of sharing in the fame and fortune to be won. When this proved disastrous and she was left an impoverished widow with four young children, she was still determined to succeed. The Earl of Leicester was a prize that many women envied, even the queen. Lettice was thirty-eight when she remarried and with Penelope then at the marriageable age of fifteen she was unlikely to have many such opportunities.

A great deal has been written about the relationship of Lettice Devereux and the Earl of Leicester prior to their marriage, much of it coloured by the anonymous libels subsequently circulated about Leicester. In these he was accused of having murdered his first wife Amy Robsart, murdering Lord Sheffield (whose wife had born him an illegitimate son before her marriage), committing adultery with Lettice Devereux whilst Walter was still alive and arranging to have him poisoned, as well as being a political tyrant who manipulated the queen.

Leicester had for thirty years, along with Lord Burghley, been one of the two most important men in England. As such and as the queen's favourite in a world of spying and intrigue he was a target for attack, the purpose of the libels being to discredit him with the queen. When these libels were published some years after the events they purported to describe they were investigated and refuted by the queen and the Privy Council. Nevertheless the scandals were taken up by historical novelists from Sir Walter Scott down.

An examination of the libels insofar as they relate to Leicester's relationship with the Countess of Essex shows that there had indeed been a suspicion that the Earl of Essex had been poisoned. Nevertheless there is no contemporaneous source connecting the alleged poisoning with Leicester. Sir Henry Sidney had examined the matter and concluded that the death was from natural causes, and reported accordingly. His official report had been accepted, but his private confirmation of the same views to his brother-in-law Leicester several months afterwards reinforces his conclusion.

Sir Henry wrote to his brother-in-law in February 1577 about the rumours:

I trust I have satisfied your lordship with my writing . . . touching the false and malicious bruit of the Earl of Essex's poisoning . . . I would not have doubted to have made Knell to have retracted his inconsiderate and foolish speech and writing; but God have prevented me, by taking him away, dying of the same disease that the Earl did; which most certainly was free from any poison; a mere flux, a disease appropriate to this country and whereof there died many in the later part of the last year, and some of mine own household, and yet free from any suspicion of poison.[10]

If the Earl of Leicester had been suspected of the poisoning, Sir Henry Sidney would not be writing to him in these terms. Sir Henry then went on to give as his opinion of the late Earl of Essex that he would have proved a 'violent enemy' of Leicester and saying he could not 'brook' the man. A very private letter indeed, meant only for Leicester's eyes. The connection of the alleged poisoning with the Earl of Leicester is of subsequent date, emanating from the later libels.

As regards the accusation of adultery, if there had been such a relationship between Leicester and Lettice whilst Walter was alive, it is difficult to explain why Leicester should abandon her after Walter's death at a time when she was almost destitute, and then reappear to marry her two years later. Had he been her lover at that time he would surely have been able to find means of assisting her. On balance the evidence goes against such a relationship whilst her husband was alive.

There was also a story about a secret wedding, later followed by the more formal but still quiet ceremony of September 1578. Philip Sidney has been credited with being one of the first people to know of the alleged earlier secret marriage because he referred in a letter to his uncle written in 1577 to 'my Lady and Aunt'.[11] However the identity of the uncle to whom the letter was addressed is not known, and it could just as easily be to one of his other married uncles, like the Earl of Huntingdon. It is not evidence of an earlier marriage. The marriage was performed at Wanstead at seven o'clock in the morning of the 21st September in the presence of only a few guests: the bride's father Sir Francis Knollys, the groom's brother the Earl of Warwick, his nephew the Earl of Pembroke, and Lord Roger North, a family friend. The reason for the secrecy is given in the chaplain's subsequent deposition as to the marriage, made three years after the event, that hints that the bride was pregnant: 'in a loose gown, as I remember'. However, nothing further was heard of a child at this time.

In his deposition the chaplain testified that the Earl of Leicester had 'signified that he had a good season forborne marriage in respect of Her Majesty's displeasure and that he was then for sundry respects and especially for the better quieting of his own conscience determined to marry forthwith with the right honourable Countess of Essex'.[12]

On the reverse side of this document is an unfinished deposition by Lord North to the same effect.

Leicester had given up all hope of marrying the queen. At the time of his remarriage he was in his mid-forties and he wanted a son and heir. His first marriage to Amy Robsart had been childless and his only child was the illegitimate son he had with Lady Sheffield.

Elizabeth had an aversion to marriage plans for any of her court, let alone for her favourite. She would not have given her consent had she been asked so that there was every reason to keep it quiet as long as possible. Lettice in fact needed the queen's consent to marry as the widow of a landowner owing the duty of knight-service to the crown. Failure to obtain this consent did not invalidate the marriage, but only involved those concerned in the payment of a fine. Marrying quietly without the queen's knowledge was the only sure way.

When Elizabeth eventually learnt the news a year later her anger was all that could have been predicted and dreaded. Lettice was banished permanently from court, though Leicester, once her initial anger with him had subsided, was able to climb back into favour.

So, by the marriage of Leicester and Lettice, the two families of Dudley and Devereux were united, but far from the way in which Walter Devereux had hoped.

Sir Philip Sidney

CHAPTER FIVE

The rich Lord Rich

During the years when Penelope was in her guardians' care, before coming up to court, her path is unlikely to have crossed Philip Sidney's. Philip during that period was either attending at court or visiting his sister Mary, now married to the Earl of Pembroke, in Wiltshire. Philip's career had been progressing in a number of ways. He had embarked on his first literary venture, a masque *The Lady of May*, a pastoral entertainment. It was composed for presentation before the queen in either May 1578 or 1579 when she visited Leicester at Wanstead, Essex, a house Leicester had recently acquired and the scene of his marriage to Lettice.

His diplomatic career too had got off to a fine start with a mission on which Elizabeth sent him in 1577 to represent her at the court of the Emperor Rudolph in Prague to present credentials to the new emperor and send condolences on the death of the late emperor. Whilst on this mission he was also to visit the other German princes as the queen's ambassador. This was a role that Philip saw himself as born and educated to fulfill. He also saw it as a stepping-stone to a greater ambition, as an opportunity to investigate the possibilities of a Protestant league and to emerge as the spokesman for the international Protestant cause.

Proud of his position, Philip would set up his coat-of-arms on a tablet wherever he stopped on his journey, with an inscription describing himself as the most illustrious and generous Philip Sidney, son of the Deputy of Ireland, nephew of the Earls of Warwick and Leicester, and Ambassador to the Emperor of the great Queen Elizabeth. He took himself and his position very seriously.

However, Philip Sidney's career as a diplomat received a set-back in the next two years (1578-9) when the proposed marriage plans for the queen with the Duke of Alençon, now Duke of Anjou, were revived. This French duke was the younger brother of Henri, the Duke of Anjou, who had eleven years previously courted the English queen. When that marriage proposal was abandoned Francis, the younger brother, then a mere seventeen-year-old, had been put forward in his stead. When Henri succeeded to the French throne, Francis became the new Duke of Anjou, known to the court in general as Monsieur, and called by Elizabeth her Frog.

Sidney, as a fervent Protestant, was strongly opposed to the marriage of his queen with a French Catholic duke. The new Duke of Anjou, who had once shown Huguenot sympathies, had become devoutly Catholic. Walsingham and Leicester both opposed the marriage. Sidney, meeting the Earl of Oxford, a supporter of the marriage, at the tennis court, found himself involved in a violent argument. The earl called Sidney 'a puppy' and Philip challenged him to a duel. Elizabeth forced him to climb down on the basis that it was unfitting for him as a mere commoner to challenge an earl.

Undeterred, Sidney wrote an open letter to the queen, setting out the arguments against the marriage and the presentation of this letter, not unnaturally, lost him the queen's favour. It was an ill-judged act which could not fail to set the queen against him. One possible explanation is that he was encouraged by his uncle Leicester to send it, as a means of expressing opposition to the marriage without himself being a party to the criticism. Even so, it was indicative of a blind spot in Philip, an indifference to the consequences to himself where matters of principle were at stake. It was a foretaste of his still more quixotic behaviour on the field of battle. He had sufficient tact to retire from court in early 1580 and did not reappear again until New Year's Day 1581, when he presented the queen with a 'whip garnished with small diamonds' in token of his submission to her will.[1] He was to spend a considerable part of the year at court.

For the seventeen-year-old Penelope her guardians' main duty now was to find her a husband. Tucked away in the north she was unlikely to find a suitable match and it was therefore important for her to appear at court. To this end the Earl of Huntingdon had spoken to the queen about his two wards and she 'was pleased last year to give me leave at times convenient to put her Highness in mind of these young ladies'. Now the queen had agreed to receive Penelope at court as one of her maids of honour. Philip Sidney was at court to welcome his aunt the Countess of Huntingdon when she arrived in January. With her she brought her beautiful ward Penelope.

The year Penelope came to court, 1581, was a particularly spectacular year for festivities and entertainments, some of them annual court events, others arranged specially in honour of the proposals for the queen's marriage with the Duke of Anjou. It was traditional to celebrate the anniversary of the queen's accession by a revival of the medieval courtly sports of jousting and tilting. The first recorded account of an accession tilt was in 1581 and that year the custom was extended to other occasions. Philip Sidney played a leading part in these, devising the entertainments and writing speeches as well as competing as a champion knight. The first of these events, with Philip as a leading contender, took place on the 22nd January. When a week later on the 29th January Penelope arrived at court with her guardian everyone would still be talking about the spectacular occasion. Soon she was herself to be caught up in all the brilliance of court society. In February, shortly after her arrival, there was a great banquet, 'finer than ever had been seen in England since the time of King Henry', on board Drake's ship, the *Golden Hind*, at Deptford, given for Anjou's secretary.[2]

By April the preparations to welcome the French visitors occupied all the queen's attention as she brushed aside state matters in order to concentrate on the arrangements for the celebrations. Even her Orders in Council reflected the prevailing interest when she issued an order that all the rich dress materials, cloth of gold, velvet and silk, were to be sold at a reduction of twenty-five per cent, to encourage her courtiers to deck themselves out in fine new clothes.

On the 20th April when the French visitors reached London there was a series of lavish banquets for them given in turn by the queen, the Earl of Leicester and other lords, with entertainments of plays and masques.

There was another great jousting event in May when Elizabeth 'most royally feasted and banqueted' the French commissioners. The elaborate speeches written for the occasion bear the mark of Sidney's authorship. As well as devising the pageant Philip, with three other knights, 'calling themselves the Four Foster-children of Desire' attacked 'the fortress of perfect beauty' (symbolising the queen), and conceded defeat at the hands of twenty-two knights guarding it. Philip also played a leading role in the third tournament in celebration of the queen's accession in November.

For Penelope, released from the constraints of her four years with her puritan guardians in the bleak north, the life of the court was a dazzling new experience. The arrival of a beautiful girl with golden hair and striking black eyes must have caused something of a stir. Although a country girl, Penelope had the presence and social graces that fitted her for the court life. Her musical talents and love of dancing would bring her early attention.

At the centre of this brave new world stood the splendid figure of Philip Sidney, the young man whom it had been intended she should marry. When Penelope arrived a week after the tournament Philip was still basking in the admiration following its success. She was naturally more than interested to meet the man whose destiny was so closely linked with her own. She was seeing for the first time as an adult the man whom her father had intended her to marry, though by the remarriage of her mother to his uncle and benefactor they had become related in a very different way.

The countess and her ward were graciously received by the queen and Penelope became one of the queen's maids of honour. From the start of her reign Elizabeth had surrounded herself with young girls of aristocratic families, many of them her relations, and it was a mark of honour to serve their queen in this way. Penelope's mother had been one of the first maids of honour. Now, the girls were very much younger than their mistress. They formed an important part of the social life at court, attending the queen at dinner, at dances, masques, plays and feasts, ready to entertain their mistress by their singing and playing, gossiping with her and at the same time performing all the little personal attentions she required. Amongst the innumerable little tasks that fell to them were 'to bear Her Highness's mantle and other furniture and to carry the cup of grace during dinner'.[3] The life of the maids of honour was not always one of pleasure. Elizabeth was a difficult mistress and would often chide her attendants 'for small neglects, in such wise as to make these fair maids often cry and bewail in piteous sort'.[4]

The truth was she could be easily aroused to jealousy if any of the ladies attempted to outshine her. The famous story of Lady Mary Howard's gown is a case in point. This gown was so beautiful that Elizabeth coveted it for herself, but trying it on and finding it too short told its unfortunate owner, 'I am mindful it shall never become thee, as being too fine. It fitteth neither well.' And so the dress was 'laid up till after the queen's death'.[5] Penelope was not so unwise as to offend Elizabeth by appearing to compete, as her mother had done. In spite of her great beauty she was sufficiently judicious in her demeanour as never to incur the queen's jealousy.

Elizabeth was determined to remain the most admired lady at her own court. As she grew older and uglier she could not bear to see herself in her glass. Yet her courtiers were expected to continue playing the role of her lovers, fighting for her at the tournaments like medieval knights paying their addresses to an idealised and unattainable mistress, impossibly beautiful, eternally young. It created a highly artificial atmosphere at court in relation to love.

Elizabeth also had very strict views on the morals and marriages of her maids, exhorting them 'to remain in virgin state as much as may be'. The penalties for disobeying the royal wishes in this were severe.

Penelope had been plunged into an entirely new world, one where she was very quickly to establish herself, but there was to be no breathing-space allowed her to settle into her new life. On her arrival at court the Countess of Huntingdon lost no time in finding a husband for her young ward and very quickly alighted on Robert Rich. Robert was the grandson of Sir Richard Rich, that successful lawyer who made both a name and a fortune for himself helping Henry VIII in the suppression of the monasteries. His main notoriety perhaps stems from having given false evidence against Sir Thomas More. Later he himself became Lord Chancellor. This was how he had climbed to success and this was the basis on which the Rich family's great wealth had been founded. Their home was at Leighs in Essex, a former priory, granted to Sir Richard by King Henry. Sir Richard Rich had made great alterations to the priory, turning it into a magnificent dwelling. In addition Sir Richard had collected other estates, mainly in Essex, from the dissolved religious houses.

On his death the title of Baron Rich of Leighs descended to Robert Rich's father, the second Lord Rich. He had been the first of the volunteers to accompany Walter Devereux in his Ulster campaign and he was also to be the first of the deserters, preferring the comforts of his home to fighting in Ireland. He died on the 27th February, 1581. Robert's elder brother had died only the previous year, leaving Robert, the second son, to inherit the title.[6] Robert Rich was thus the third generation of the new aristocracy.

Robert does not appear to have inherited, along with the great wealth, the brains and abilities of his lawyer grandfather. Instead he seems to have taken more after his own father, for he too was time and again to disappear when there was trouble or danger.

Unlike Penelope's brothers, Philip Sidney and other sons of the nobility, Robert Rich did not receive a university education. Indeed his education was more limited than Penelope's own. Whilst she was fluent in French, Italian and Spanish, he had no knowledge of languages, 'a poor man of no language', he described himself, although he acquired a smattering of French during a visit to France in his middle years.[7] Again in his adult years he received some legal training at Gray's Inn for service as a Justice of the Peace, a position which his father and grandfather had held before him.[8] Apart from his undistinguished service as a J.P., Robert did not in fact make his mark in any career or enterprise. His main claim to fame, aside from his marriage, was as the rich Lord Rich.

At the age of twenty-one Robert had become a great landowner in Essex. He immediately began asserting himself in a most unpleasant manner, bullying and harassing his tenants. One of his first actions was the forcible eviction of a family from their home. Robert's grandfather had given to William White, a park keeper, the right to occupy the old lodge at the great park of Pleshey in Essex. Robert's father had subsequently confirmed this grant. On coming into the title Robert had seen fit to deny the grant, but instead of going to law in the proper way, decided to take the law into his own hands. He used violence to have White and his family evicted from their home. So much force was used that Rich was accused of endangering their lives. He had besieged the family for a week, they had run out of food and were starving. Because of this harassment the Sheriff of Essex was on the 20th December 1581 asked to intervene. The Privy Council requested Rich to show some charitable consideration towards the White family, but if he would not, ordered him to put his case before the proper court of law and not use violence.[9]

Despite this early brush with the law, Robert Rich was himself appointed to serve as a local magistrate. Because of his position as a great landowner he became a Justice of the Peace, sitting on the bench at the quarter sessions and assize courts in Essex. The duties involved dealing with minor transgressions of the law, quarrels between neighbours, poaching and other such misdemeanours. As a J.P. Rich took statements from the witnesses and, after hearing the case with the other members of the bench, gave judgement, fining wrongdoers, or binding them over to keep the peace, or in the more serious cases committing them to the Sheriff. It was worthy work, much of it dull and routine, but necessary.

However, even at this level Robert Rich was accused of incompetence. His name heads the list of justices in the reports of cases, but if this gives the impression that he had been appointed chairman on merit it is misleading. As a baron he took precedence over the other members.

The accusation of incompetence was levelled at him, along with much more, by the Vicar of Felsted. This vicar, William Rust, had been given the benefices of both Felsted and Rayleigh in Essex by Robert's grandfather and he had held them for twenty-four years. In 1582, the year after he came of age, Robert in another burst of aggression deprived the vicar of the Rayleigh benefice.

The vicar's reply was to launch a verbal attack on Lord Rich, on several fronts. First he accused Rich, with justification, of depriving him of his living: 'if Lord Rich might have his will to put men out of their benefices he would keep their livings and have some serve the cure for little or nothing'. His next ground of attack might be mere abuse, but does not suggest that Rich was exactly popular: 'there were none of Lord Rich's neighbours but would be glad if he were further from them'. The third barb was thrust at Rich the Justice of the Peace: 'Lord Rich was in the commission of the peace but as a cipher in agreement, for he could do nothing.'

Ten years later Lord Rich was again to be abused in court by two defendants aggrieved at being brought before him after having already been discharged by a higher court. These men, George and John Raye, not only exhibited 'a very arrogant, inconsiderate and slanderous bill of complaint' to Lord Rich and the other justices present but also 'very unreverently demeaned themselves (especially George) in the face of the whole court'. The exact form this took is not dwelt on. Their father too was in trouble at the same Sessions, when he contemptuously tore up a warrant from Lord Rich and the other justices.[10]

From these glimpses it is apparent that Lord Rich was far from being a respected or popular figure in the local life of Essex.

Robert's main preoccupation at about the time of his wedding to Penelope was with the puritan religion. His father had been a leading

Essex puritan and Robert continued in the same vein.

Puritanism had begun to take hold as a growing movement of dissent amongst those who believed that the reformed church did not go far enough in stripping away ritual and ceremony. Puritan ministers denounced in their sermons indulgence in pleasure in all its forms, play-going and card-games, music and even 'the horrible vice of pestiferous dancing', in fact many of the pleasures to be enjoyed in the life of the court. The very pleasures Penelope most enjoyed.

The holding of non-conformist religious services was not permitted but enforcement action against puritan meetings depended upon the strength of feeling against the movement of the individual bishops. The Bishop of London at this time, Bishop Aylmer, whose diocese included Essex, was a fervent anti-puritan.

It came to the queen's ears that 'there were disorders practised in Essex and in particular in the house of Lord Rich' and Aylmer was told that it was her 'command to him to forbid them'. He told the queen

> that he had many great storms with the late Lord Rich and that now lately the present Lord Rich and his bastard uncle and another came into his house at Fulham to solicit him to licence Wright to preach in his diocese, and he had refused to do so, but that the Lord's aforesaid uncle did hereupon so shake him up that . . . he was never so abused at any man's hands since he was born.[11]

Robert Wright was an irregular preacher who has often been mistakenly identified with that Robert Wright who was tutor to the Earl of Essex.[12] Because he had been ordained at Antwerp and not in England he had no licence to preach and in fact denied he needed one. He believed that the congregation should elect its own minister, never used the Prayer Book and boasted his ignorance of its contents. Lord Rich supported Wright in his views, inviting him to form a congregation at Rochford Hall, one of his two residences in Essex. There they held 'nightly catechizing, announced by the ringing of a bell', and many of the local people went there rather than the parish church.[13] Lord Rich had tried to bully Bishop Aylmer into granting Wright a licence. The Bishop refused but when the services went ahead could hardly, as he said 'send a power of men to fetch him out of a nobleman's house'.

Instead the matter was brought before the ecclesiastical court. On the 17th October 1581, only two weeks before his wedding, Lord Rich, his uncle (and later Wright) appeared before the Bishop of London's court at Weston.[14] Wright was found to have had the temerity to criticise the celebration of the queen's accession day, asking 'if they would make it a holy day and so make our queen an idol'.[15] He was committed to the Fleet prison for his offences and Rich's uncle to the Marshalsea prison. Lord Rich himself was fortunate to escape with a stern warning. His impending marriage to the queen's maid of honour could well have tipped the balance in his favour. Robert was always to show due respect for Penelope's powers of influence.

Only eleven days after Robert succeeded to the title, the Earl of Huntingdon was writing from Newcastle to Lord Burghley about a proposed marriage between Robert and Penelope, at the same time writing to Sir Francis Walsingham, the queen's principal secretary. He informed them that the late Lord Rich had 'left to his heir a proper gentleman and one in years very fit for my Lady Penelope Devereux' and asking their assistance so that 'with the favour and liking of Her Majesty' a match might be arranged.[16]

Robert Rich was very enthusiastic about the proposed marriage to the beautiful and vivacious Penelope, daughter of an earl, making a special trip to Cambridge to win the favour of her brother, the fourteen-year-old Earl of Essex. He took the boy off on a trip and together they left Cambridge without the young earl having asked his guardian's permission. In a letter of apology written to Lord Burghley in Latin in August 1581 Robert asked his guardian's pardon for the escapade, describing it as 'honest pleasure', and he wrote glowingly of Lord Rich who 'most kindly called on me at the University' as 'very dear to me'.[17] Rich had been responsible for getting his future brother-in-law into trouble, but Essex loyally took the blame.

Shortly afterwards the young earl was removed from Cambridge, partly because of the great debts he had run up there and partly because it was noted that there was interference with his studies.[18] It was not specifically stated who was the main culprit. His tutor Wright had been negligent, but Robert Rich was clearly at least in part responsible for keeping Essex from his studies.[19]

Her mother does not appear to have played a prominent part in arranging the marriage. Lettice no longer had any legal control over the matter since the Earl and Countess of Huntingdon were Penelope's guardians and were responsible for her. Nevertheless a woman of her strong temperament could no doubt have exercised influence. The choice had been made by the family, for the family, since Walter had given the care of his daughters and younger son to the earl as his nearest male kinsman. The all-important financial considerations outweighed everything else. Although Lettice herself was no longer poor after her marriage to Leicester, she could not expect to use his estate to assist her first family, so that Penelope's own financial situation had not changed. Besides, women were expected to sacrifice their personal feelings in marriage for the good of the family and many women did just that.

Lettice herself was far away from her daughter at the time, living in Staffordshire and cut off from the court. It was she who had born the brunt of the queen's anger at the marriage of her favourite Leicester. She had been banished for ever from court and the queen did not relent. Leicester however had been returned to favour and forgiven. At this time Lettice was at the age of forty-one pregnant with her and Leicester's son, the future Lord Denbigh. For Elizabethan women giving birth was a danger at the best of times, and at her age it was a greater hazard. Her life was no doubt fully occupied with the birth and her new baby. The child was in fact to live for only three years.

Penelope does not seem to have blamed her mother for the choice. Indeed she named her first child after her mother. If anything she became closer to her mother after her marriage, when she chose to spend a great deal of time in her mother's house in preference to being with her husband.

What did her earlier proposed suitor feel about the marriage negotiations? Philip Sidney was certainly around the court at the time the wedding was being arranged. He had reappeared at court on New Year's Day 1581 and Penelope arrived at court with her guardian, his aunt, at the end of that month. He had become a member of parliament and attended the sessions of the House of Commons regularly from January to March and during the summer he participated in the events at court. This was therefore the time when they first got to know each other. As we later learn, he did not fall in love with her at first sight, but he certainly liked her at first meeting. Philip, with a youthful eagerness to please the uncle he so admired, may even have helped in the marriage arrangements. As it was a family wish to have Penelope married off quickly, it would not have occurred to him initially to do other than assist his uncles and aunt. It may even have been his suggestion that Robert Rich might be a possible husband for her. He was later to torment himself that he had been responsible for his own unhappiness.

Philip's personal prospects had received a severe blow. The birth of a son to Leicester and Lettice that summer had materially affected his future. As a result of the birth he was disinherited from the glittering prize of being the Earl of Leicester's heir. Far from hiding his disappointment, Philip drew dramatic attention to it. His motto was 'Spero' (I hope), and he appeared at the November 1581 tilts with this device on his shield: 'SPERAVI' (I have hoped), crossed through, to show his hopes of inheriting had gone.[20] Philip could turn anything into pageant material.

Money continued to be an increasing problem for the Sidney family, just as it was for the Devereux. On the 10th October 1581 Philip Sidney wrote to Lord Burghley asking for a grant of a hundred pounds a year from the queen for relief 'being wholly out of comfort, asking for some token, that his friends might see he had not utterly lost his time'.[21] Such were Philip's preoccupations at the time.

All Penelope's relatives and friends had either concurred or acquiesced in the marriage proposal, though she herself never consented to the arrangements.

The necessary consent of the queen was obtained. Robert Rich did not attract her jealousy. From a practical point of view he was an asset to the Devereux family. Penelope would cease to be a financial burden to the family, once her dowry had been paid, and Elizabeth herself would then stand a better chance of recovering her debt from them. The marriage had been recommended by her advisers, Lord Burghley and Sir Francis Walsingham, as well as by the Earl of Leicester, now back in her favour. Robert's social status was not on a par with Penelope's but it was counterbalanced by his wealth.

All was now set, with only the bride herself remaining to be convinced. We know what Penelope's feelings were from a later source, and though the words are Lord Mountjoy's (later to become her lover) the description of the situation must come from her: She

being in the power of her friends, was married against her will unto one against whom she did protest at the very solemnity, and ever after; between whom, from the first day, there ensued continual discord, although the same fears that forced her to marry constrained her to live with him.[22]

The marriage has been dated from a letter written by Richard Brakinbury, gentleman usher at court, to the Earl of Rutland on the 18th September 1581:

In London seventy-five died of the plague last week . . . My Lady and mistress will be married about All-hallowtide to Lord Rich. Though your Lordship is mindless of beauty, our maids are very fair.[23]

A nicely oblique compliment to Penelope. All-hallowtide was All Saints Day, the lst November 1581.

After the wedding ceremony there would have been a great feast, with music and dancing for the honoured guests. If the puritan Lord Rich suffered any qualms about such festivities he would have had to put aside such feelings for the time being in order to make himself acceptable to Penelope's family and so secure his bride. We cannot doubt that the young couple received some lavish wedding presents. One of the gifts, given to her by Lord Roger North, a wedding guest, was a silver cup 'to give to my Lady Penelope on her marriage'.[24] It was entered in his household book for 29th October 1581 and cost £11.16s, a substantial sum, exceeding the value of the New Year's gift North presented to the queen.

The wedding was an important occasion, uniting as it did two prominent families, more particularly on the Devereux side. It was somewhat overshadowed by a great public event for it so happened that it coincided with the arrival in London of Francis, Duke of Anjou, the queen's suitor.

CHAPTER SIX

'He did Study in all Things to Torment Her'

After her marriage Penelope Rich remained at court and continued her attendances on the queen. Her home had become Leighs Priory, Lord Rich's house in Essex, but during the course of her marriage she was to live with her husband as little as possible. Instead she managed to spend her time at court or in her brother's houses, or with her mother, returning to her husband's home only when he insisted.

Why she did this is clear. She had never wanted to marry Lord Rich and marriage did nothing to lessen her initial dislike. Philip Sidney was to accuse Lord Rich of 'foul abuse' of Penelope. Much later Lord Mountjoy was to write in not dissimilar terms of Rich. 'He did study in all things to torment her,' is one of his accusations.[1] These attacks must have had some justification even though both accusers were Penelope's champions and devoted to her. Lord Rich had certainly shown a fondness for bullying in other areas of his life and it would be true to type for him to have tried similar tactics in his relations with Penelope.

Lord Rich had been forewarned and yet still went ahead with the marriage. He has been described as 'rough and uncourtly in manners and conversation, dull and uneducated', and as such he was not likely to endear himself to Penelope.[2] Above all he was a puritan, hostile to every form of pleasure.

Penelope had escaped from one puritan household, that of her guardians, to the pleasures of the life of the court. On her marriage she resisted, so far as she could, being sent back again into a similar environment, to a house where there was 'nightly catechizing', with a husband who expected her to conform to the puritan ideals, of obedience and submission.

To have an idea of the standard of behaviour a man like Lord Rich would expect from his wife, we can turn to another contemporary puritan marriage. Katherine Stubbs, wife of the moralist, married at fifteen and died in 1590, before she was twenty. Her husband lamented her death, as well he might, praising her because '"she obeyed the commandment of the Apostle, who biddeth women to be silent and to learn of their husbands at home". She was in every way a model wife, never quarrelling, never going out when her husband was away, sober, humble, taking neither delicate food nor strong drink, never swearing, a good housekeeper, loyal to her husband, merry when he was merry, sad when he was sad, never crossing him but rather persuading him with wise advice.'[3]

If Lord Rich hoped for such qualities in a wife, Penelope must have been a disappointment. Penelope showed no natural inclination towards the puritan notion of female subservience. Faced with the situation in reality, she was not prepared to subordinate herself to Lord Rich. He had failed to win her respect, let alone her love. The puritan ideals for women, imposed upon them by men, became anathema to her.

It must have been almost immediately after her marriage that Philip Sidney fell in love with her. Until that moment Sidney had viewed marriage in the accepted way of his time, as a matter of family alliance. He was brought up to regard marriage in that light, and up to this point he had always done what was expected of him. In his particularly privileged position there were opportunities open to him to form an important political alliance by marriage. One of the proposals made to him had been marriage with a princess of the House of Orange. If this proposal had proceeded his royal bride would have brought him as her dowry the states of Holland and Zealand, and made him a major Protestant ruler in Europe.

Sidney's letter to the queen against her marriage to the Duke of Anjou had caused him to retire from court in 1580. Since his hopes for advancement in a political career lay at court, it effected a change of direction for him, away from the political arena and further towards the life of a poet.

The year 1581 in particular marked a turning point in his life, when three events of the deepest significance to him occurred: the birth of an heir to his uncle, the Earl of Leicester thereby disinheriting him; the death of his great friend and mentor Hubert Languet; the marriage of Penelope Devereux to Lord Rich.

We know very little about the details of Philip Sidney's romance with Penelope Rich. That it was no mere figment of his poetic imagination is clear. It is also apparent that it began after her marriage. Philip was an earnest young man, grave and grown up even as a child. His friend Fulke Greville said of him; 'though I lived with him and knew him from a child, yet I never knew him other than a man'.

Elizabethan children were expected to behave as miniature adults but it must have been present in Philip to a remarkable extent and contributed to the way he was treated seriously even when very young. He recognised his over-earnestness as a fault. 'I am ready to admit that I am often more serious than my age or pursuits require.'

Initially the vivacious Penelope may have found her step-father's nephew rather a daunting figure. To a young country girl he would appear enormously self-assured, even proud and haughty. As they got to know each other better she would find him a kind and sympathetic listener and a passionate crusader against injustice. Once he felt that she had been wronged by the forced marriage he became her champion. Thereafter it was a short step to fall in love with her. This high-spirited girl would not have allowed him to be always so grave. In her company he could be young and light-hearted for the first time.

Sidney had returned to court at the New Year of 1581, offering his gift of a jewelled whip to the queen. He was present at court during most of that year, as was Penelope Devereux, arriving with her guardian in late January. He remained at court until about six weeks after her wedding on the 1st November. He left court in mid-December to spend Christmas with his family and did not return to London until the following March, when he was at court for two or three months before going to spend the summer with his father at Hereford, near the border of Wales. It was probably in that summer of 1582 that he wrote a series of poems around his relationship with Penelope, *Astrophil and Stella*. This means that the events it describes, insofar as they are factual, must have taken place over a very short period, almost immediately before they were written. Certainly the poems relate to Penelope as a married woman, Lady Rich, and so do not pre-date the wedding of the previous November.

There are a hundred and eight sonnets and eleven songs in the sequence. Sidney, though not merely writing a verse diary, makes it abundantly clear that they are autobiographical. He chose as his theme the events of his own immediate experience and identified himself explicitly with Astrophil, the lover. Less directly but just as clearly, he identified

Penelope Rich with Stella. The autobiographical element of the work is inextricably part of the poetry and cannot be ignored.

Sidney did not write the poems for publication. They were intended for private presentation to the woman whom they celebrated. Some perhaps may have been privately circulated, with the greatest discretion, to a few of his closest friends. He was not writing, as his later imitators were, for a patron but to a woman who was his social equal. Writing freely, he chose to make the identities plain, revealing himself and Penelope as lovers.

The first requirement is to establish that the lovers are indeed Philip and Penelope. There is ample evidence for this, so much so that one wonders why there have been doubts. Astrophil's name means 'lover of the star', and Stella 'star'. 'Phil' as well as meaning 'lover' is, of course, an abbreviation of Philip. Sidney thus identifies himself with Astrophil. He also does this in other ways, most directly in Sonnet 30 where he speaks of 'my father' and refers to his father as having 'half-tamed Ulster'. As we know Sir Henry Sidney had indeed played a role in Ulster and had been governor of Ireland three times. Again, in Sonnet 65 he refers to his own coat of arms, directly speaking of himself, Sidney, rather than of Astrophil as a separate person. Stella also has her coat of arms clearly identified as the Devereux arms in Sonnet 13. She is beautiful, black-eyed and golden-haired, like Penelope. (The poet Henry Constable referred to her 'black sparkling eyes' and her hair as 'waves of gold'.) She is married and her name is Rich. These facts emerge from reading the sonnets.

Confusion as to her identity arose in two ways. Firstly, the first publication of the poems, which occurred after Sidney's death, omitted the three sonnets most clearly identifying Stella with Penelope Rich (sonnets 24, 35 and 37). Secondly, the confusion of Stella with Frances Walsingham (daughter of Sir Francis Walsingham, the queen's principal secretary) whom Sidney later married, seems to have been either as a courtesy to his widow after his death when the poems were published, or as a form of censorship on the part of commentators reluctant to reveal that the aspiring Protestant leader could be deeply in love with another man's wife.

Three sonnets (24, 35 and 37 – set out in the Appendix) identify Stella as Penelope Rich by punning on the name Rich. Sonnet 24 contains the most powerful invective against Lord Rich. He is:

that rich fool, who by blind fortune's lot
The richest gem of love and life enjoys,
And can with foul abuse such beauties blot

In Sonnet 35 Sidney neatly tells us that Stella's name is Rich: 'Fame' he says, 'Doth even grow rich naming my Stella's name.'

In Sonnet 37 he asks us a riddle and himself supplies the answer. It is a paean of praise to his mistress, rich (the word is repeated seven times) in so many gifts, but who

Hath no misfortune but that Rich she is.

Her only misfortune is to be Lady Rich. These three sonnets, clearly identifying Stella as Lady Rich, were the ones discreetly omitted from the first publication of the poems after Sidney's death.

That Astrophil is in love with a married woman is clear from Sonnet 78. He complains of the monster who infects their love and asks in the final line, the rhetorical question:

Is it not evil that such a devil wants horns?

The horns are the horns of the cuckold. The point that she is married is made again in the Eighth Song where he says:

Her fair neck a foul yoke bore.

It is the yoke of matrimony, what Sidney himself had so lightly referred to as the 'chains of matrimony' in his letter to Hubert Languet four years previously.

He goes to add:

In his sight her yoke did vanish.

She could forget she was married when she was with him. This shows that he comforted her after her unhappy marriage, and it was out of this that their love developed.

Once these facts have been established we do not need to go one stage further and expect every incident in every poem to be autobiographical. Sidney is using a basis of reality on which to build his sonnets. Astrophil and Stella are dramatic alter egos of himself and Penelope. In some poems they have merged completely with their creator and his own mistress, in others, particularly some of the songs, they are separate entities, at times a shepherd and his shepherdess. But Sidney does not expect us to believe that this is a simple shepherd speaking, he wants us to see the additional figures of himself and his mistress alongside their dramatic counterparts. This was the intended effect of a complex and subtle poet, to give additional layers of feeling and undercurrents of meaning.

Three sonnets (nos. 2, 30 and 33) are of particular interest as illuminating the personal lives of Philip and Penelope.

Sonnet 2 (set out in the Appendix) is particularly revealing. It traces the development of Sidney's love directly reflecting his own experience. It begins:

> Not at first sight, nor with a dribbed shot,
> Love gave the wound, which while I breathe will bleed;
> But known worth did in mine of time proceed,
> Till, by degrees, it had full conquest got.
> I saw, and liked; I liked, but loved not;
> I loved, but straight did not what Love decreed:

('dribbed' means ineffectual or random)

Sidney had not fallen in love with Penelope at first sight. In his case, real life contradicted convention. Marlowe was later to ask his famous rhetorical question: 'Whoever loved that loved not at first sight?' echoing a universal sentiment. Sidney's line, unromantic by comparison, reflects a truth personal to him. There would be no particular point in saying he did not love at first sight unless he was using his own experience. His first sight of Penelope may have been at Chartley in the summer of 1575.

Whether then or later, he did not fall in love on sight but gradually, as he grew to know her worth. The period when he saw and liked, 'liked but loved not', must have been the time when she was preparing for her marriage to Lord Rich. Penelope's attractions for Philip were by no means just the obvious ones of her beauty and charm, for all her undoubted physical appeal. He was at pains to insist that he liked her long before he fell in love with her and that his liking grew out of knowing her value. For Penelope to be courted in this way, praised not only for her beauty but for her 'known worth', was the very antithesis of the treatment she had received at the hands of Lord Rich. It would be difficult to imagine two more different men than the chivalrous Sidney and the 'rough, uncourtly' Rich.

Sonnet 30 (set out in the Appendix) is important both for dating purposes and for showing us in concrete terms Sidney's changed attitude to world events once he has fallen in love. The poem refers to seven topics of international importance which were current in the summer of 1582. Sidney, world-traveller and international diplomat that he is, is asked by 'busy wits' for his views on weighty political questions affecting Turkey, Poland, Russia, France, Holland, Ulster and Scotland. He tries to answer 'But know not how: for still I think of you' he tells her.

For the man who saw himself as the figurehead of the international Protestant cause to speak in these terms would no doubt diminish him in the eyes of the politicians had they been likely to read it. The sonnets as we have noted were in fact never widely circulated, let alone published, in Sidney's lifetime, so personally revealing were they.

This is no mere poetic platitude of the conventional lover giving up the world for his mistress. Once it is expressed in these specific terms Sidney ceases to see himself as a wholly serious politician. This attitude reflects a turning point in his political career, which indeed never fulfilled its earlier promise.

Sonnet 33 (set out below) is the most poignant of all the sonnets. It is a poem of intense regret for the marriage that might have been between Penelope and himself.

> I might! – unhappy word – O me, I might,
> And then would not, or could not, see my bliss;
> Till now wrapt in a most infernal night,

I find how heav'nly day, wretch! I did miss.
Heart, rent thyself, thou dost thyself but right;
No lovely Paris made thy Helen his;
No force, no fraud robb'd thee of thy delight,
Nor Fortune of thy fortune author is;
But to myself myself did give the blow,
While too much wit, forsooth, so troubled me,
That I respects for both our sakes must show:
And yet could not, by rising morn foresee
How fair a day was near: O punish'd eyes,
That I had been more foolish, or more wise!

It begins with a heartfelt cry. He is torturing himself with the thought of what might have been. The simplicity and directness of the first two lines come from a deep well of feeling. There is irony in the line:

No lovely Paris made thy Helen his.

If the parallel were taken literally, Sidney would be Menelaus, the deceived husband in the triangle, but it is Lord Rich who has this role in real life whilst Sidney himself was the Paris who was trying to steal her. Instead, Sidney seems to cast himself in the role of her true husband, since he was intended for her by her father and under the marriage treaty that was never fulfilled.

He goes on to torment himself with the thought that he was himself responsible for his own misery. It was not force, fraud, or fortune that was responsible:

'But to myself myself did give the blow'.

The implication in this is that Philip himself assisted in the arrangements for Penelope's marriage to Lord Rich and failed to take his opportunity, which gives added poignancy to his suffering. The main people concerned in the wedding plans were his uncles Leicester and Huntingdon so that this explanation is a likely one.

The reference in the lines:

> And yet could not by rising morn foresee
> How fair a day was near

is to his first meeting with her, when she was very young, perhaps at Chartley, when he was unable to appreciate her or what she would become. Although he blames himself for his lost happiness, her extreme youth when the marriage treaty was made clearly contributed.

After the earlier sonnets depicting the turmoils of a young man in love, there is a central group of sonnets showing the struggle between virtue and love. Astrophil/Sidney is demanding a physical expression for their love. Paradoxically it is Stella/Penelope who is concerned for his honour and eventually, 'passion-rent', he parts from her.

The final evidence that Philip and Penelope were lovers comes not from the poems but from life, long after the event. It was to be at his death, as famous as any in English history, that the vision of Penelope Rich was to haunt him in his last moments.

By then the affair was long since over and Philip himself had in the meantime married. Matrimonial plans for Philip began again after Penelope's marriage. In December 1581, a month after her wedding, he wrote to Francis Walsingham, the queen's principal secretary, with whom he had stayed whilst in Paris and now a close personal friend, sending 'humble salutations . . . to yourself, my good Lady, and my exceeding like to be good friend'.[4] 'Friend' in Elizabethan terms meant wife or lover, so that as early as this date, when Frances herself was only fourteen, it appears a marriage between Philip and Walsingham's daughter was contemplated. However, it is not heard of again until February 1583, when several references to it appeared in correspondence.

The other marriage proposal for him about this time was to Penelope's younger sister, Dorothy. With Penelope disposed of, Leicester began making plans for Dorothy Devereux. At the end of January 1582, he drafted a will to make provisions for his baby son, Lord Denbigh, and added that as there had been 'some talk of marriage between my well beloved nephew Philip Sidney and the Lady Dorothy Devereux' and as 'my hearty and earnest wish was and is that it be so, for the great good will and liking I have to each party . . . I do most heartily desire that such love and liking might be between them as might bring a marriage.'[5] We note, this time, the saving clause that there should be 'love and liking' between the couple, so singularly absent from Penelope's marriage. He made provision for a dowry of two thousand pounds over and above her father's bequest and also agreed to provide a yearly income for the couple. However, nothing came of this proposal.

Although Philip was performing diplomatic missions for the queen again he was not particularly in her favour. She knighted him in 1582, not for any special service of his, but for reasons of protocol, since he was required to be of that rank to perform a proxy for which he had been nominated. By February of 1583 the plans for his marriage to Frances Walsingham, left in abeyance for over a year, came to the fore again. The queen, who had not been informed, took offence, as she so often did when her courtiers and ladies attempted to pair themselves off. She did not actually forbid the marriage, although she continued to be displeased with it. The marriage took place on the 21st September 1583. Thereafter we have no knowledge as to whether Philip Sidney saw Penelope Rich again and certainly by then the affair was over.

It was in 1585 that Sidney finally entered the field of active service which he had so desired, fighting for the international Protestant cause against Philip of Spain and the threat of a Catholic league. The battlefield was the Netherlands, Leicester was in overall command, and Sidney was appointed by the queen as governor of Flushing. This was the first official employment the queen had given him for eight years. He had waited a long time for the chance to prove himself as a man of action. For this was what he wanted to be above everything else. He had turned to writing to while away the time until he was called.

The battle at which Sidney was wounded took place at Zutphen on the 22nd September 1586. Leicester, Sidney and their men, 550 in all, found themselves facing a Spanish convoy of 3,000 foot soldiers and 1,500 cavalry. Bravado and chivalry seem to have been the English reaction to the situation. Amongst the many acts of bravery on the field, we note the young Earl of Essex, Penelope's brother, who shattered his lance on the first Spaniard he met and yet rode on at the head of his troop, hacking with his axe.

The most heroic act was Sidney's. He had fully armed himself, but noticing that the Marshall of the Camp was only partially armed and not wishing to have an advantage, he removed his thigh-pieces. Philip was acting by the same code of honour as he would if at the court tournaments, bringing onto the battlefield the manners of the chivalric knight. He was to pay dearly for his quixotic behaviour which indeed cost him his life, for it was in the thigh that he was wounded. His magnanimity at this moment is immortalised:

> He called for drink, which was presently brought him, but as he was putting the bottle to his mouth, he saw a poor soldier carried along who had eaten his last at the same feast, ghastly casting up his eyes at the bottle. Which Sir Philip, perceiving, took it from his head before he drank and delivered it to the poor man with these words "Thy necessity is yet greater than mine."[6]

His death was a prolonged one. During this period his wife Frances, pregnant with their second child, joined him. He made his will and the preachers gathered round him. Amongst the preachers was George Gifford and it is his account of the last days of Philip Sidney that reveals the final death-bed confession and repentance on Philip's part for his affair with Penelope Rich. As previously with references to Lady Rich in the *Astrophil and Stella* poems, there were attempts to delete the offending reference. The account reads:

> He added further: I had this night a trouble in my mind. For, examining myself, me thought I had not a sure hold in Christ. After I had continued in this perplexity a while, observe how strangely God did deliver me (for indeed it was a strange deliverance that I had). There came to my remembrance a vanity wherein I had taken delight, whereof I had nor rid myself. It was my Lady Rich. But I rid myself of it, and presently my joy and comfort returned within a few hours.

There is another expurgated version of the passage omitting the words 'It was my Lady Rich'.[7] The reason for the deletion is apparent: to protect Sidney's reputation. The cult of Sidney as hero of the Protestant cause necessitated the suppression of any scandal.

If Philip's relationship with Penelope were entirely innocent, as some of his admirers wished to believe, it makes no particular sense to find it so troubling him on his death-bed that he could not find peace. Repenting of 'vanities' at death was common enough at this period, especially when attended by the clergy encouraging one to do so, as Sidney was. Philip had ample time to reflect on his past during the twenty-five days he lay dying.

What amounted to a 'vanity' might differ according to the individual conscience. For a highly sophisticated, worldly man it would be naive to regard his death-bed repentance other than as an admission of adultery.

Sir Philip Sidney died on the 17th October 1586, at the age of thirty-two. He was buried with great pomp and ceremony at St Paul's Cathedral on the 16th February 1587. Both his parents had died shortly before him and his impoverished estate could not afford the expense of so costly a funeral. This seems to have been the explanation of the delay of four months between his death and burial. In the end the cost of the funeral was largely borne by his father-in-law.

His funeral was as grand as that of any prince and he was publicly mourned as 'the worthiest knight that ever lived'. Astrophil had worn stars on his armour in deference to Stella and from a pictorial record of his funeral we can see that Sidney too had adopted them as his personal symbolism. They were engraved on the gloves and helmet of his armour. A pennant from his battle array carried in the funeral procession shows a fish looking up at the stars, with the motto 'Pulchrum propter se' (beauty for its own sake).[8] The key to the star symbolism is Stella, 'the Star, whereby his course was only directed' (Sidney's own words).[9]

He had also chosen for himself a motto which appeared twice on his standard carried at his funeral: 'Vix ea nostra voco', (I can scarcely call these things my own.) The words come from Ovid's *Metamorphoses* (Book 13) where Ulysses debates with Ajax as to which of them shall have the arms of the dead Achilles. The choice of this motto indicates Sidney's desire to succeed on his own merits and not merely rely on his illustrious family for fame. He had achieved that wish.

At another level, by choosing the motto, Sidney had taken for himself the words of Ulysses, exiled husband of Penelope.

Just as in his poetry Philip Sidney had dramatised himself in the role of the courtly knight, so in life itself he had consciously shaped his presentation of himself. He had indeed played the part in real life, performing in the tournaments at the court of Elizabeth and living out the image to the ultimate in his heroic death. By the use of his personal symbolism and his deliberate cultivation of the role of knight in shining armour he had created his own image in the modern sense.

If the picture seems impossibly idealistic it is partly because that is what history has left us, the paragon without the warts. Part also of the explanation is Sidney's conscious striving to eliminate everything in himself that was unworthy of his reputation and his own heightened self-image. So successful was he in this that the real Philip became merged in the idealised one. It comes as something of a relief to find him human after all, with a chink in the shining armour, and one chapter of his life still on his conscience as he lay dying – his love-affair with Penelope.

He chose as his heir for the role of champion of the Protestant cause Penelope's brother the Earl of Essex, and signified this by bequeathing to him his best sword. Four years later Essex was to complete the symbolic link by marrying Philip's widow.

Lady Dorothy Devereux. Note the parrot on her left hand, a visual pun on the name of her first husband, Sir Thomas Perrot. On her second marriage she became Countess of Northumberland. The portrait is incorrectly labelled 'Lettice Knollys'.

CHAPTER SEVEN

'The Idle Housewife'

The love affair between Sir Philip Sidney and Lady Penelope Rich had long since been over when Philip renounced her on his death-bed. It had begun almost immediately after her marriage and lasted for a very brief period, an idyllic interlude that could have no future. By the summer of 1582 Philip had retired from court and joined his father at Hereford, there to write the *Astrophil and Stella* poems. They had to resign themselves to their respective duties.

In Penelope's case her duty lay in being a good wife and mother and this she appears to have been in spite of the odds against it. Resilient by nature, she was not given to brooding about misfortune but instead began to find ways to lead a fulfilling life notwithstanding her unwanted marriage. In any event, her daily life was fully occupied in having a large family as well as playing an active role in court life.

This was the period when the first of her many children were born. Her first child was a daughter named Lettice after her mother, and her next, also a daughter, named Essex after her late father and her brother. Then came her first son, an heir for Lord Rich, Robert, born the 19th March 1587 named surely after her adored brother even if Rich considered the child named after himself. A third daughter was baptised on the 26th November 1588 but died soon afterwards. Her second son Henry was baptised on the 19th August 1590 and was her last child by Lord Rich. In all, she was to have eleven children, nine of whom survived; in itself an impressive fact since infant mortality was very high. She also suffered at least one recorded miscarriage.

Temperamentally Penelope and Lord Rich were an ill-assorted couple. Their interests lay apart. He was a puritan, against the theatre, music, dancing and pleasure whilst she revelled in the court life enjoying the social events, plays, dances, masques. Whilst he involved himself in local affairs in Essex she took a lively interest in the political intrigues at the centre of things, at the court.

Leighs Priory, her matrimonial home, had been the Rich family seat
since Robert's grandfather had acquired it from Henry VIII and turned the
old Priory into a fine home. Robert's mother, the dowager Lady Rich, had
moved out of Leighs and into another of their houses in Essex, Rochford
Hall, to make way for the new Lady Rich on her son's marriage. Penelope
was now mistress of Leighs.

Penelope showed no particular wish to devote her life to household
tasks, especially not to the daily grind and sheer drudgery of which there
was a never-ending supply to absorb the energies of the Elizabethan
housewife. The domestic virtues were too much a part of the puritan
ethos, which she had rejected so energetically and so early. Already by the
age of nineteen she had flouted the three cardinal virtues of puritanism:
chastity, obedience and submission. The lesser virtues of prudence and
domesticity were hardly likely to commend themselves to her.

By marrying a wealthy man Penelope was at least able to escape much
of the dull routine of women's work. With a large establishment to run she
would not be expected to do the work herself. She must, however, see that
it ran smoothly and as every home had to be self-sufficient there was a
great deal to be done. She would have to select suitable servants and
supervise their work, see that proper household accounts were kept, that
the house and its furnishings were properly cleaned, the daily food
prepared, stores maintained, preserves and cures laid down, as well as
seeing that the children were properly cared for and their early education
provided. That she had an aptitude for organisation is apparent and now
she was to develop her management skills. There is also no doubt that she
took a deep personal interest in her servants and their problems. She wrote
a number of letters of recommendation for servants which show her as
putting her sympathy for misfortune above practical considerations. Such
warmth and generosity elicited a devoted response.

Her success at arranging for things to be done rather than doing them
herself did not meet with her mother's approval. Lettice no doubt
regarded her daughter as a shocking modern woman, half-critical, half-
admiring her for getting away with so much. It became her custom to
write teasingly about Penelope to her brother as 'that idle wench your
sister' or 'the idle housewife'. Penelope was determined not to become a
slave to domestic routine.

Her primary duty was of course to provide Lord Rich with a son and heir. This she did not achieve until six years after the marriage, with the birth of their third surviving child. When their second son was born three years later the line of succession was well secured.

Penelope had her last child by Lord Rich in 1590, their second son Henry, baptised on the 19th August.[1] Her duty as a wife to secure the line of inheritance was now amply fulfilled. After the birth of this child, though she and her husband maintained outward relations, they did not live together as man and wife. She continued to perform other duties for him, nursing him when he was sick and coming at his bidding, but putting off the day until the last possible moment.

Though Penelope did not overburden herself with domestic duties there is evidence to show that she was a concerned and careful mother. Her own mother, writing to her brother the Earl of Essex, teasingly depicted Penelope as fussing over the health of one of her children, 'her best beloved daughter'. Robert had gracefully bowed out of a family party and his mother replied: 'Your excuse is so reasonable, sweet Robin, as it must be taken, but if you had come this night you had found a knot of good company here together and the idle housewife your sister in one of her worst humours, solemnly disposed in doubt that her best beloved daughter should be a little sick.' Her children were indeed her greatest source of pride. John Florio described how Lady Rich when 'invited to show your richest jewels, would stay till your sweet images (your dear-sweet children) came from school'.[2]

It was Penelope, not Lord Rich, who was to prove the practical one, scheming for the advancement of her family. In a letter of 1588 to Lord Burghley she wrote requesting the guardianship of a rich orphan, which was a way of getting the profits from his lands during his minority. As we have seen Lord Burghley's position as Master of the Court of Wards gave him the power to sell off the rights to receive the benefits from land during the minority of its heir. The practice was based upon the medieval idea that land was held from the crown in return for feudal services rendered. These services included the duty to fight for the sovereign, but if the owner died and his heir was a minor, during his minority these services would not be given. The land therefore temporarily reverted to the crown, and the crown's interest was protected by selling off the benefits from it to the highest bidder.

From the viewpoint of the day, this was good practical sense, only remarkable that it came from the wife not the husband. The Earl of Leicester had initially raised the matter with the queen on Penelope's behalf. Penelope wrote her letter to Lord Burghley only six days after Leicester's death, clearly in some concern that it would be overlooked. She was heavily pregnant at the time (with her third daughter who died soon after baptism) and pleaded:

> I would have been glad to have waited on your Lordship myself if I might have done you any service but my burden is such as I am fitter to keep the house than to go any whither, wherefore I hope your Lordship will pardon me for this time.[3]

The picture we gain of Lord Rich after his marriage continues to show him in an unattractive light. In an age when men were expected to fight for their country courageously he seems to have avoided such service whenever possible. He accompanied his brother-in-law Essex to Cadiz but managed to be absent at the strategic moment, missing the fighting. The contrast between her brother's and her husband's conduct is marked. Sir Christopher Blount, writing to Lady Rich (by then his step-daughter) on the 5th July 1596 described how her brother was the first man to set foot on shore at Cadiz. He sent his greetings to her husband and deplored Lord Rich's absence, wishing he had been ' a partaker of all the glory those shall enjoy (who have) been doers in this action'.[4] Shakespeare's *Henry V* is thought to have been inspired by the Earl of Essex's expedition to Cadiz. There is indeed an echo of Henry's great speech before Agincourt in these words of Blount, with Rich as one of those 'gentlemen in England, now a-bed', though no doubt relieved rather than one of those thinking themselves 'accursed they were not here'.

In an age of adventure Lord Rich got as far as volunteering for the expedition to the Azores, again along with his brother-in-law and Lord Mountjoy (as well as men like Walter Ralegh, Admiral Lord Howard and the poet John Donne) but had to be put ashore at the outset suffering from seasickness. Severe gales had forced the ships to turn back to Plymouth and in his report Essex classified his brother-in-law as amongst those unwilling to undergo again the inconveniences of a sea-voyage. A postscript to his letter at the time to the queen reads, 'I have enforced my brother Rich and your Majesty's servant Carew Reynolds to stay for if I had carried them to sea, they would have been dead in a week.'[5]

In an age when men of spirit and drive sought to make their way at court, he kept away as much as possible, busying himself in local matters. Because he had no influence at court, when he needed a favour it was Penelope who would make the arrangements for him, exercising powers which her husband lacked.

Lord Rich preferred to be an important man in local affairs rather than seek to make his way at court in competition with more able men. Though Rich avoided court life from preference, he was ready enough to accept any rewards which could be steered his way without taking any risks himself. Over and above his attitude to public life, his private behaviour, as revealed in contemporary accounts, indicates an ungenerous and unpleasant personality.

By the standards of the day for Penelope to have a husband like Lord Rich, whom she could neither like nor respect, was a misfortune to be borne with patience. Penelope was too strong-minded to accept the situation. She was not prepared to lead a life of pretending to love a husband for whom she had never cared. Far more attractive to Penelope was the life at court. She had come to court under the auspices of her powerful stepfather and by her own beauty and accomplishments found favour. With the arrival of her brother her position was enhanced further.

This welcome event took place when Robert was seventeen. Before that he had for a time been placed under the control of the Earl of Huntingdon, from whose stern guardianship Penelope had then so recently escaped, in the hopes of curbing his extravagance. The financial problems that had hounded his father had started early for him. Each year his expenditure exceeded his income; in 1581, for example, he was overdrawn by more than six hundred pounds. Against the accusation of prodigality it must be remembered how very young he was to have such spending power.[6]

Even his puritan uncle's influence could not keep him entirely out of debt. At Michaelmas 1584 he was at Lamphey, his Welsh estate, keeping open house: 'and there did very honourably and bountifully keep house with many servants in livery and the repair of most gentlemen of those parts to attend his lordship'.[7]

His mother would not allow him to remain in the country for long, away from the court where the key to advancement lay. Banished from court herself following her marriage to Leicester, she was determined that her son should make his mark. The revival of the Devereux family fortunes depended upon his success at court. After the death in 1584 of the only child of her second marriage Lettice again concentrated all her hopes and ambitions on her elder son. When, in 1585, he presented himself at court he did indeed find favour with the queen.

In the same year Penelope's old home Chartley Manor in Staffordshire became the scene of an extraordinary plot that eventually led to the execution of Mary Queen of Scots. Mary had been imprisoned at Tutbury, about twelve miles east of Chartley, and her custodian was seeking a more fortified place for her. Chartley lent itself to the purpose because of its moat; Elizabeth remembered it from her visit as 'strong, in that it is enclosed with water'.[8]

It was still Robert's main home, and its requisitioning would leave him homeless for the duration. Already they had begun to cut down trees on the estate. In desperation he wrote to his grandfather, Sir Francis Knollys, Treasurer of Her Majesty's Household, appealing to him to do what he could to prevent the appropriation, pointing out that it was 'the only house of him which must, if that be taken, live at borrowing lodgings of his neighbours'. Knollys sent the letter to Walsingham, the queen's secretary, adding in the margin his own plea, astutely intended for Elizabeth's eyes: 'It is no policy for her Majesty to lodge the Queen of Scots in so young a man's house as he is.'[9] In the event Robert embarked for the Netherlands with Leicester, believing that his home would not be used. With his grandfather's objection no longer applicable, Mary was transferred to Chartley in his absence.

Walsingham proceeded to concoct an ingenious plot to trap the Scottish queen by intercepting secret letters with the aid of the brewer who supplied Chartley with its ale. Mary believed that a safe line of communication had been established via the beer barrels and letters were smuggled in and out in water- (or beer-) proof containers, all of which were scrutinised by Walsingham's men. Thus was the Babington plot detected. It was from Chartley that Mary was soon to be taken to Fotheringay Castle and to her death.

With her husband and son in the Netherlands Penelope's mother evinced an urge to travel that had been absent during her first marriage. Being the Earl of Leicester's wife was an unforgivable sin and Lettice succeeded in infuriating the queen yet again by the news that she was joining her husband with a full train of courtiers that rivalled the queen's own entourage.

Whether the story was true or not, it was certainly used to discredit Leicester during his absence and to stir up once again Elizabeth's jealousy of her cousin, the woman who had dared to marry her favourite.

The queen was told that Lettice would be joining her husband in the Netherlands: 'with such a train of ladies and gentlewomen and such rich coaches, litters and side saddles as Her Majesty had none such; and that there should be such a court of ladies as should far pass Her Majesty's Court here.'

All this was relayed to Leicester in the Netherlands to explain to him the real cause of Elizabeth's fury with him. The writer hastily went on to add:

> This information (though most false) did not a little stir Her Majesty to extreme choler and dislike of all your doings there, saying, with great oaths, she would have no more courts under her obeisance but her own, and would revoke you from thence with all speed.

To placate the angry queen, Leicester was advised to 'bestow some two or three hundred crowns in some rare thing for a token to Her Majesty'.[10]

As for Lettice there was now no possibility of joining her husband after the story had reached the queen's ears. All she could do was to deny it and remain quietly out of sight.

In the meantime a second Devereux daughter had also come to court. Lady Dorothy Devereux was two years younger than her sister Penelope. Both girls had come under similar influences during their formative years, going after their father's death to live with their puritan guardians, the Earl and Countess of Huntingdon. We have seen the way Penelope reacted to the constraints of an unwanted marriage. Dorothy's revolt took a different form, but revolt she did.

We last heard of Dorothy in connection with a proposed marriage between her and Philip Sidney in January 1582, about the time when he was falling in love with her newly-married elder sister. It is not difficult to account for Philip's lack of interest in the proposal. One sister did not replace the other. As for Dorothy, she had learned enough from her sister's unhappy marriage to want to choose for herself. She had seen the results of the conventional method of finding a husband, by allowing one's friends and family to arrange it, and learned not to trust to this.

At one time according to the Spanish ambassador and spy Mendoza, Leicester was proposing to marry Dorothy to King James of Scotland. Elizabeth, learning of the proposal, was reported by Mendoza to have exclaimed that she would 'rather allow the king to take her crown away than see him married to the daughter of such a she-wolf'.[11] However, stories from such a source have to be treated with circumspection. It is without corroboration and could well be one of the stories fabricated by foreign spies in order to have something to report to their masters.

Dorothy forestalled any attempts to make her a pawn in the marriage market by choosing for herself. The man she chose and eloped with was Thomas Perrot, son of Sir John Perrot, a Lord Deputy of Ireland. The Perrot family owned lands in Pembrokeshire, South Wales, near Lamphey where the Devereux children spent their childhood summers. Tom Perrot might well have been Dorothy's childhood sweetheart.

Dorothy had come to court at the age of seventeen, becoming one of Elizabeth's maids of honour. The queen's attitude to her maids of honour was well known. She was especially strict with them and they were not expected to have admirers when Elizabeth herself was there to be admired. Above all, they must not marry without her permission and this she was reluctant to give. The result was that they feared to ask her consent and usually ended up in worse trouble through not knowing what to do for the best, since nothing would please her.

Dorothy failed to obtain either the queen's consent or that of her family except for her sister Penelope. In June 1583, Tom Perrot wrote to Penelope seeking her help in support of his suit for her sister's hand. A draft of his letter has been preserved and it shows the immense pains he had taken with its composition, so full of scorings out and amendments is it. He wrote:

I know my Lady Dorothy to be worthy of all titles that may be given to any lady, and one whom the greatest and proudest minded in England may think himself happy to serve . . . Undoubtedly it is an assurance of my own worth that makes me dare to aspire to her love.

He went on to make it clear that Penelope had given her blessing to the match: 'I understand by my cousin Taseborow how great a happiness it hath pleased your ladyship to wish me.'[12]

Penelope's role in her sister's love-match shows her warm-heartedness. Herself deprived of such good fortune, she was generous enough to give Dorothy her blessing and support. No one else in the family was informed, otherwise the marriage would have been prevented. Penelope kept quiet about the secret and the next thing we know is that on the 17th July 1583 the couple took out a marriage licence, issued by the Bishop of London, in which they were described as 'Thomas Perrot, Gent. and Dorothy Devoraxe, spinster of City of London'.[13] Armed with the marriage licence they eloped. There were garbled accounts of the event, and certainly it seemed to have been a very strange wedding indeed. Dorothy had been staying at Broxbourne in Hertfordshire. The clergyman described as 'a strange minister' who afterwards turned out to be the Perrot family minister, had agreed to marry them and approached the vicar of the local church asking for the keys of the church. When he was refused, the wedding party broke into the church and the marriage took place with two men guarding the door with swords and daggers under their cloaks. Their angry relatives arrived on the scene too late.[14] How different from Penelope's own wedding scene two years earlier, but in its way it shows an equal independence of spirit.

Dorothy also was to suffer for her unconventionality. The couple found themselves not only with the severest wrath of the queen and their families to contend with, but financial problems as well. In a letter written in September 1583, two months after the elopement, Dorothy asked Lord Burghley to intervene on her behalf with the queen. Her husband had been sent to the Fleet Prison for eloping with her and she thanked the Lord Treasurer for getting him out of prison as well as their 'poor chaplain'. She begged him to help her to obtain her fortune (the £2000 her father had left her). She also asked him to try to persuade the queen to send a gracious letter to Sir John Perrot, her father-in-law, so that he 'will do like a father' and send them some Michaelmas rent 'otherwise not to be had; this by your Lord's favour being presently provided will hit this time most right'. She thanked him for helping her to obtain her marriage money:

For our infection is like a pleurisy that have need of present remedy and though other in right or to be preferred before us, yet I think that willingly they will give place to our undeserved necessity. I am loath to trouble your lordship with my disgraceful fortune but I have a great hope of your lordship but that worse than it is it cannot be.[15]

She was confident of getting her way, direct and eloquent, not to be suppressed.

The following month she was again writing to Lord Burghley (29th October 1583) about her financial problems:

If I may be so bold with your lordship's good acceptance as to put your lordship in mind once again of the effects of my last letters my necessity calling every day on me . . . I thought it not amiss to be my own solicitor once again unto your lordship beseeching your lordship to have a favourable care of me concerning the well payment of my marriage money . . . Mr. Perrot's fortune is so unfriendly as unless it be released at this time with the marriage money it will be a double damage to us both. He had a piece of land in mortgage to one Mr. Barnes which unless it be redeemed presently does bid him a farewell for ever and his debts have been so long deferred by promises of his marriage as his creditors think he does but mock them and will no longer be delayed; besides our present estate that is too full of lacks; but it is the part of base minds to make an anatomy of their necessity, therefore I present the consideration thereof unto your honourable mind which hath been and is the chief staff that my father's children depend on.

She that owes all honour and duty to your lordship

D. Perrot.[16]

It is an effective piece, basically very respectful in its pleading, but at the same time leaving the reader aware that she would go on until she got her way. When she wrote it she had just turned eighteen.

There is a delightful and beautiful portrait of Dorothy at Syon House, Middlesex. It has been wrongly catalogued as 'Lettice Knollys' but is clearly of her younger daughter.[17] Syon House became the property of Dorothy Perrot on the death of her father-in-law, Sir John and her husband Tom Perrot and it is appropriate that her portrait should hang at Syon. The real clue to the identification lies in the parrot which she holds on her left wrist. With the usual Elizabethan variance of spelling 'Perrot' was often spelled 'Parrot'. It is a delightful visual pun which would have been taken very seriously at that time. Coats of arms were often based on such play on words. Dorothy's portrait shows her as a bold and vivacious beauty, proud, not in the haughty manner of her mother, but proud of herself, of her parrot (for parrots were a great rarity at that time) and of the identity link.

After her elopement Dorothy was not permitted to appear at court. On one occasion the queen was staying at the country house of Lady Warwick who had also asked the Earl of Essex and his sister Dorothy to stay. Walter Ralegh, arch-enemy of Essex, was able to make an issue out of Dorothy's presence, seeking to cause a rift between Elizabeth and her favourite by persuading the queen that Dorothy's presence was a deliberate sign of disrespect on his part. Elizabeth ordered Dorothy to keep to her room. Essex was furious, defending his sister and lashing out against Ralegh and his influence over the queen. The quarrel grew more heated and Elizabeth went on to attack his mother, Lettice. The dispute ended in Essex storming out, sending Dorothy home with an escort (it was almost midnight) and himself riding off to go and fight in the Dutch war. Elizabeth by this time had calmed down and sent her emissary to bring him back. So they were reconciled.

The queen bitterly mourned the death of the Earl of Leicester in September 1588 shortly after the defeat of the Spanish Armada. Even before this, Essex had already begun to replace his stepfather in her affections. The death left Lettice a widow for the second time. Again she suffered the consequences of lack of male support. This took the unpleasant form of being forcibly ejected from her home at Drayton Bassett. John Robinson had taken Drayton Bassett by force and kept out

Lady Leicester 'to her injury' until her son was able to send aid. On 8th November 1588 the Earl of Essex wrote from court to Richard Bagot, his neighbour at Chartley, (itself nearby to Drayton Bassett) asking Bagot to help the sheriff get Robinson out. A note on the letter in Bagot's hand asks someone to meet him at 5 a.m. with four or five men to go to Drayton to meet the sheriff.[18] Clearly Lettice needed the protection of a husband and within the year after Leicester's death, she was married for the third time, to Sir Christopher Blount, who had been Leicester's master of horse. He was a kinsman of Charles Blount, her daughter Penelope's future lover, but has often been mistakenly referred to as Charles's younger brother.[19] He was in fact seven years older than Charles though still much younger than Lettice. Christopher Blount had been a loyal follower of Leicester and appears to have retained a most respectful attitude to his late master's widow even after he married her. He never referred to her as his wife, nor she to him as her husband, instead referring to him as her 'friend' and retaining the title of Lady Leicester.

The third of the Devereux children to marry was Walter who, in 1589, married Margaret Dakins, an heiress. Margaret had been brought up in the household of the Earl and Countess of Huntingdon, just as Walter and his two older sisters had been. Margaret was her father's sole heir and so a good marriage catch in financial terms. It was to be a short-lived marriage, and there were no children.

The last of the Devereux to marry was the Earl of Essex himself. In 1590 he married Sir Philip Sidney's widow, Frances, still only twenty-two years old and with a daughter Elizabeth aged five. Essex was suffering severely from financial problems which could no doubt have been alleviated by a wealthy match. Though Frances was her father's sole heir (he had died in the same year as her re-marriage) he left large debts which included the funeral expenses of Sir Philip Sidney. Frances was indeed badly off when Essex married her. It was a remarkable romantic act to marry the widow of the great hero of chivalry who had bequeathed to him 'his best sword'.

The marriage was concealed from the queen for six months in the hopes of avoiding, or at least postponing, her anticipated displeasure. Elizabeth's predictable anger turned, as so often, against the wife rather than the husband. Frances was excluded from the court but as she was content to lead a private life, this does not seem to have been any real hardship for her. For most of the time she lived quietly with her mother either at Walsingham House in Seething Lane or Barn Elms in Putney, keeping away from the queen just as Essex's mother had to do. However both those houses were on the Thames and so were easily accessible to her husband who could come to her by boat from Essex Stairs.

Frances and her sister-in-law Penelope became close friends and when in January 1591 Frances was about to have her first child of the marriage, it was Lady Rich who stayed with her and looked after her. The child, a daughter, was called Penelope.

The Earl of Essex had started his military career young and his brother Walter was even younger when he joined the earl at Portingale in 1589. His military career was to be extremely brief. Two years later he again accompanied the Earl of Essex to France and was the first victim to fall, mortally wounded, at a skirmish outside Rouen.

The death of their youngest member at the age of only twenty-one was a severe blow to the Devereux family. Essex himself was stricken with grief, lamenting that he had 'lost my dear and only brother, half arch of my house'.[20] His brother was, he said, 'dearer to me than ever I was to myself'.[21] When the queen summoned him home he begged leave to remain at Rouen in order to avenge his brother's death.

After his death, Walter's young widow came to London, lodging at the Earl of Huntingdon's house. As a wealthy heiress she was clearly a very bright marriage prospect and the plans for her remarriage began offensively soon for the Devereux family's liking. The negotiations for her hand began only a fortnight after her husband's death. Part of the haste was because of a rivalry of suits, between Sir Thomas Sidney (youngest brother of the late Sir Philip and of Sir Robert Sidney) and Thomas Posthumous Hoby (son of Sir Thomas Hoby, the translator into English of that influential book, Castiglione's *The Courtier*).

The short-term winner of this marriage race was Sir Thomas Sidney, though when he died four years later Margaret married for the third time, to the loser of this particular contest, Thomas Hoby.

Margaret's second marriage took place only three months after Walter Devereux' death. A young widow certainly needed protection, but her speed was unseemly even by the standards of the day. To the mourning Devereux, stunned by the early death of their youngest member, it must indeed have seemed as it did to Hamlet that

A beast that wants discourse of reason
Would have mourned longer

How deeply wounded the Devereux family had been by his widow's over-hasty remarriage is apparent from the fact that it still rankled four years later. At that time, when Margaret was about to remarry yet again, her third husband-to-be found Essex still 'highly offended with the gentlewoman with whom I seek to match'. Hoby tried to find excuses for her conduct to try to expel from Essex 'all former dislike from his honourable breast' for his former sister-in-law. Whilst Hoby admitted that such a hurried remarriage was 'evil' he hoped to 'excuse the gentlewoman's sudden marrying at that time of her first widowhood'.[22]

The rift between the Devereux family and Walter's widow was to be in evidence yet again at a much later date in their history, at the time of the Essex rebellion when Margaret, along with so many relatives and former friends, coldly disassociated herself from them.

CHAPTER EIGHT

'Love the Reward of Love'

Amongst the Earl of Essex's many rivals for the position of queen's favourite was Charles Blount, the man who was to be the great love of Penelope's life.

Charles Blount was born in 1563, the same year as Penelope, the second of three children, his elder brother William being the heir to the Mountjoy title. The Blount family lived mainly at Canford Manor in Dorset. Charles attended Oxford University but came down 'not well grounded'.[1] He then went up to London to study at the Inns of Court. There is a well-known story of him going to Whitehall when he was about twenty to see the queen at dinner. Elizabeth noticed the handsome young man and asked who he was, whilst Charles, conscious of her attention, blushed. The queen called him to her and told him, 'Fail you not to come to the court and I will bethink of myself how to do you good.'[2] Encouraged by this beginning, Charles took up the royal invitation and became one of the favoured young men about the court.

Charles's family was an ancient and noble one whose fortunes had been depleted, a familiar story, but in this case caused not so much by extravagance or wars as by his father's addiction to the study and practice of alchemy. The object of the study was to increase the family's wealth, by finding the secret of turning base metal into gold, but instead it almost bankrupted him. As a younger son he had to make his way in the world. In 1585 during his first military campaign in the Netherlands he was, like Philip Sidney a year later, wounded in the thigh. He fought at Zutphen with Sidney, was knighted by the Earl of Leicester in 1587 for his services in the Netherlands and again fought for his country against the Spanish Armada in 1588. The queen continued to show him favour, granting him a succession of offices, such as Keeper of the New Forest, with which to support himself and in 1589 gave him the security of a permanent income by making him one of her Gentlemen Pensioners. In 1594 he was granted the office of Captain of the Town and Island of Portsmouth and in the same year, on the death of his elder brother without an heir, he inherited the title of Lord Mountjoy. Like Penelope's father, he made his career as a soldier and like both her father and brother, Ireland was to be a major battleground for him. Of the three, Charles Blount, Lord Mountjoy was to be easily the most successful, achieving a great military victory over the Irish.

We have a very detailed description of Charles from his secretary who observed him meticulously. He was tall and handsome with black hair and beautiful large eyes, also black, like Penelope's and with a remarkably cheerful and amiable face. He was very neat, loving cleanliness in both clothes and food. He ate only the choicest foods and drank the best wine but never in excess. He was a modest man of a scholarly disposition, studying cosmography and mathematics in particular, enjoying discussions about natural philosophy, but his favourite subject of study was divinity. He had an excellent memory and could read French and Italian, but was shy about speaking them. He was not flirtatious.

Some further details about him suggest a quiet retiring man and also give us some idea of an Elizabethan's way of relaxing.

He loved private retiredness with good fare and some few choice friends. He delighted in study, in gardens, a house richly furnished and delectable rooms of retreat; in riding on a pad to take the air (i.e.: walking), in playing at shovelboard or at cards, in reading play books for recreation, and especially in fishing and fishponds.[3]

Essex had initially regarded Charles Blount as a rival. There was a famous quarrel between the two young men which took place in the year of the Armada. Blount had distinguished himself at tilting and the queen sent him a golden chess piece queen, richly enamelled, as a reward. Blount fastened the piece on his arm with a crimson ribbon to wear as a favour in the style of a medieval courtly lover. This was just the sort of compliment that the ageing Elizabeth appreciated from her handsome young courtiers. Essex, jealous of the queen's attentions to a rival, was heard to observe, 'Now I perceive every fool must wear a favour'.[4]

Blount, according to the code of the day, considered it proper to challenge Essex to a duel. The two met in Marylebone Park and Blount disarmed Essex, wounding him slightly in the thigh. The queen, no doubt exhilarated to have two such handsome young men fighting over her favours, proclaimed it fitting that someone should take Essex down and teach him better manners. Thereafter the two became friends.

Elizabeth continued to favour Charles and liked to have him about her at court. When, needing advancement, he sought military experience abroad, she stopped him from going, saying:

> You will never leave it until you are knocked on the head, as that inconsiderate fellow Sidney was. You shall go when I send you. In the meanwhile see you lodge in the court, where you may follow your books, read and discourse of the wars.[5]

We do not know exactly when Penelope and Charles Blount first met, though this is likely to have been soon after his arrival at court. Their personal circumstances make it highly unlikely that their paths could have crossed before that date. However, there is a story that they were secretly engaged before Penelope's marriage to Lord Rich. The story is a fabrication, the reason for which is clear. It arose from an attempt to exonerate William Laud, the chaplain who many years later was to perform an illegal wedding ceremony for the lovers, after Penelope's divorce from Lord Rich. Laud was afterwards to become Archbishop of Canterbury and his ministers rushed to defend his conduct. The story of a prior engagement between Charles and Penelope before her first marriage may initially have emanated from the couple themselves in order to persuade Laud to marry them, but was certainly used to whitewash Laud's part in the affair. There is no evidence that they even met before her marriage.

There is a beautiful little portrait of Charles Blount from about the time he first fell in love with Penelope. This is the lovely miniature by Nicholas Hilliard of 1587 inscribed, 'Amor Amoris Premium' (Love the Reward of Love). It shows a handsome and kind face and accords with the description we have of him at this time as 'brown-haired, of a sweet face and a most neat composure, tall in his person'.[6]

Nicholas Hilliard was the greatest artist of the Elizabethan age. John Donne recognised his qualities when in the poem *The Storm* he wrote:

> a hand or eye
> By Hilliard drawn is worth an history
> By a worse painter made.

Donne wrote the poem during the expedition to the Azores of 1597, the Islands Voyage, in the company of the Earl of Essex and Lord Mountjoy himself.

The fact that the greatest painter of the day expressed his art in miniature is significant of the period. Indeed, if we consider that one of the highest forms of literary perfection was the sonnet, we can see the parallel between the two forms. Just as the sonnets of Sidney and Shakespeare were expressing private emotions and were not intended for publication, so the miniature portraits were for private viewing, to be worn perhaps on a chain round the neck of the owner, hidden in a jewelled case and to be admired in private. Men as well as women might wear them. They were love tokens and would have particular appeal to parted lovers. Elizabeth herself kept a miniature of a frog in her Bible to remind her of Alençon. Many of them appear to have been painted at about the time of the engagement or marriage of their subjects, just as today we would have engagement and wedding photographs taken. The miniature of Charles Blount is clearly such a love token with its amatory inscription. We can well believe that Penelope kept the miniature as a treasure to look at when they were apart, as they often had to be.

It was not unusual to have a Latin motto inscribed on the portrait and this was an additional intimate feature, not to illuminate but almost to obscure the meaning to intrusive eyes. The meaning would be clear to the recipient of the miniature, but not to the rest of the world. The result was a perfect form of exclusive art.

So far as the portrait of Charles Blount is concerned we can only speculate. The Latin tag is a simple one at least on the face of it. Love is the reward for love, a message of reciprocity. It would not be unreasonable to suppose that Charles possessed a companion portrait of Penelope. We know that Nicholas Hilliard was befriended by Penelope Rich and named his daughter, born on 31st October 1586, after her. We also know that Nicholas Hilliard painted Penelope Rich's portrait on at least one occasion and probably several times. Henry Constable, a contemporary poet, addressed one of his sonnets 'To Mr. Hilliard upon occasion of a picture he made of my Lady Rich'. Constable was to write more than twenty sonnets to Penelope Rich, as well as one on the impending birth of a child to her. This child was her third daughter, baptised on the 26th November 1588, who died soon afterwards.

The Nicholas Hilliard miniature of Penelope has disappeared and the only picture we have of her is the one at Lambeth Palace. It is labelled on the reverse side 'A Countess of Devonshire' and the story is that it was placed in Lambeth Palace by Archbishop Laud as a reminder to him of his sin in performing an illegal marriage service for Penelope and Charles.[7] If we compare this picture with the Syon House portrait of her sister Dorothy, we can recognise a strong family likeness: the golden hair with its reddish glow; the round face with its broad forehead and high cheek colour; the dark eyes that look boldly at the viewer with their direct gaze. Nevertheless, the Lambeth portrait of Penelope does not do justice to her legendary beauty. It is interesting to note that in her hand she holds what appears to be a miniature. We can only surmise that it was the portrait of Charles Blount.

In his sonnet on the Hilliard portrait of Penelope, Constable managed to pay an elaborate compliment to both painter and sitter. He had ample opportunity to examine the miniature before celebrating it in his poem, since he was entrusted with the task of carrying it to King James VI of Scotland.

The delivery of Penelope's portrait to King James was in 1589 and in connection with her first attempt at political intrigue. Penelope was to take a much more active part in politics than other women of her day, and it is about this time that she appears to have first become politically involved.

It was a matter of national concern that Elizabeth's successor had not been named and she was now past the age of producing an heir herself, even if she was still to marry, though the time for this too seemed to have passed. The uncertainty this gave led in Penelope Rich's case to scheming on behalf of her brother. In the autumn of 1589 she began writing letters to

King James VI of Scotland to secure his favour for the Earl of Essex. Jean Hotman, son of the Huguenot jurist, Francis Hotman, and secretary to the Earl of Leicester from 1582 until Leicester's death in 1588, was her emissary. A letter which she wrote to Hotman at this time shows a light flirtatious touch, rather than a serious political stance at this stage. It runs:

> Je baise en toute humilite les mains de ma cherre Clarté et a Monsieur de Buzenal. Je luy souhaite les bonnes graces de sa maistresse et a Monsieur Palevesin bon vant, et a Monsieur de Sydnye, qui ne croye pas tout ce que l'on luy dict, et a Monsieur Constable qu'il ne suit plus amoureux et a vous mesme d'aymer bien votre femme et a tous d'etre constrans jusques a vendredy.
>
> La plus constante de ceus, qui sont nommez en ce papier, hors mis une,
>
> Penelope Riche.[8]

This translates as:

> I kiss in all humility the hands of dear Clarté and to Monsieur du Buzenal. I wish him in favour with his mistress and to Monsieur Palevesin good reputation and to Monsieur Sidney, who does not believe everything he is told, and to Monsieur Constable that he should stop being amorous, and to yourself that you love your wife well, and to everyone that they hold on until Friday.
>
> The most constant of those who are named in this paper, with one exception,
>
> Penelope Rich

Her letter suggests that Constable had fallen in love with her. Others involved in the intrigue were Buzenal and Robert Sidney, Philip's younger brother (both mentioned in the letter quoted above: the M. Palevesin mentioned was Sir Horatio Palavicio who had been Elizabeth's ambassador to Germany on behalf of Henry of Navarre).

On October 7th, Lord Burghley's Edinburgh's spy, Thomas Fowler, reported Hotman's arrival from London, bringing letters to King James from Essex and his sister.[9] Hotman had several private meetings with the king and according to Fowler seemed pleased with the result. Then on October 20th it was reported that 'young Constable' also had had several meetings with the king. Like Hotman, he had a commission from Essex and from Lord and Lady Rich and brought with him Lady Rich's picture. This was the miniature painted by Nicholas Hilliard.

Penelope clearly enjoyed her part in the intrigue, showing imagination and a sense of humour in devising it. She had a nickname for everyone involved, and there was a long scroll of these names in the possession of Richard Douglas, nephew of the Scottish ambassador in London, Archibald Douglas, who was the chief link with the Scottish Court in the affair. The queen was 'Venus', King James 'Victor', the Earl of Essex 'the weary knight' abbreviated to 'TWK', Penelope herself 'Ryalta', Jean Hotman was 'VSP', Henry Constable was 'Sconsolato'. Thomas Fowler reported to Lord Burghley:

> She is very pleasant in her letters and writes the most part thereof in her brother's behalf, so that they shall be showed to the king (here Lord Burghley has written 'Victor') which they were, and the dark parts thereof expounded to him. He commended much the fineness of her wit, the invention and well writing.[10]

The participants seemed to have been concerned to secure their own positions in the event of James's succession which was then believed to be imminent. Nothing much seems to have been accomplished, perhaps owing to James's preoccupation with his marriage as well as to his natural caution. Nevertheless, it was a first taste of dabbling in political intrigue for both brother and sister, and a lighthearted forerunner of the grimmer events to follow.

Sir Charles Blount, Lord Mountjoy, Earl of Devonshire by Nicholas Hilliard. Inscribed with the motto 'Amor amoris premium' ('Love the reward of love') Dated 1587.

Robert Devereux, 2nd Earl of Essex by Isaac Oliver.

CHAPTER NINE

'This Rich Praise, that you alone are you'

On the 17th November 1590 at the tournament to mark Queen Elizabeth's accession day, Sir Charles Blount, a brilliant figure dressed in blue and gold, rode out to the tilts wearing Lady Rich's colours as his courtly favour, as proudly as he had worn the queen's gold chess-piece. The poet George Peele described the occasion, punning on the Rich name:

> Comes Sir Charles Blount . . .
> Rich in his colours, richer in his thoughts,
> Rich in his fortune, honour, arms and art.

Penelope had acquired a new champion.

At what point they became lovers it is difficult to say precisely but the 1590 tournament marked an open indication of his feelings for her. That she returned his passion at an earlier date, before she had born Lord Rich his second son, has previously been believed. This was based upon the understanding that their first child, their daughter Penelope, was born in October 1589. As the last of the children she bore to Lord Rich, Henry, was born after this, the implication has been that there was an overlap between the two families of children.

It would be uncharacteristic of Penelope not to have made a clean break from physical relations with Lord Rich after her love affair with Charles began. There is now conclusive evidence that this is true since her daughter Penelope was in fact baptised on the 30th March 1592, two and a half years after the date previously believed to be correct. This accords with the statement at the time of their divorce that Lord Rich 'had not for the space of twelve years enjoyed her.' The dating of her daughter's birth in 1589 seemed incontrovertible, for it was based on her age at her death engraved on her tombstone. She was the first wife of Sir Gervase Clifton and her gravestone recorded that she died on the 26th October 1613 aged twenty-three years. However when I discovered from the unpublished records of St Clement Danes Church that she was baptised there on the 30th March 1592 I became convinced that the tombstone was incorrect. Without a doubt there would not have been a gap of two and a half years between birth and baptism. On the contrary the baptism would have been arranged for as soon as possible after the birth because of the risk of the child's dying without having been received into the Church. Lady Rich would have been particularly conscious of the danger as her last daughter had died soon after baptism.

The explanation for the apparent enigma is to be found in the events of her daughter Penelope's own life. Under the terms of her father's will she stood to gain her inheritance of five thousand pounds at the age of eighteen. In 1608 her hand was sought in marriage by Sir Gervase Clifton. If she were only sixteen, as the baptism record indicated, she would have had to wait another two years before inheriting the money. With both her parents dead she or her husband-to-be must have succeeded in convincing the trustees of her father's estate that she was two years older than her real age and so obtained her fortune. She was, alas, not to enjoy it for long and after her very early death her husband, a consummate fortune hunter, went on to marry six more wives.

Her birth probably took place at Essex House since she was baptised at St Clement Danes Church just opposite.[1] It was at Essex House, her brother's London home, that the relationship between Charles and Penelope seems mainly to have been conducted. This was the great house in the Strand, formerly Leicester House, with its gardens leading down to the Thames and its own landing-stage, Essex Stairs. It was maintained in great style and attended by a hundred and sixty servants. There Penelope had her own apartment, Lady Rich's chamber, always ready for her. It had a particularly splendid bed all in black, gold and silver, with a black velvet canopy trimmed with gold and black damask, and with black bed curtains trimmed with gold lace, a lovers' bed rather than a matrimonial one. One cannot imagine the puritan Lord Rich sleeping in such a bed. The chairs and stools were also of black velvet with gilt frames, and the cushions were of cloth of silver.

At Essex House Penelope, Charles and her brother formed the centre of a group more congenial to her than the husband to whom she still owed obligations. There she could meet Charles not clandestinely (which went against her open nature) but amongst friends who welcomed her in her own right as a celebrated member of what was the most brilliant circle of its day. The Earl of Essex offered lavish hospitality to his guests, providing great banquets, theatrical entertainments and grand parties.

At Christmas-time there were the Revels, those elaborate entertainments provided by the Inns of Court. Because they were costly they did not take place every year on an equally elaborate scale, but the two famous ones were the Grays' Inn Revels of Christmas 1594 and the Middle Temple Revels of 1597. Penelope attended both. For the 3rd January 1595 Penelope was accompanied not only by her brother and her husband but by her lover. For the 1597 Revels, the Middle Temple invited its great neighbours at adjoining Essex House to share its celebrations, with Penelope a dazzling central figure in the audience. The writer Bartholomew Young described how her 'honourable presence . . . graced and beautified those sports.' He played the part of a French orator and it was Lady Rich, with her 'perfect knowledge' of the language, of whom he confessed to being most in awe.[2] As well as the grand public celebrations there were private occasions for the lovers to enjoy together, like the intimate little suppers given for Lady Rich. The household accounts show such casual items as 'For supper for the Lady Rich at Essex House that night she came thither 42s.', an occasion that was enjoyed, we can only imagine, by Charles and Penelope à deux.[3]

Their first child Penelope was given the surname Rich and treated as part of the Rich family until many years later, just as the other children were to be. Clearly this was done with her husband's acquiescence. Lord Rich tolerated the situation because it was to his advantage to do so, to have as his brother-in-law the most influential man at the queen's court. He was too much of an opportunist to risk losing that advantage. In any case, Rich was not the man to have a direct confrontation with his wife's lover. It would be uncharacteristic of him, for example, to have challenged Charles to a duel (as Charles had challenged Essex) and so put himself at risk. Instead, he seems to have confined himself to snide remarks, at least to his brother-in-law. In a letter to Essex written in 1595, he complained about 'Lords of the Council [who] are freely privileged to receive writings from other men's wives without any further question and have full authority to see every man's wife at their pleasure'. He had not the courage to speak his mind plainly but only hinted in a petulant whine at the cause of his annoyance. Behind the veiled blustering he was complaining about his wife's lover.

He ingratiatingly signed himself 'Your lordship's poor brother to command in all honesty.[4] Self-interest and self-protection are his main concerns and for them he is prepared to forego any shreds of dignity remaining to him. He cuts a pathetic figure and there is little to admire in him.

Charles had by then succeeded to the title of Lord Mountjoy. He had never expected to be more than a younger son, with his own way to make in the world, at which, thanks initially to his good fortune in attracting the queen's notice and thereafter to his own endeavours, he had been remarkably successful. When in 1593 his father died, his elder brother William succeeded to the title. Then only a few months later William himself died without issue and in 1594 Charles unexpectedly found himself the new Lord Mountjoy. Suddenly he had not only his own career to make but the honour of his house to maintain. He was then aged thirty-one and he could not but have been aware of the importance of securing the lineage by having a family of his own. Indeed he had adopted as his motto: 'To rebuild the ancient house'. His secretary Fynes Moryson who knew him well emphasised how ambitious he was to re-establish the family's honour and wealth. Now that he was Lord Mountjoy the whole weight of that obligation fell upon him. It certainly extended to a duty to secure the succession. In spite of these pressures Charles remained constant to Penelope. Once he had given his devotion it was hers for life. Resoluteness of purpose was a strong element in his make-up, one that was later to play such an important part in his success in Ireland. In his relationship with Penelope, once he had committed himself to her he was unswerving.

At about the time he succeeded to his title Penelope was again pregnant but lost this child in a miscarriage: 'My Lady Rich hath not gone out her time but I hear she is reasonable well again,' wrote Sir Robert Sidney to his wife Barbara in May 1594.[5] In all there were to be six children of this second family, five of whom survived: three sons, Mountjoy, Charles and St John, and two daughters, Penelope and Isabella.

Mountjoy did not join Essex's expedition to Cadiz in 1596 since the queen forbade him to go. Lord Rich duly set off with his brother-in-law but managed to miss the fighting. Penelope and Charles therefore had at this time a quiet interlude before what was to be a turning point in their lives.

Penelope was again pregnant and it was probably in January 1597 that their first son was born. It was now that they made what was to be the final decision that indicated they had bound their lives together permanently. They chose to give their son the Christian name of Mountjoy, a name that left no doubt as to who the father was. When their daughter Penelope was born the situation had been quite different since she had generally been assumed to be Lord Rich's daughter. This was a proud, or brazen, announcement, depending on the viewpoint. In fact it took a good deal of courage for Penelope to do this since it opened up the knowledge of her adultery to a wider circle. If it was indiscreet, it showed a fine disregard of public opinion. Again the child took the surname Rich and again Lord Rich accepted the situation.

This was indeed a momentous year for Penelope, crammed with events, not all of them pleasant ones. That April, a few months after the birth, she fell ill, suffering from smallpox. The news was, 'They say the smallpox has much disfigured Lady Rich.' Later however came the happy news: 'My Lady Rich is recovered of her smallpox without blemish to her beautiful face.'[6]

In July Mountjoy set off with her brother on the Islands Voyage, with Lord Rich accompanying them until he had to be sent back suffering from seasickness. They returned towards the end of October and again this was to be a euphoric period since Lord Rich went off to France.

Penelope had a second child that year, a son Scipio, baptised on the 8th December 1597 at Essex House. This child must have died soon afterwards and considering Penelope's illness at the time of her pregnancy this would not be surprising. (He does not appear ever to have been mentioned in any book of reference or elsewhere, but I have noted his baptism record in the unpublished Parish Register of St Clement Danes Church.)[7]

Again the naming of the child, Scipio, is telling. Charles was spoken of as another Scipio but it is also interesting to recall Sir Walter Ralegh's tribute to Sir Philip Sidney as 'the Scipio, Cicero, Petrarch of our time'. In any event no one thought of Lord Rich as another Scipio. Another son too was to be named after his father, this time directly, by the unambiguous name of Charles.

The fact that the parents chose these names for their sons shows a pride in their family and a refusal to behave furtively. On the other hand this did not mean that they wished to flaunt their liaison to the world at large. On the contrary, assisted no doubt by Lord Rich's time-serving acquiescence, they were able to maintain a degree of discretion.

This was the remarkable situation at Essex House during the 1590s: the scene of the creation of this extraordinary second family, brought up in the husband's name but with the sons' forenames at least bearing witness to their parentage. Her brother had opened up the doors of his home for the lovers to meet. There they could openly enjoy each other's company as well as the society of their close friends to whom their secret was known.

This could not have been achieved without the co-operation of Penelope's brother. As head of the Devereux family he was ostensibly in a position to exercise some control over a recalcitrant female member of it, but there was never any suggestion that Robert did otherwise than accept the relationship. In fact he rarely if ever attempted to interfere in the lives of those three determined older women, his mother and two elder sisters, whose wills were more than a match for his own.

Robert had a particularly close relationship with Penelope, valuing her as a friend as well as a sister. His was a complex personality and they understood each other. He could 'hit her humours right', just as she could his.

Only two of Essex's letters to his sister Penelope have survived. They are remarkably revealing of the complexities of his nature. To her he could write openly about his moods, knowing that she would be understanding and receptive. The letters are unusual because of their personal nature. Unlike most extant letters they are not concerned with affairs of state nor are they merely confined to domestic matters. The fact that Essex wrote to his sister in this vein is in itself interesting since it reveals something about the closeness of their relationship. They are also fascinating to read as a living instance of the language on which Shakespeare drew when depicting his aristocrats. Although we have no direct evidence of a connection between Essex and Shakespeare we know that there was indeed a relationship via the Earl of Southampton. Though neither letter is dated they appear to have been written about the same time. The first letter, as its final sentence indicates, must have been written in church whilst waiting for the preacher to begin his sermon. It reads:

Dear Sister,
Because I will not be in your debt for sending of a footman I have directed this bearer to Leighs to bring me word how you do. I am melancholy, merry, sometimes happy and often unfortunate. The court is of as many humours as the rainbow hath colours, the time wherein we live more inconstant than women's thoughts more miserable than old age itself and breeding both people and occasions like to itself that is violent, desperate and fantastical. Myself for wondering at other men's strange adventures, have not leisure to follow the ways of mine own heart but by still resolving not to be proud of any good that can come because it is the favour of chance nor to throw down my mind a whit for any ill that shall happen because I see that all fortunes are good or evil as they are esteemed. The preacher is ready to begin and therefore he shall end this discourse though upon another text.
Your brother that dearly loves you.
R. Essex.

The second, written when he is ill, which he described as a 'fantastical letter', is more than a letter, it is an imaginative essay on 'affections'. It reads:

Dear Sister,

I would have made more haste unto you but that yesternight I was surprised with a fever, and this morning I have such a humour fallen down into one side of my head as I dare not look out of my chamber. This Lady hath entreated me to write a fantastical letter but I am so dull with my sickness and some other more secret causes as I will rather choose to dispraise those affections with which none but women, apes and lovers are delighted. To hope for that which I have not is a vain expectation, to delight in that which I have is a deceiving pleasure, to wish the return of that which is gone from me is womanish inconstancy. Those things that fly me, I will not lose labour to follow. Those that meet me I esteem as they are worth, and leave when they are naught worth. I will neither bray of my good hap nor complain of my ill for secrecy makes joys more sweet, and I am then most unhappy when another knows that I am unhappy. I do not envy, because I will do no man that honour to think he hath that which I want, nor yet am I not contented because I know some things that I have not. Love I confess to be a blind god more for the poets' sakes that were his godfather than for any power I see that he hath. Ambition fit for hearts that already confess themselves to be base. Envy is the humour of him that will be glad of the reversion of another man's fortune and revenge of such fools as in injuries know not how to keep themselves aforehand. Jealous I am not for I will be glad to lose that which I am not sure to keep. If to be of this mind be fantastical then join me with the three that I first reckoned, but if they be young and handsome with the first.

And so I take my leave being not able to write more for pain.

Your brother that loves you dearly,

R. Essex.[8]

Strange letters to write to one's sister, perhaps. There is a whiff of the poseur in them, as though he were seeking to impress her, knowing her to be a critical reader who expected something imaginative from him. She had after all been the recipient of the most famous love poetry of its day. Robert too wrote poetry and she would be a natural audience and critic for his literary ventures.

Essex now occupied the position at court of queen's favourite, so long enjoyed by his stepfather before him. Nobody approached the queen except through him and all her time was spent in his company. The two would play at cards together until the early hours of the morning.

In times of stress, Essex became ill and unbalanced, lacking in judgement. However, the atmosphere which surrounded him in the court with its dangerous intrigues might well have unsettled the judgement of a much more stable person. There were dangers to him from all sides, from men like Walter Ralegh, another ambitious schemer on the one hand, and the shrewd civil servant Cecils, Lord Burghley and his son, Robert, on the other. Elizabeth enjoyed playing off one against the other as much to maintain her own authority and power as from the satisfaction she derived from keeping her favourites always in a state of submission to her. Her political and personal motives are hard to distinguish because their outlet took the same form on so many occasions. Her storms of jealousy were perhaps partly motivated by personal feelings, partly by the need to inspire complete loyalty and dedication in her subjects.

Essex maintained his position as the queen's favourite only with immense effort. Of his many enemies none was more dangerous than Walter Ralegh. Each of these two arch-opponents had his own supporters. On the one hand there was the Essex party with his friends like the Earl of Southampton, patron of Shakespeare, and the Earls of Bedford and Rutland, a powerful and influential group with strong literary as well as political interests. Essex's followers also included a number of writers, in particular men with special knowledge of foreign affairs. Amongst them were John Florio, Southampton's Italian tutor and translator of Montaigne, the two Bacon brothers, Anthony and Francis, and for a short period the Spaniard Antonio Pérez.

Ralegh's friends were avant-garde intellectuals concerned with philosophic and scientific studies but at the same time reputed to be atheists and dabblers in 'the black arts' (i.e. magic). Amongst the members of this group was Thomas Harriot, celebrated mathematician, the poets Marlowe and Chapman and the Earl of Northumberland, known as 'the wizard earl', a keen student of astrology and alchemy. It was into this circle that Penelope's younger sister Dorothy was to enter by what turned out to be a misalliance as infamous in its way as Penelope's own. After ten-and-a-half years of marriage, her husband, Sir Thomas Perrot, died in

1594. Only one child survived out of the numerous births to the couple, a daughter named Penelope, after her sister.★

Dorothy was eventually to inherit substantial amounts of land from both her husband's and his late father's estates. Sir John Perrot, Dorothy's father-in-law, had been convicted of high treason, wrongly as he maintained, and imprisoned in the Tower where he died in 1592. Because of the alleged felony, his lands were forfeited to the Crown on his death instead of passing to Thomas, his son and heir. When Thomas himself died less than two years later, any rights in the forfeited lands passed to his widow so far as it could be shown that the Crown was not entitled to them. Essex tried to restore to his sister the forfeited lands now held by the queen because of the alleged treason, and Dorothy had to go to law to claim them. This was a time-consuming business and in February 1597, Rowland White writing to Sir Robert Sidney remarked that Essex's

> keeping in is noted of all men, but I hear that what troubles him greatly is certain lands of Sir John Perrot's which is now again called in question for the Queen who since his death by due court of law was adjudged to be the right of my Lady Northumberland [as Dorothy had now become].[9]

★It has been alleged that Dorothy remarried during the lifetime of her first husband and the story is still repeated with the writers being unable to find any evidence of a divorce. It is then suggested that the marriage was annulled because Sir Thomas Perrot was unworthy of Lady Dorothy Devereux (by a legal action of 'disparagement' as it was called). These allegations do not accord with the facts.

For a start, an action for disparagement was a means of protection for a ward to prevent the ward from being married off against her will beneath her status. Dorothy's own letters after her elopement show her as happy with her marriage. Any complaints on her part related only to her financial position.

Secondly, Sir Thomas Perrot though not of so aristocratic a family as Dorothy herself, was by no means undistinguished. He was one of the honoured knights who walked in state by the coffin of Sir Philip Sidney; his father had been appointed by the queen as Lord Deputy of Ireland; he had fought bravely for his country and distinguished himself at Zutphen with Philip Sidney.

Thirdly, the marriage lasted until his death in February 1594 as can be seen from his will made only a few days before when he left his estate to his 'well beloved wife'.

They included the lease of Syon House, Middlesex and lands in Wales.

As a young widow of means with only one child (a girl who would not inherit if her mother were to remarry and have a son) Dorothy was an eligible prize in the marriage market. Her brother Essex seems to have played a part in finding his sister a husband from the aristocracy. Her second husband was Henry Percy, ninth Earl of Northumberland, marrying for the first time at the age of thirty-one. The marriage was about a year after Perrot's death. The wedding guests were afterwards entertained at Essex House to a theatrical performance for which her brother duly paid the players the sum of ten pounds.[10] Unfortunately, we do not know what play was performed for the occasion.

Being an heiress and marrying an earl do not however seem to have solved Dorothy's financial worries. In a letter written to Essex by Sir Christopher Blount in 1597, his then stepfather said:

I am entreated by your sister to let you know that she hopeth your care will be no less for her means of living ladylike than your endeavour has been earnest to bestow on her a ladyship.[11]

The Earl of Northumberland chose Dorothy more for her wealth than her beauty or character. He later wrote an *Advice* to their son in which he related how he specifically looked for a wife who could 'bring with her meat in her mouth to maintain her expense'. Lord Henry Howard had this to say about the earl's attitude to marriage:

He came to her without any other affection than a Flemish jade comes to a courser mare desiring only an heir male to prevent the brothers that are next whom he hates damnably and protesteth to some of his friends that next to his wife he abhoreth them above any.[12]

Any illusions Dorothy had about the delights of becoming a Countess were shortlived. The Earl was renowned for his very hot temper and more than once issued challenges to a duel. In early 1597 he quarrelled with the Earl of Southampton and challenged him. From the start of their marriage the couple quarrelled fiercely. Dorothy was as headstrong and outspoken as the other Devereux women, her mother Lettice and her sister Penelope. Their clash of personalities was undoubtedly exacerbated by Dorothy's continuing loyalty to her brother and the Essex circle.

It was indeed a fascinating group that congregated at Essex House. There was her brother's friend and follower the Earl of Southampton, who in September 1595 began paying court to their first cousin, Elizabeth Vernon. Like most of the group he was a patron of poets and had already by the early 1590s given his patronage and friendship to the emergent dramatist William Shakespeare. Shakespeare had come to London probably in the late 1580s and had by then written his earliest plays. With the theatres closed because of the plague from August 1592 to April 1594, he turned to writing poetry, dedicating his two long poems, *Venus and Adonis* and *The Rape of Lucrece,* his first published works, to the Earl of Southampton.

His growing friendship with Southampton would have brought Shakespeare into close contact with the Essex circle. The Earl of Essex himself was the foremost patron of poets of the day. Lord Mountjoy too was an important patron and Penelope in turn became a patroness of literature not only because she was Essex's sister but also in her own right. Once she became known as Sidney's Stella and as an influential court figure sympathetic to writers the dedications began to flow. At least eleven authors wrote or dedicated works to her. She was a most generous patron as several writers had cause to remember. Bartholomew Young called her 'so high and excellent a patroness' and Alexander Craig, addressing her as 'liberal Penelope', wrote of her raining 'showers of gold' on him.

Shakespeare would have appreciated the enormous value to be gained by an alliance to this circle. Even from the standpoint of patronage such a connection was highly important for him. Apart from the material considerations, the impact of this elitist group upon the highly perceptive mind of Shakespeare must have been immense. Shakespeare stored up impressions absorbing them into the stream of his creative processes, so that we can rarely trace directly back to its source any particular character or event from his own experience, of which indeed very little is known.

The first publication of *Astrophil and Stella* in 1591 triggered off a vogue for sonnet-writing amongst the poets of the day, including Shakespeare. At first Penelope Rich's identification as Stella would only have been known to a select few, since the first two editions in that year omitted the three sonnets punning on the name Rich that clearly identified her. When in 1598 the whole sequence was published it would have been common knowledge. With the Elizabethan relish for double meanings, felicitous references to Lady Rich became the popular literary pastime of the day. A pastime with a purpose, since the aim was to secure patronage, or at least the hope of repeating Sidney's success by imitation not only of his themes but his model. A graceful pun was a good disguise for flattery.

Amongst these endeavours was a work by the poet Gervase Markham called *Devoreux* after the Essex family, and a panegyric to them. It was published in 1597 and dedicated to Lady Rich and her sister. In the prose introduction Markham acknowledged her as Sidney's Stella by a rather laboured pun on that name: 'with the beams of your gracious eyes . . . the worst of my pen's earthiness doubtless shall be stellified.' Fortified by this effort, Markham went on in the poem itself to hammer home the more obligatory pun. In Stanza 18 he addressed Penelope as

> thou rich Rich, richest did ere compile,
> The only history shall eternal stand.

Stanza 16 is marked in the margin: 'The Countess of Northumberland and the Lady Rich'. It begins:

> But you, O you, you that alone are you.

and goes on to praise the two sisters as the seat of all virtues.

Markham clearly saw the Essex circle as the foremost source of literary patronage and indeed had already dedicated poetic works to other members of the group. In 1595 he had dedicated *Sir Richard Greville* to Lord Mountjoy, with a verse dedication 'To the Fairest' that appears to be dedicated to Penelope Rich and including a sonnet adressed to the Earl of Southampton. In 1597 Markham went with Essex, Mountjoy and Southampton to the Azores, perhaps composing at least some of the numerous verses during the voyage and probably finishing and publishing the poem soon after their return. The lengthy eulogy was a massive bid for the invaluable patronage of the Essex circle.

Through his patron Southampton, Shakespeare must have known a good deal about the Essex circle, including the great love affair taking place at Essex House. Even he seems to have joined in the references to Lady Rich.

One of the groups of his sonnets is concerned with a 'rival poet', someone who was competing with him for Southampton's patronage and affection. Theories as to the identity of this rival abound, with Robert Gittings cogently arguing the case for his being Gervase Markham. Whether he was Markham, Chapman, Marlowe or another poet is not the subject here.

If we look at the first two lines of Shakespeare's Sonnet 84 concerning the rival poet we see:

Who is it that says most, which can say more
Than this rich praise, that you alone are you?

The second line is more than merely reminiscent of Markham's line in Stanza 16 of *Devoreux*. As well as the exact quotation, the use by Shakespeare of 'rich' in this context can only be a play on words. The pun, once established continues in his next sonnet, number 85.

My tongue-tied muse in manners holds her still
While comments of your praise richly compiled.

'Richly compiled' should, in the context, mean 'compiled to the Lady Rich'. So, whoever was the rival poet of Shakespeare, addressed verse to Lady Rich as well as to Southampton.

In an earlier sonnet there is an apparent allusion to the love affair between Penelope and Charles, locked in the imagery. Sonnet 52 begins:

So am I as the rich whose blessed key
Can bring him to his sweet up-locked treasure,
The which he will not every hour survey,
For blunting the fine point of seldom pleasure.

When he wrote this sonnet Shakespeare must have been aware that he was sharing his mistress with his patron. He compares himself to 'the rich' who do not spoil their pleasure by frequent enjoyment but keep it fresh by occasional visits. The words 'rich' and 'blunt', occurring together in the same image, carry with them, for the initiated, resonances of Penelope Rich and Charles Blount (frequently spelt Blunt).

At the end of his book *Shakespeare's Rival* Gittings finds inexplicable 'Markham's utter silence for twenty-seven years about the group to which he dedicated all the fruits of his Muse up to 1597'. He suggests that it must have been caused by 'some personal wound . . . The personal passions involved may have been concerned with someone very much in the forefront of the group such as Lady Rich. We cannot tell', he concludes.

I believe that he is right in suggesting that it concerns Lady Rich and that the explanation is to be found in the events of Penelope's life during 1597. Gittings has called her 'the most notorious member of the Essex circle'. The question to ask is, when did she become notorious? The answer must be, after 1597, when she became the mother of a son whose illegitimacy would have been no secret to those familiar with the group at Essex House.

Markham's views on women were very much the puritanical ones. He later wrote a book entitled *The English Housewife* in which the puritan virtues loom large, beginning of course with chastity. It could well be that Markham was shattered when he realised the truth about the woman on whom he had lavished his most effusive praises. Not even necessarily shocked at her behaviour, but at her and Mountjoy's refusal to cover up their tracks. It was from just this sort of moral fervour coupled with hypocrisy that Penelope and Charles were to suffer so devastatingly several years later.

Another of the punsters was Markham's friend Everard Guilpen. In *Shadow of Truth* published in 1598 he wrote teasingly of his friend Markham:

So though his plot be poor, his subject's rich

This was a quibble calculated to appeal to Elizabethan taste – the subject may be poor but paradoxically is rich because it is about Lady Rich. 'Plot', alternately spelt 'platt', meant the theme or subject of a literary work.

Other prospective candidates for Shakespeare's rival, like George Chapman, came from the Ralegh group. Chapman was later, in a bid for patronage, to dedicate his translation of seven books of Homer's *Iliad* to the Earl of Essex when it came out in 1598. Four years earlier in the dedication of his work *Shadow of Night* he extolled the intellectual attainments of members of the Ralegh circle and made slighting remarks about 'idolatrous platts for riches'. It was another of the popular puns on Penelope Rich's name, this time from someone who regarded the cult of sonnet writing as overrated.

Chapman in his dedication of *Shadow of Night* singled out Dorothy's new husband the Earl of Northumberland for praise as a 'deep-searching' scholar. The earl was something of an essayist, who had apparently been forced to try his hand at love poetry in order to please his lady, but was only too relieved to abandon the attempt. Some time after his marriage to Dorothy he wrote an essay *On the Entertainment of a Mistress being inconsistent with the Pursuit of Learning,* brought to light by Frances Yates. In this essay he reminds his lady how he won her by writing 'platts' to her, recalling Chapman's complaints about 'idolatrous platts for riches.' Northumberland, after deep investigation of the subject, has decided it is all a farcical waste of time and plainly tells his lady so.

The earl describes how he is unable to concentrate on his study because thoughts of his mistress keep intruding. The book to which he is trying to give his attention is a study on the subject of light. He recalls how in order to win her he had to write contrived 'platts' to her. Like the scientific man he is, he weighs up the relative merits of the pursuits and comes down heavily in favour of scientific learning as against sonnet writing.

Frances Yates has ingeniously shown the connections between the earl's essay and Shakespeare's *Love's Labour's Lost*.[13] This play, written for private performance probably about 1594 with later revisions, is generally recognised to be full of allusions to contemporary persons and events and almost certainly to people and ideas from the Essex circle.

The theme of the earl's essay is reversed in *Love's Labour's Lost* where the young king and his courtiers begin by renouncing love with the intention of devoting themselves absolutely to study and then have to abandon the attempt because each has fallen in love. By criticising sonnet writing to ladies Northumberland was attacking not only his wife but her sister Penelope and the poet Philip Sidney. The ladies and the dead poet needed a champion and this was undertaken by Shakespeare as poet of the Essex/Southampton circle. *Love's Labour's Lost* was his riposte.

There is a very clear theme running through the play presented by Berowne. In the first scene he tells the king and the other lords that truth is not found in books. He tells them this at some length with many references to 'light' and 'eyes'. When they have all admitted that they are in love he expands on this theme in a long peroration in which he insists that true inspiration comes from the eyes of women. This long speech is at the heart of the play.

We note that Rosaline, Berowne's mistress, has black eyes:

two pitch balls stuck in her face for eyes.

Berowne defends her blackness to the king, just as Sidney had defended the blackness of Stella's eyes in Sonnet 7 of *Astrophil and Stella:*

That, whereas black seems beauty's contrary

She even in black doth make all beauties flow.

Rosaline is:

born to make black fair.

Northumberland's decision to abandon love and dedicate himself to study is paralleled, even parodied, in the behaviour of the King of Navarre and his courtiers. When Shakespeare in *Love's Labour's Lost* wrote:

As painfully to pore upon a book
To seek the light of truth, while truth the while
Doth falsely blind the eyesight of his look,

we can well believe that it was of Northumberland and his laborious studies he was thinking. The fact that Northumberland particularly chose the study of light is reflected in the play by the constant references to light, as well as sun, moon, stars. The obsession with eyes recalls a similar mesmerism in Sidney's sonnets with Stella's eyes.

Direct allusion was not Shakespeare's style but, set in their historical context, apparently isolated pieces of a jigsaw begin to build up a picture of topical events and the current talking points of the day, with the ladies of the Essex circle led by Penelope very much at the centre of things.

The extent of the influence of the Essex circle on Shakespeare is a matter of pure conjecture. It is interesting to consider the characters of the heroines he was creating in the 1590s and compare them with his later creations. The 1590s saw the first of his great heroines, Kate the Shrew, Rosaline of *Love's Labour's Lost* and Beatrice of *Much Ado*. Of all Shakespeare's women, these early portraits are the most high-spirited and exuberant, before the lines had softened into the gentler characters of his later heroines. Shakespeare's vivacious, practical, witty heroines did not spring fully formed out of their maker's mind. They must have had a basis in reality. Whether he had met the Devereux sisters or not, he must have heard tell of their exploits and sayings, and something of their personalities must have filtered through into his creations.

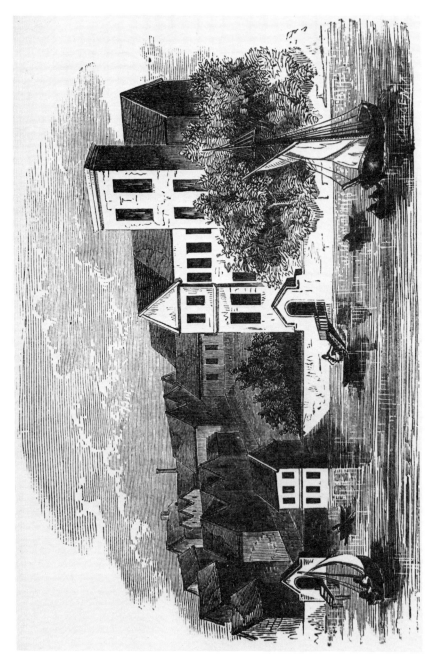

Essex House. Formerly Leicester House. A view from the Thames showing Essex Stairs. Penelope Rich had an apartment there.

CHAPTER TEN

'My Lady Rich's desires are obeyed as commandments'

Not all Penelope's life in the 1590s was spent around the court. During this period she divided her time between the court, her brother's houses at Chartley in Staffordshire, Wanstead in Essex, Essex House in London, visits to her mother at Drayton Bassett in Staffordshire, and her husband's home, Leighs Priory in Essex. Much of her travelling was probably accomplished on horseback, the way the queen preferred to travel. Coaches, first introduced to England in 1555, had become highly fashionable after the queen acquired her first one in 1560. They were cumbersome contraptions and not the most comfortable way to negotiate the muddy, pot-holed roads of deepest Staffordshire. Penelope's mother expressed her feelings about the discomforts, complaining about the 'foul travelling' and asking her son to 'send some coach horses to fetch me for my own will never be able to draw me out of the mire'.[1]

Such journeys could be hazardous with thieves and vagabonds lying in wait to rob unwary travellers and it was customary to break the journey into short stages. Despite the discomforts, travel was the best way for an adventurous woman like Penelope to avoid being housebound. Penelope was almost as insatiable a traveller as the queen. There was nothing she liked better than paying visits, to see her friends and family.

Wherever she went the promise of a visit from her set in motion the sort of flurry of activity, on a minor scale, that preceded the queen's progresses. In June 1592 she was due to visit Blithfield, the home of the Bagot family, near neighbours to the Devereux at Chartley. Anne Broughton, née Bagot, who had married Richard Broughton, Essex's steward at Chartley, was away from home at the time. She wrote urgently to her mother Mary Bagot to make sure that everything should be ready for Lady Rich. If Penelope arrived before her own return her mother must take whatever was needed from her house.[2] On another occasion, news that 'the ladies' were soon to arrive at Chartley caused 'uproar', as William

Trew wrote to Walter Bagot.[3] We can imagine the commotion as bed linen and mattresses were shaken out and aired, floors cleaned and fresh rushes strewn, meats and pies baked, jams and jellies prepared.

Gregarious by nature Penelope would often take a large group of her women friends with her for company. In 1593 Richard Broughton, wrote that she had asked his wife to go to Leighs with her and that her mother, sister and Lady Essex 'as well as many good gossips would accompany her.'[4] Taking her own company with her was a form of self-preservation, a way of standing up to Lord Rich and his puritan friends and diluting the pious atmosphere at Leighs. It was an assertion of her own identity. Alone she would have found it extremely difficult not to be drawn into his world. She may also have been genuinely afraid of being alone with him, bearing in mind his violent temper. She was plainly reluctant to return to Leighs, putting it off as long as possible.

From time to time Lord Rich needed her and if he insisted on her return she must obey. On one occasion he particularly required her help, when he was engaged in a lawsuit over some land. Seriously worried that he was going to lose a large part of his estate he summoned Penelope, who was staying at Chartley at the time, to Leighs to assist him. She had the influence that he lacked, so she must act as his 'solicitor' in the case. Penelope wanted to take her friend the Countess of Southampton with her and busily began arranging everything to her liking, or at least to make the best of a bad situation. In a letter of the 8th July, 1599, the countess explained it all to her husband:

My Lady Rich will needs have me send you word how importunate my Lord Rich is with her to come to London, fearing he shall lose most of his land, which my Lord Chamberlain hopes to recover, but he thinks if she were near London she would make means to have the suit not proceed till her brother's coming home, which else he fears will go to his loss before that time. Therefore go to him needs she must. She is she tells me very loth to leave me here alone and most desirous I thank her to have me with her in Essex till your return unto me and tells she has written both to you and her brother that it may be so . . . she desires that you will write a letter to my Lord Rich that I may do so [i.e. go with her] and she has sent to her brother to do the like, for she says she knows his humour so well as he will not be pleased unless that course be taken. She will be gone before Bartholomew Day [24th August].[5]

Penelope's letter to the Earl of Southampton followed. She wrote:

My Lord Rich so importunes me daily to return to my own house as I cannot stay here longer than Bartholomewtide which I do against his wish and the cause of his earnest desire to have me come up is his being persecuted for his land as he is in fear to lose the greatest part he hath this next term, who would have me a solicitor to bear part of his troubles and is much discontented with my staying so long. Wherefore I beseech your Lordship to speak with my brother since I am loth to leave my Lady here alone and if you resolve she shall go with me into Essex, which I very much desire, then you were best to write to me that you would have her go with me, which will make my Lord Rich the more willing though I know he will be well contented.[6]

Penelope still had obligations to her husband. He found it most useful to have a wife whose personal influence so clearly exceeded his own and she must have been successful in her suit for nothing further is heard of Lord Rich's losing his lands. Again we see her as the great organiser telling them all how best to arrange things so that she and her friend, the Countess of Southampton, can remain together. She is happier having company with her than going back on her own, whilst at the same time protective of her friend. Lord Rich is revealed as most pedantic about formalities. He must have letters from both the Earl of Essex and the Earl of Southampton giving their consent to the arrangement.

Lord Rich was more deeply committed than ever to the puritan views that had led to his arrest a decade earlier but by now he had learnt discretion. Penelope had opposed these views from the start and indeed there was even a suggestion that she went to the other extreme.

The practice of Catholicism was an even more subversive activity than the holding of puritan services since it carried with it political connotations of sympathy with enemy Spain. One of Lord Rich's neighbours in Essex, William Wiseman of Broadoaks (or Braddocks), was secretly a Catholic and used his home for sheltering Catholic priests from time to time. One of these was the famous Jesuit priest John Gerard who prided himself on the number of converts he had made and was a wanted man. He was in hiding at Broadoaks in March 1594 and a special hiding place was constructed for him in the wall below the fireplace in the chapel. A Protestant spy in the household informed on him but although his pursuers knew he was in the house they could not find the secret hideout. Father Gerard had scrambled into the tiny space just as the search-party entered the house with only 'a biscuit or two and a little quince jelly' to sustain him. On this meagre diet he managed to hold out for four days whilst the search continued. They combed the place for him, even lighting a fire in the fireplace above his head, but at last retired, defeated.[7]

Father Gerard boasted in his autobiography how he had come near to converting Lady Rich to Catholicism. Whilst staying at Broadoaks in March 1594 his host's mother had told him that a great lady, sister of the Earl of Essex and married to the greatest lord in the county, wanted to see him. He went openly to the Rich house, pretending to bring a message from another great lady, a relative of hers. He dined at her table and afterwards talked to her privately for three hours. She was, according to the priest's account, ready to be instructed how to prepare for confession. But:

> There was a nobleman in London who loved her with a deep and enduring love. To him she wrote to announce the step she proposed to take, intending perhaps to break with him. But she roused a sleeping viper. At once he rushed down to see her and began to talk her out of her resolve for all he was able. He was a Protestant and was well read and cleverly persuaded her to ask her 'guide' the answers to certain doubts he himself had about the faith. He assured her that if he was convinced, he too would become a Catholic. Meanwhile, he begged her to take no irrevocable step – unless she wanted him to commit suicide.[8]

Charles, with his love of theological argument would no doubt have enjoyed setting difficult questions for the priest to answer. 'He received all his answers', Gerard assures us, 'and long ones at that, but he did not reply'. He had no intention whatsoever of becoming converted, as the priest ruefully realised. Gerard saw it as a ruse to postpone Lady Rich's conversion and eventually dissuade her altogether. If so, it was successful.

The story, coming from a not impartial source, is worth examining further. For a well-known Catholic priest in hiding to come openly into a strong puritan household was inviting trouble. The hope of gaining the Earl of Essex's sister as a convert might be an irresistible prize but the risks involved for him were great. If he had indeed abandoned caution he may have been led on by Penelope for her own entertainment.

Pregnant at the time (she was to suffer a miscarriage two months later) and no doubt bored, she may well have regarded the episode as a diversion. Her early distaste for the moral fervour of puritanism may have drawn her towards at least hearing the Catholic point of view, with the added attraction of indulging her pronounced taste for flirting with danger. She both enjoyed intrigue and had a sense of humour and may well have relished the thought of Lord Rich's horror at having unbeknown to himself a Catholic priest actually dining at his table and trying to convert his wife. If the 'nightly catechising', to which Lord Rich was so partial, was beginning to try her patience, what better way to retaliate than by this mischievous escapade?

The threat of suicide on Charles's part if she went through with it is too melodramatic for him ever to have made. It would be more in character for her, whiling away the time when she and Charles were parted and fretting against the rigours of the puritan Leighs household, to liven things up in this way, even getting Charles to participate by preparing his pages of knotty theological problems.

It was in fact not uncommon for allegations of Catholicism to be made in connection with all sorts of unlikely people including Lord Rich himself. Years later, the Venetian Ambassador in Savoy, writing to the Doge and Senate of Venice in 1612, referred to Lord Rich as a 'good Catholic' who visited their church daily and even twice a day.[9]

Gerard was writing his autobiography for his fellow-Jesuits, as an education for the novices under his direction and was especially interested in converts from the noble and wealthy families. At about the same time Penelope was befriending another Catholic priest Father John Bolt, whom she had met at court and with whom she shared musical rather than religious interests. He had been a highly talented musician at court and left to become a Catholic, living with Catholic families where he taught music and practised his religion. He was arrested at Broadoaks also in March 1594 and was about to be tortured when Penelope intervened on his behalf and managed to secure his release and he escaped to the Continent. Gerard's own interest in Lady Rich may well have stemmed from this episode.

It is from letters that we can piece together something of the domestic lives of Lady Rich, her friends and family. There is a wealth of information about them to be gleaned from the correspondence between Rowland White and Sir Robert Sidney. He was the younger brother of Philip, who kept up a friendship with Penelope, particularly through his wife Barbara whom Penelope befriended during his long absence fighting in the Netherlands. Rowland White was his agent at court who looked after his interests while he was away and proved to be a most informative correspondent.

The letters are fascinating, containing insights into current events and at the same time providing a wealth of detail about their day-to-day concerns. There is a lighthearted group of letters where the event of the moment is the purchase by Lady Rich of some 'hangings'. These hangings was the arrases familiar to us from *Hamlet* through which Polonius was stabbed. They served to keep out draughts from chilly Elizabethan houses and were also highly decorative. This little group of extracts from letters dating from September to December 1595 (all from Rowland White to Sir Robert Sidney unless otherwise stated) show Penelope as moving about from Staffordshire, to London, on to Essex and back to London, all within a period of three months, a surprising degree of mobility considering the state of the roads at the time, which were especially bad in winter.[10]

23rd September 1595
Rowland White writes to say that Lord Rich is not in town and his lady is in Staffordshire with her mother. Letters for Lord Rich were enclosed with letters in a packet and directed to her which may be the reason he did not get the packet as soon as Sir Robert Sidney desired.

27th September

My Lord Rich is looked for daily in town. I will attend him and let him know your Lordship's care of his hangings.

8th October
Lord Rich has not yet come to town. I have left a letter for him at Essex House.

15th October
Lady Rich desires that if the hangings you write of are not gone, she would like a piece or two of the story of Cyrus and money will be sent to you.

7th November
The Earl of Essex is infinitely troubled with a printed book the Queen showed him. My Lady of Northumberland is with child. Lady Leicester and Lady Rich are yesterday come to London and Lord Rich will write to you about his hangings; if they do not answer a note he sent to Bloq, they will not serve. There is a rumour Spanish forces are landed in Britanny. (The book that so disquieted Essex was 'A Conference about the Next Succession to the Crown of England', printed in English at Antwerp and concerned the succession to the English Crown and Elizabeth's right to the throne. It was dedicated to Essex, with the intent of bringing him into discredit).

9th November
Lady Rich thanks you for the hangings. Some say my Lord of Oxford is dead.

13th November

Lady Rich likes the piece of hanging but wishes her husband to see it. Lady Leicester thought the price high, but wishes you had sent her friend Sir Christopher some.

Same date: Sir Robert Sidney to Lady Sidney (his wife).
I sent twelve boar pies to you with a piece of hangings for Lord Rich . . . You must not forget that your two chief gossips must be my Lady Rich and my Lord Mountjoy. (Gossips were the godparents for the child that Lady Sidney was expecting).

16th November
I send your Lordship the hanging. My Lord Rich says the border is too deep. Lady Leicester said that if it be above ten shillings the stick it is too dear. I answered that it seemed hangings were good cheap when she bought any. Sure I was that your Lordship would buy them as good cheap for my Lady Rich as for yourself and so was my Lady Rich answered who liked the hangings very well. I showed the piece to Mr Mainard who sent for an arras man who thinks it well worth sixteen or seventeen shillings the stick . . . My Lord of Essex and my Lord Treasurer have their boar pies and this day the rest are presented, my lady reserving none for herself, bestowing her two upon Sir Robert Cecil in hope he will be careful for your leave.

22nd November
The boar pies are all delivered and specially much commended for their well seasoning.

29th November
I sent by Will of the scullery the hanging Lord Rich saw and marvel what is become of Will.

Then on the 1st December there was an important event in Sir Robert Sidney's life, the birth of a son to his wife Barbara. The child was born safely but both mother and son had measles. Penelope had agreed to be godmother and, impulsively, was prepared to risk infection so as not to postpone the christening. Rowland White begged her:

to take a long time to think on the danger which she did till afternoon and then coming to Essex House she told me she was resolved.

Lord Mountjoy was to be godfather and was particularly pleased to be told that Lady Rich was godmother. At this time he was living at his house in Holborn.

Two weeks later before the christening had taken place, Lady Rich was in Essex evidently attending her husband. Her return was awaited for the christening date to be fixed and she arrived on St Stephen's Day, 26th December, 1595, having spent Christmas with her husband at Leighs. She put off the christening until New Year's Eve, which Rowland White suspected was because of a spot 'on her fair white face that keeps your son from being christened'. Too much rich Christmas food perhaps.

Barbara was by now anxious to have her son christened but what Lady Rich said clearly carried weight: 'My Lady Rich's desires are obeyed as commandments.' She even chose the name: 'They named him Robert, my Lady Rich's desire.' The godparents generously gave 'three very fair standing bowls all of one fashion that may be worth £20 apiece'.

Sir Robert Sidney had been hoping to return to England to see his wife and new son. The queen repeatedly refused his requests for leave. By March 1597, the letters had begun to focus on less domestic matters. The Earl of Essex wanted the post of Warden of the Cinque Ports which the queen refused him, telling him that she was giving it to Lord Cobham. Essex resolved to leave the court and had his horses prepared, when the queen sent for him and offered him instead the post of Master of Ordnance which he accepted. (These official posts were a valuable and much needed source of income).

Sir Robert Sidney then became interested in the vacant wardenship. As he was away on service and the queen had refused him leave to return, he had to rely on friends for assistance with his candidature. Penelope could be influential in the scheme both as Essex's sister and because of her own position at court where she was very popular.

Penelope's influence over her brother was recognised at the start. 'Lady Rich has undertaken to appease the Earl of Essex,' Rowland White wrote. Essex was still sensitive to the fact that he himself had been refused the post. Penelope, though her brother's interests came first, was ready to help a friend when his interests did not conflict with her brother's, who after all had now accepted an alternative post.

Sir Robert was careful to seek Essex's advice and so tactfully draw him to his side. He sent Essex his all-important letter of application for the post, and Essex thought it was a very good one, suggesting Lady Warwick as the best person to deliver it to the queen. She was unable to do so and Rowland White found himself going from person to person, trying to find someone suitable to deliver it. It was a nightmare task for him, responsible for this all-important delivery. He spent the whole day combing the court and going further afield, taking the boat to court and then back to Baynards' Castle, the Earl of Pembroke's town house at Blackfriars. At one point, he almost gave up when he was informed that the post had already gone to Lord Cobham. All the influential people he asked could not help him for one reason or another. Finally, he sought out Lady Rich who told him how sorry she was to hear that the queen would not allow Sir Robert to return to England. She took him aside and related this incident: The queen recently asked her what news and she replied she was glad to hear the queen's good choice of a Warden of the Cinque Ports, naming Sir Robert Sidney. The queen denied she had yet made the appointment. Penelope had thus established that the post was still open.

Rowland White asked her to deliver Sir Robert's application to the queen. She took the letter, kissed it, and without reading it put it in her bosom, assuring the exhausted and grateful Rowland White that it would be read by the queen that night or tomorrow. It was done with grace and charm.

The queen however, in her usual way, put off making a decision. Lord Cobham's friends gathered at court to assist him and Essex, who regarded Lord Cobham as an enemy, fell sick at the strategic moment, which led Rowland White to suspect that Lord Cobham had somehow had private access to the queen, a privilege Essex regarded as his sole prerogative. The observation suggests an interesting awareness of the psychosomatic nature of Essex's illnesses.

Penelope then became ill herself. She, who had withstood the threat of measles and spots, now fell a victim to smallpox. Lord Rich was no great comfort to Penelope in her illness as a letter he wrote to her brother indicates:

Your sister being loath to send you any of her infection hath made me an instrument to send this enclosed epistle of Dutch true or false love wherein if I be not in the right I may be judged more infected than fitteth my profession and to deserve worse than the pox of the smallest size. If it fall out so I disburden myself and am free from such treason by my disclosing it to a councillor who as your lord well knows cannot be guilty of any such offence. Your lord sees by this care of a fair maid's beauty she does not altogether despair of recovery of her own again which if she did assuredly envy of others' fairness would make her willing to send infection amongst them. This banishment makes me that I cannot attend on you and this wicked disease will cause your sister this next week to be at more charge to buy a masker's visor to meet you dancing in the fields than she would or hoped ever to have done. If you dare meet her I beseech you preacheth patience unto her which is my only theme of exhortation.
Your lordship's poor brother to command
Robert Rich
Written from St Barts 16th April 1597.[11]

The letter was written from St Bartholomews, Lord Rich's London home in Smithfield. Usually when in London Penelope lived either at court or at Essex House but enough was known about infection for her to isolate herself at St Bartholomews with her husband, so that he too was unable to attend on his brother-in-law in person. Because of the risk of infection Penelope was unwilling to write directly to her brother and had asked

Lord Rich to forward a letter from a girl she was assisting. Lord Rich, distrustful of the girl, made a heavy-handed joke about venereal disease: 'If I be not in the right I may be judged more infected than fitteth my profession and to deserve worse than the pox of the smallest size,' i.e. the great pox or syphillis.

It is a distasteful letter. His suggestion that Penelope would deliberately infect another 'fair maid' if she thought that she would not recover her own beauty is hardly to be taken seriously. It is indicative only of the unpleasantness of Lord Rich's own nature.[12]

There is malice in the suggestion that she will need to cover her once beautiful face in a mask before dancing, which she loved, and then only in a field with her brother. This is the puritan in Lord Rich coming out, but he is afraid to say too much to his brother-in-law who himself enjoyed the pleasures of court life.

Later, however, there came the happy news of her recovery, her beautiful face unblemished.

This was the summer when Essex, Lord Mountjoy and others set off to the Azores, on the Islands Voyage and Lord Rich had to be put ashore suffering from seasickness. Not very many of Penelope's own letters survive, and where they do (apart from letters of recommendations for favours) they are mainly concerned to obtain news of her brother when he was away. He was the person about whom she 'infinitely longs to hear'. No doubt news of Mountjoy would be equally welcome but here discretion had to be maintained.

In September Penelope wrote to Sir Robert Cecil in her politest style:

I will only now entreat you to do me the favour to let me hear from you when you have any news of my brother, since I infinitely long to hear that all the troubles of this voyage are past and some hope of his speedy return.[13]

When Essex did return safely it was to be reprimanded by the queen for an unsuccessful voyage. Mountjoy however was honoured for his part in the adventure and in the following year (1598) was created a Knight of the Garter.

Another correspondent of Penelope's was Anthony Bacon, elder brother of Francis, who had taken up residence in Essex House. He was her contact with events at court whilst she was away. In May 1596 she wrote asking for news, of her brother of course, but she also wanted serious information about world affairs:

To my especial friend Mr Bacon at Essex House.

Worthy Mr Bacon,

There are many respects which leads me to an extraordinary estimation of your virtues and besides your courtesies towards myself increaseth the desire I have to requite your friendship and so do you all honour, praying you to believe my words, since your merits doth challenge more than I can acknowledge, although I do with much affection esteem your worth and while I am in this solitary place, where no sound of any news can come, I must entreat you to let me have something of the world from you, especially of my brother, and then what you know of the French affair, or whether there go any troops from hence to their aid, and so wishing you all contentment I remain,

Your friend, very affectionate,

Penelope Rich.

I would fain hear what becomes of your wandering neighbour.[14]

The 'wandering neighbour' was Antonio Pérez, the flamboyant Spaniard, who clearly intrigued Penelope.

Another correspondent of Anthony Bacon referred to a supper attended by Pérez, Lady Rich and others. His letter shows Penelope as making the most of her position as a married woman whose husband was often in the country and with the most influential man at court for her brother to enjoy freedoms not open to other Elizabethan ladies. Penelope is seen moving about in society with a degree of independence remarkable in a male-dominated society. She attended the supper unchaperoned, the other guests being Pérez, Sir Nicholas Clifford and the writer of the letter Anthony Standen. Her brother arrived with Sir Robert Sidney and when Penelope learnt that Essex would be dining at Walsingham House the following day and on the way visiting Anthony Bacon, she proceeded to invite herself along. In a practical manner she then organised the transport arrangements, clearly used to taking charge.[15] Here is a woman at ease in a man's world. Part of the confidence she needed for this came from her position as Essex's sister, part from the security she had finally found in an enduring relationship with Lord Mountjoy. The rest came from her own dominant personality.

Her brother was a little uneasy about these signs of independence. He asked Pérez to keep a watchful eye over her, as the same letter makes clear: 'My lord hath provided him here with the same office those eunuchs have in Turkey, which is to have the custody of the fairest dames.'

Antonio Pérez himself wrote to Lady Rich in a highly intimate manner. The over-blown compliments, as when he addressed her, Frances and Dorothy as 'the three sisters and goddesses,' is conventional enough. More surprising is the tone of sexual innuendo, under the guise of metaphors from gardening, and the teasing threats of blackmail. All three women were clearly pregnant at the time and Pérez knew Penelope's secret. The letter that follows was written to Lady Rich in March 1596 in Spanish and translates as follows:

Señor Wilton hath given me news of the healths of your ladyships three sisters and goddesses and in particular that all three have amongst yourselves drunk a carouse unto Nature in thankfulness that she gave you not those delicate shapes to keep them idle, but rather that you should push forth unto us here many buds of those divine beauties. To those gardeners I wish all happiness for so good tillage of their grounds. Sweet ladies mine, many of those carouses. O what a book I have full of secrets of the like tillage and trimming of gardens. If I return again to England I shall have no need to seek my living of any body for my book will serve my turn, but I will not be so good cheap this second time, my receipts will cost dearer. Wherefore let everyone provide.[16]

On one occasion Pérez sent Lady Rich some gloves made out of dog-skin, abasing himself in his accompanying note: 'The gloves, lady, are of dog. Not of me, though I hold myself a dog – Your ladyship's flayed dog.'

The correspondence between the Devereux family itself is a delight to read, full of warmth and affection, light-hearted and teasing in tone.[17] In particular, the adoration of the three women, Lettice and her two daughters, for the young head of the family shines out from their letters. It makes nonsense of the statement of one biographer of the Earl of Essex that all the Devereux children were 'emotional cripples'.[18] It is far more likely that the strength of feeling of these three powerful women had a smothering effect on Robert. If he suffered, it was from too much love rather than too little.

Lettice, whose usual style was plain and perfunctory, wrote rapturously to her son. She addressed him as 'sweet Robin' and invariably ended with such phrases as 'your mother infinitely loving you'. In one letter, written when he was about to embark upon an expedition, she reminded him that, though she would not want to 'persuade your invincible courage to cowardice', a great commander does not risk his own person. She was anxious for his safety, yet at the same time trying to be tactful, and above all proud of him.

In another letter she reminded him that

You are much beloved and greatly honoured in this desolate corner, not according to the fashion of your courtly mistresses but in our true country sincerity we will ever pray for the height of your happiness.

We catch a few glimpses of Penelope from these letters. In one, her mother teasingly wrote:

the idle wench your sister threatens revenge on you for hitting her humours so right . . . sweet Robin I mean to bring your sister as far as Weston, Mr Sheldon's house, about three weeks hence if leisure might serve you to cross us there . . .

Dorothy's letters to her brother are also light-hearted, full of warmth and affection.

Penelope's own letters to her brother are few, since she was often in his company. They mainly concern recommendations for offices that have fallen vacant or assistance that she was seeking for her friends or acquaintants. It is clear from these letters that she had a generous nature and performed frequent services of this kind. She was usually torn between not wanting to trouble her brother unduly and her compassion. In one letter she pleaded for a wife whose husband had been 'subject to franticness through his troubles' and 'in such despair as his wife's infinite sorrows makes me satisfy her again who thinks that none will pity her misery and her children if you do not'. In another letter she recommended her former steward for a position 'because of his suffering,' telling her brother 'and I hope also he will be able to do you service', signing the letter: 'Your sister that most infinitely loves you, Penelope Rich'.

Her warmth and generosity contrast with Lord Rich's coldness. In a letter Rich wrote to his brother-in-law, he refused to employ a man recommended to him by Essex as a language secretary, being as he admitted, poor in languages. Penelope had clearly got hold of the letter before it was sent and from her additions to it, meant only for her brother's eyes, her broad sense of humour can be gleaned. After her improvements it read:

'myself, as your lordship well knoweth, am a poor man of no language only in the French [disease] having therein but a little oversight [amended to undersight] [with coming over] to attend my Lord of Shrewsbury [at] which being now performed, I look not for like occasion.

She has also added a postscript: 'You may imagine my Lord Rich hath no employment for a language secretary except he has gotten a mistress in France.'

Lady Leicester's main complaint was that she did not see her beloved son often enough. If he could not be spared from court and his many other duties to 'grace this ill-favoured cottage', as she called her home, she must try to visit him. The journey between Staffordshire and London was hard, particularly in winter, but in spite of the 'unseasonable time' (it was December 1597) she was ready to brave the

foul travelling . . . especially if matters stood so well as you might hope to obtain some favour for us, then would I come also presently up, otherwise a country life is fittest for disgraced persons but if you find reason to wish my coming then you must presently send some coach horses to fetch me for my own will never be able to draw me out of the mire.

The country life did not suit her, in spite of trying to make the best of it, (incidentally echoing her first husband's words shortly before his death in Ireland). She was clearly longing for the excitement of court life especially at the Christmas and New Year festivities.

On this occasion she did get down to London, taking care not to come within too great a distance of the court to avoid offending the queen. At any rate she was able to enjoy one spectacular party at least, given at Essex House on St Valentine's Day 1598 with her whole family present, her son and his wife, her two daughters and Lord Mountjoy as well as many other guests. They had 'a very great supper', followed by 'two plays which kept them up till one o'clock after midnight'.[19]

It was Lettice's dearest ambition to be reinstated at court and she was prepared to lavish any amount on gifts to the queen to secure this. On the 1st March 1598 Rowland White wrote to Sir Robert Sidney:

I acquainted you with the care to bring Lady Leicester to the Queen's presence; it was often granted, but the Queen found occasion not to

come. Upon Shrove Monday, the Queen was persuaded to go to Mr
Controller's at the Tilt End, there was my Lady Leicester with a fair
jewel of £300. A great dinner was prepared by my Lady Chandos, the
Queen's coach ready and all the world expecting Her Majesty's own
coming; when upon a sudden she resolved not to go and so sent word.
My Lord of Essex that had kept his chamber the day before, in his
night gown went up to the Queen the privy way; but all would not
prevail and as yet my Lady Leicester hath not seen the Queen. It had
been better not moved, for Lord Essex by importuning in unpleasing
matters loses opportunity to do good to his friends.[20]

By the following day:

> My Lady Leicester was at Court kissed the queen's hands and her
> breast and did embrace her and the Queen kissed her. My Lord of
> Essex is in exceeding favour here.

In fact, the Queen had not really undergone a change of heart towards her
cousin for whom there was still to be no place at court.

In July 1598, the Countess of Leicester was deeply concerned about
her son. She wrote:

> Sweet Robin,
> Yourself have given us such a taste of some strange matter to be
> looked for as I cannot be quiet till I know the true cause of your
> absence and discontentment, if it be but for Ireland I doubt not but
> you are wise and politic enough to countermine with your enemies . .
>
> if it be but men's matters I know you have courage enough, if
> women's you have meetly well passed the pikes already and therein
> you should be skilful . . .

By February 1600 Lettice was begging her son for news in 'this most
dangerous time'. Essex's fortunes had plummeted. He was a prisoner
about to be tried for his life, but his mother was still entreating him:

to bestow some time a few idle lines on your mother who otherwise may grow jealous that you love her not so well as she deserves, which blot I know you will take away. And, as she hath made you the chief comfort of her life, so I doubt not of your noble nature but that you will be careful to maintain it with all childlike kindness.

At such a time letters like this can become cloying, even suffocating. She still saw him as a boy, though he was by now thirty-three.

His mother and sisters continued to lavish their affection on him. However, all the concern and love of these women could not protect and support Essex through the trials to come.

A letter written by Lady Penelope Rich 'To Mr. Donnall' at the time of her brother's arrest. For a transcription of this letter see Page 128.

CHAPTER ELEVEN

'The storm continues'

The Earl of Essex had reached the height of his reputation with Cadiz in 1596. His military campaigns in Portugal and Spain and his expedition to the Azores, the Islands Voyage of 1597, had plunged him further into debt adding to his ever-increasing personal expenditure which since his boyhood had invariably exceeded his income. His accounts for the years 1593-8 show debts to the astronomical figure of £30,000.[1] Amongst his sources of income was the lease of all the sweet wines imported into England which the queen had granted to him in 1590, previously the perquisite of his stepfather Leicester. By the mid-1590s he had even mortgaged this, borrowing £4,000 on the security of the sweet wine lease.

In 1598 two events occurred that were to prove the beginning of the deterioration in Essex's close relationship with the queen. On the 1st July at a meeting of the privy council Essex in anger turned his back on the queen and in her fury the queen boxed his ears. Equally enraged he reached for his sword but an intervention at this point prevented the matter becoming more serious. Such an incident would not be easily forgiven or forgotten and thereafter there was a marked coolness between them.

In the same year another serious rift occurred between the queen and Essex over a matter which might be thought objectively to be of no direct concern of either. This was the love affair between Essex's great friend, Henry Wriothesley, Earl of Southampton, and Elizabeth Vernon, one of the queen's maids of honour and Essex's cousin. Southampton had in February 1598 requested the queen's permission to marry Elizabeth Vernon, which the queen refused. Instead, she gave him permission to travel for two years. He set off for France on 10th February, leaving behind him 'a very desolate gentlewoman who have almost wept out her fairest eyes'.[2] When Elizabeth Vernon found she was pregnant she told her cousins and Essex had Southampton brought back from France. At Essex House the couple were married in secret, Southampton quietly returning to France afterwards. Elizabeth stayed with her cousins at Essex House and then went to Leighs with Penelope for the baby's birth.

The news reached the queen's ears and via Cecil she expressed her outrage that Southampton had married one of her maids of honour without her consent. He was ordered to return home at once and await her orders, but the letter was delayed and Essex had to send money to his friend for the journey. When eventually Southampton did return, he was immediately arrested and put in the Fleet Prison. Essex set about securing his friend's release.

On 8th November, whilst Southampton was still in prison, his countess gave birth to a daughter. Lady Rich was the godmother and the baby was called Penelope after her. Essex gave the family a set of rooms at Essex House and from this time onwards the countess spent as much time as possible with Penelope either at Essex House or Leighs or at Chartley. Essex also assisted his cousin financially.

The queen's anger turned against Essex for helping the couple. The marriage of a maid of honour without her consent was not a matter to be taken lightly, and her resentment against Essex was not easily forgotten.

Essex was anxious to find some great cause into which he might plunge himself and repair his waning fortunes. Ireland was once again a seething trouble spot and Elizabeth vacillated as to whom she should send. Elizabeth favoured appointing Mountjoy as Lord Deputy of Ireland. This proposal seems to have stirred up in Essex his old jealousy of Mountjoy, dating back to the gold chess-piece incident. Though Mountjoy's close friend, Essex advised against his appointment on the grounds that Mountjoy was insufficiently experienced in military affairs, was too bookish, had too few followers and too small an estate to undertake such a great enterprise. By enumerating the necessary qualifications for the leadership it was evident that he himself was the prime candidate and he thus drew upon himself the appointment which was to be one of the first steps to his ruin. Essex was reluctant to leave court but nevertheless felt he must go.

At the beginning of 1599 Essex was finally given the commission of leading the English against the Irish to try to reconquer and pacify Ireland. He took with him his friend Southampton, so recently in disfavour, but was expressly forbidden to make him Master of the Horse as he wished. Another of his company was Sir Christopher Blount who had become his stepfather on Lettice's marriage soon after Leicester's death.

During her brother's absence Penelope went to stay at Chartley, Essex's Staffordshire home, taking with her Frances, her sister-in-law, and Elizabeth, Countess of Southampton. It seems likely that her correspondence at this time came under scrutiny. Two of her letters to the Earl of Southampton ended up in Cecil's hands. They were in fact about personal rather than political matters, with Penelope sending reassuring family news: 'Your Lordship's daughter is exceeding fair and well, and I hope by your son to win my wager.'[3] Southampton had no heir and in spite of Penelope's bet, Elizabeth later had to break the news that she was 'not now in that happy state'.

When Lord Rich insisted that Penelope must return to Leighs to assist him in his lawsuit over his land she was determined to take Elizabeth with her and set about making the arrangements. After disposing of the problem of Lord Rich she expressed her sympathy for Sir Henry Danvers who had been shot in the face, relieved that it would not spoil his looks.[4]

Essex's Irish campaign was not a success. Tyrone, the Irish rebel leader, eluded Essex and the climate made him ill. He appointed Southampton Master of the Horse in open defiance of the queen and further outraged her by dispensing knighthoods liberally to keep up morale. He received angry letters of recrimination from the queen and finally agreed an ignominious truce with the rebel Tyrone. Elizabeth had expressly commanded him not to agree any terms with Tyrone until he had submitted them to her, but by then he had already done so. He was in an impossible situation.

Essex was now desperate and seriously considered leaving Ireland and marching home to seize the court. Southampton urged him on, whilst Christopher Blount recommended him to refrain from violence. Had he remained in Ireland he might have saved himself. Alternatively, if he had decided to march on London, supported by a powerful army, he might have overpowered all opposition. Instead he did neither, but left his post of command and, taking a mere handful of friends, landed in England and rode at speed to the court, then at Nonsuch Palace in Surrey, where he arrived at about ten o'clock on the morning of the 28th September 1599.

On his arrival he burst in on the queen unannounced, his face and clothes muddy and unwashed. The queen was not yet dressed and he found her without her wig, her jewels, her make-up. She disguised her alarm and hid her fury. Essex had not properly thought out the net result of his behaviour. He fell on his knees and kissed her hand. She led him to believe he had been received with 'a sweet calm'. Later in the day, however, he found her 'much changed in that small time'. That night, between 10 and 11 o'clock an order came from the queen that he should 'keep his chamber'.[5]

Penelope had been given the news of her brother's return. She lost no time in returning to London, in her haste not even bothering to pack any day clothes. She moved back into Essex House whilst Frances went to Walsingham House to be with her mother. A distraught Essex now appealed to his sister for help.

There is a letter of Penelope's undated but written at midnight, to 'my especial friend Mr Donnall' which relates to a most urgent and secret appeal she had received from her brother to come to him at court, in the morning, early. Though she was ill and in her night clothes she would go and Mr. Donnall was asked to take her there very early and smuggle her in.

This is the letter:

> Dear Mr Donnall,
> This bearer tells me my brother would have me come to the Court in the morning early. I am here scarce well and in my night clothes, having nothing else here, but yet I will come and desire not to be seen by any but himself, wherefore I pray you come for me as early as you think good, and design how I may come in very privately.
> In haste, this midday night.
> Your most affectionate friend,
> Penelope Rich.

> If it had not been for importuning my brother's rest I would have come in the night, to have kept myself from any other's eyes. Good Mr Donnall, let me not fail to see you early. I would not write to my brother because I thought he would be asleep before the messenger come.[6]

Because of its conspiratorial nature the letter might be thought to belong to a later date, to the events of the rebellion. However this cannot be so as the request is to come to her brother at court and this was to be the last time he was ever at court. The court was at whichever palace the queen was staying, in this case Nonsuch, about seventeen miles south of London. The whole tone and import of the letter places it at this traumatic moment. It was to Penelope that he turned for advice and at risk to her health she willingly responded to his appeal.

The following day the Privy Council drew up the list of charges against Essex relating to his conduct of the Irish campaign and his reckless return. Essex was sent to York House, home of the Lord Keeper, to be kept a prisoner. His wife Frances had, on the 30th September, two days after his return given birth to a daughter but he was not allowed to see the child. He was to remain imprisoned at York House for the next six months, during which time he fell seriously ill.

After her hasty return from Chartley Penelope did not stay long at Essex House for, on the 11th October, she and Lady Southampton were reported to have 'gone to the country to shun the company that daily were wont to visit them in town', and so 'gave offence to the Court'.[7] Her brother's illness was a great anxiety and for the next few months all Penelope's energies were concentrated on trying to secure his release or at least his removal to his own house. She would appear at court dressed in mourning, to draw dramatic attention to her brother's plight. Rowland White writing to Sir Robert Sidney on 8th December 1599 reported:

> The Earl continues very sick at my Lord Keeper's. Yesterday the Queen removed to Richmond. The two ladies Northumberland and Rich all in black were at court; they were humble suitors to have the Earl removed to a better air for he is somewhat straitly lodged in respect the Lord Keeper's household is not great. The Lord Mountjoy after the holidays must be gone; the Earl of Southampton and Sir Henry Danvers go with him.[8]

The queen now wanted Lord Mountjoy to be appointed to go to Ireland to replace Essex. He was reluctant to go and indeed had never sought military honours in the way Essex had. However, the queen insisted on his accepting the Lord Deputyship of Ireland, which he did at the end of November 1599 although he did not set out for Ireland until the following February, postponing his departure as long as possible. He was to fulfil the queen's prediction for him 'that it would be his fortune and his honour to cut the thread of that fateful rebellion and to bring her in peace to the grave'.[9]

As Christmas drew near, Penelope was again at court, bringing all her influence to bear on her brother's behalf. Alarmed at his illness she used this to make a dramatic plea: 'Her Majesty spake with her and used her very graciously. Her humble suit was to have leave to see her Lordship-brother before he died.'[10]

Essex was indeed so ill that prayers were said and the 'bell tolled for him'. This again gave offence to the queen, to whom it was explained in mitigation that

> the preachers who prayed for him were all Cambridge men of which University he was Chancellor and they were bound by ancient custom to pray for their Chancellor. The bell only tolled for him in one place, St Clement's Church, over against his house . . . to signify the Earl lay dying.[11]

Meanwhile at court there was 'dancing, plays and Christmas pies'. The queen's determination to enjoy herself was feverish, as if she were trying to forget all about her former favourite. It was reported:

> Her Majesty comes much abroad these holidays, for almost every night she is in the presence [chamber] to see the ladies dance the old and new country dances, with tabor and pipe. [She] graced the dancing and plays with her own presence; and played at cards in the presence [chamber] at primero, with the Lord Treasurer, Mr Secretary and the Lord North. The court was great and full of Lords and Ladies.[12]

For Penelope in her mourning there were no Christmas celebrations that year. In happier times she would have been at the centre of the festivities, thoroughly enjoying the dancing and the plays and the mince pies. Now she stayed in the background, for once impatient for the Christmas celebrations to be over in order to renew her suits to the queen for leave to see her brother.

New Year's Day was the traditional time for the exchange of gifts between queen and courtiers and in the hopes of reminding Elizabeth of former happier such days when her brother was in favour, Penelope chose this moment to write a long and impassioned letter to the queen on her brother's behalf. She followed it up with gifts and jewels.

Penelope was desperate, as her letter to the queen of the 1st January 1600 shows. It had been left to her to intercede on her brother's behalf and she proved an impassioned advocate. It was well-known that the queen disliked reading long letters – twenty-two lines was considered the maximum she would normally take. This was a letter with a difference, every word was carefully read.

There is an air of breathless frenzy about the letter and it is extravagant and over-blown, quite unlike her usual simple style; yet it is an eloquent plea for her 'unfortunate brother, whom all men have liberty to defame'. Penelope accused her brother's enemies of conspiring against him: 'those combined enemies that labour on false grounds to build his ruin'. She warned the queen that once these enemies have succeeded in bringing down her brother they would then turn against the queen herself: they 'will not only pull down all the obstacles of their greatness but when they are in their full strength like the giants make war against heaven'. These were dangerous words – the imagery does not disguise the accusation – but in the face of her beloved brother's predicament she was fearless, regardless of her own safety.

There is an even more powerful image of the danger in the second long paragraph when she moves on from classical mythology to biblical allusion. Her brother's enemies 'understand one another too well' and will grow more dangerous 'if God do not hinder the work as the tower of Babel and confound their tongues'. She reminds Her Majesty of her father's death in Ireland, imploring her not to allow two members of the family to perish through service in that country. Lavish in her compliments to the queen, at the same time she does not hesitate to speak out against 'partial judges' and 'those that lie in ambush'.

The text of the letter follows:

Early did I hope this morning to have had mine eyes blessed with your Majesty's beauty, but seeing the sun depart into a cloud and meeting with spirits which did presage by the wheels of their chariot some thunder in the air, I must complain and express my fears to the high majesty and divine oracle from whence I received a doubtful answer. Unto whose power I must sacrifice again the tears and prayers of the afflicted that must despair in time, if it be too soon to importune heaven when we feel the misery of hell or that words directed to the sacred wisdom should be out of season, delivered for my unfortunate brother, whom all men have liberty to defame as if his offence was capital and he so base dejected a creature that his love his life his service to your beauties and the state had deserved no absolution after so hard punishment, or so much as to answer in your fair presence, who would vouchsafe more justice and favour than he can expect of partial judges or those combined enemies that labour on false grounds to build his ruin, urging his faults as criminal to your divine honour, thinking it a heaven to blaspheme heaven; whereas by their own particular malice and counsel they have practised to glut themselves in their own private revenge, not regarding your service and loss so much as their ambition and to rise by his overthrow; and I have reason to apprehend that if your fair hands do not check the courses of their unbridled hate, their last courses will be his last breath, since the evil instruments that they by their officious cunning provide for the feast, have sufficient poison in their hearts to infect: the service that they will serve shall be easy to digest till it be tasted, and then it will prove a preparative of great mischief, concealed among such crafty workmen as will not only pull down all the obstacles of their greatness, but when they are in their full strength like the giants make war against heaven.

But your Majesty's gracious conclusion in giving hope of a voider is all the comfort I have, which, if you hasten not before he take a full surfeit of disgrace, they will say the spots they have cast on him are too foul to be washed away, and so his blemished reputation must disable him for ever serving again his sacred goddess, whose excellent beauties and perfections will never suffer those fair eyes to turn so far from compassion, but that the least if he may not return to the happiness of his former service, to live at the feet of his admired mistress, yet he may sit down to a private life, without the imputation of infamy: that his posterity may not repent that their fathers were born of so hard a destiny, two of them perishing by being employed in one country, where they would have done you loyal service to the shedding of their last blood, if they had not been wounded to death behind by faction of them that care not on whose necks they unjustly build the walls of their own fortunes, which I fear will grow more dangerously higher than is yet discovered if God do not hinder the work as the tower of Babel, and confound their tongues that understand one another too well. And lastly since out of your Majesty's own princely nature and unstained virtue there must needs appear that mercy is not far from such a beauty, I must humbly beseech you make it your own work and not suffer those to take advantage that lie in ambush thinking so soon as they discover a relenting and compassion in your worthy mind, to take the honour upon them as means of our salvation, not out of charity but pride, that all must be attributed to them and your sacred clemency abused by forcing us to go through purgatory to heaven. But let your majesty's divine power be no more eclipsed than your beauties which hath shined throughout all the world, and imitate the highest in not destroying those that trust in your mercy, with which humble request I presume to kiss your sacred hands vowing all obedience and endless love of your majesty.

Your majesty's most loyal and obedient servant,
Penelope Rich[13]

This outspoken letter, far from pacifying the queen,was the cause of serious trouble for Penelope herself.

On the 2nd February 1600, Rowland White was writing to Robert Sidney:

My Lord Mountjoy is not yet gone. This day sennight my Ladies Leicester and Rich were at Mr Beck's house upon Richmond Green and were humble suitors to Her Majesty to have access unto her; but they returned back again without comfort. I heard that my Lady Rich was called before my Lord Treasurer or Mr Secretary for a letter she had written to Her Majesty; what it was I know not. The Earl of Essex is well again and walks up and down the house and garden with my Lord Keeper; small hope of grace or liberty appears.[14]

With Essex's recovery, plans for his trial were resumed. The earl's friends were relying on Mountjoy's support for their leader and with the power of the army behind him Mountjoy now became the key figure in the Essex group. Before he left for Ireland Mountjoy, no doubt under Penelope's influence, promised his support for a plan to use the army to secure Essex's release, obtaining Essex's oath that nothing would be done to harm the queen. He also insisted that King James of Scotland's agreement should be obtained to the proposal. James delayed giving his reply and when it eventually came it was evasive.

Penelope was now called before the Privy Council to explain her bold letter. If this body of dignitaries had expected to overawe her she was not easily daunted. She refused to withdraw her letter but firmly stood by what she had written. By the sheer force of her presence and her cool demeanour Penelope was able to convince the privy council of her loyalty to the queen. She had written a postscript to the letter which must have been added by her at the time of interrogation. It read: 'This letter being showed at the Council table and willed to make exposition thereof and what she meant by it, I answered presently that what I meant I wrote and what I wrote I meant. P.R.'[15] Her courage and resoluteness had won the day.

Penelope appeared to be in the clear and Mountjoy could no longer postpone his departure for Ireland. He left on the 7th February 1600, the day before Essex's trial was due to begin. In the event the hearing did not take place and it was perhaps with some prior knowledge of an adjournment that Mountjoy departed. On the following day Dudley Carleton reported: 'My Lord of Essex came not to the Star Chamber on Wednesday, as was expected . . . The Lady Rich has written again to Her Majesty, but in other kind of language.'[16]

Mountjoy's restraining influence on Penelope can be felt, as his last piece of advice before his departure, in the sending of this second conciliatory letter. Penelope was, however, far from out of difficulty. On the 22nd February John Chamberlain wrote to Dudley Carleton: 'The Lady Rich hath been called coram [i.e. publicly] again about her letter, but she excused herself by sickness.'[17] Worse was to follow. Penelope's New Year's Day letter was now printed without her knowledge and made public. On the 25th February, Rowland White was writing to Sir Robert Sidney:

> The Earl of Essex is little spoken of at court. Mislike is taken that his mother and friends have been in a house that looks into York Garden where he uses to walk and have saluted each other out of a window. My Lady Rich is commanded to keep her house; the cause is thought to be that by her means certain copies of a letter she writ to the queen is published abroad. She denies it; Lady Leicester has in hand a gown she will send the queen which will cost her £100 at least.[18]

Penelope's denial was not of the letter itself but that she had in any way been responsible for its printing or publication. On the 3rd March Rowland White was writing:

> Yesterday the Countess of Leicester sent the Queen a most curious fine gown . . . Her Majesty liked it well but did not accept or refuse it only answered that things standing as they did it was not fit for her to desire what she did . . . Her Majesty's displeasure is nothing lessened towards the Earl of Essex.

However, there was then a rumour that Essex was about to be released. On 8th March Rowland White reported:

> All this week the lords have been in London and passed away the time in feasting and plays . . . there was an expectation that Lord Essex

should have come to his own house; it is conjectured that Ladies
Leicester, Southampton, Northumberland and Rich assembled
themselves at Essex House to receive him, which hindered it.

We can imagine the women preparing for the homecoming only to be
thwarted again by the queen's contrariness. Essex did return to his own
house on the 22nd March, but as a prisoner under house arrest.

Penelope now tried to make herself as inconspicuous as possible and
on the 29th March Carleton reported to Chamberlain: 'Lady Rich, once
more summoned to answer about her letter, feigns sickness and has stolen
into the country.'[19]

However, both her and her brother's cause received a further setback
with the publication of a letter the Earl had written to Anthony Bacon two
years earlier. In this letter, referred to as the earl's apology, Essex had
favoured the continuance of war with Spain at a time when Lord Burghley
had supported peace. Now, on the 28th May, Chamberlain reported that
this 'apology was lately printed with the Lady Rich's letter in the end and
some few of them sold, but they were presently suppressed and upon
search, found not to be done so much upon friendship or faction as upon
hope of gain: the poor Lady is like to have the worse of it, being sent for
and come up to answer and interpret her riddles.'[20]

Finally, in June, it was decided that instead of a formal trial in the
Court of Star Chamber, Essex should be interrogated by eighteen commissioners sitting at York House. The case against him, based on the
earlier charges, was drawn up by the Attorney-General Sir Edward Coke
and Essex's former protégé Francis Bacon. After the Attorney-General
had dealt with the charges against Essex he went on to refer to Lady Rich's
letter to the queen which 'was pressed with very bitter and hard terms'. He
called it 'an insolent, saucy, malapert action'.[21] The hearing lasted the
whole day, from 8 a.m. in the morning till nearly 9 p.m. at night, but still
no decision was reached.

Penelope's own interrogation followed. Sir Robert Cecil left the
conduct of this to the Lord Treasurer, Lord Buckhurst, but gave explicit
instructions on how the questioning should be conducted. Penelope
proved more than a match for Lord Buckhurst. First of all he had some
trouble in finding her, though she had been ordered to remain at Leighs

under her husband's control. When eventually he did catch up with her she had no difficulty in convincing her interrogator of her sincerity and repentance. Buckhurst's report to Cecil of the 13th August on the result was brief:

> It was Tuesday before the Lady Rich came unto me, for she was gone to Barn Elms and thither was I fain to send for her. I took that course with her which your letters prescribed. She seemed very glad of this riddance and prayed me to give Her Majesty most humble thanks for her favour, which she acknowledged with her follies and faults committed and assured that this should be a warning to her for ever not to commit the like; concluding still with her most humble desire to have the happiness to see Her Majesty, until which she should never enjoy a day of comfort to her heart.[22]

Cecil's answer was lengthy and he clearly took the matter very seriously indeed. First of all he dwelt on the queen's personal interest in Lady Rich's answers, which she had closely studied. Then on the queen's behalf he reprimanded the Lord Treasurer for his delay in dealing with Lady Rich and that 'you were still so apt to excuse my Lady's course in her former answers by imputing that to fear only in her of giving further offence, which rather showed a proud disposition and not much better than a plain contempt of Her Majesty and yourself that was used in the cause.'[23] Cecil had warned Buckhurst not to be too readily charmed by Penelope and was angry that in spite of this the Lord Treasurer had so easily melted.

However, the queen was ready to accept Penelope's contrition: 'Her Majesty hath noted in her declaration her sorrow for Her Majesty's displeasure, her fear to offend further, her humble and obedient spirit to satisfy all doubts and her great desire to recover Her Majesty's favour.'

The Lord Treasurer was to deliver this answer to Lady Rich:

> that it is true Her Majesty was displeased, as she had cause, to see that she, being a lady to whom it did not appertain so to meddle in such

matters, would be so bold to write in such a style to her, especially when . . . her former careless and dry answers showed how little she valued Her Majesty's commandments; but . . . she is pleased now . . . to give her leave to dispose herself as may best agree with her own health or other respect.

In spite of the preamble of stern warnings, Penelope was thus acquitted. The queen could not, however, resist a few further barbed remarks (via Cecil), pointing out that though Penelope might not have intended the printing of her letter yet she had been 'negligent that others might come by it' and that 'shrewd circumstances might be inferred upon such a voluntary negligence if it were not that by her sincerity of obedience she hath sought to make amends'.

Finally, having passed on Her Majesty's messages, Cecil got to the point that had obviously been deeply concerning him. In her New Year's Day letter Penelope had not actually given the names of her brother's enemies. That letter had caused enough of a furore but in spite of all the risks Penelope had written a further letter, for the queen's eyes alone, this time naming names. So seriously had Elizabeth taken this that she had burnt the letter without showing it to a single person, not even telling Cecil himself the names. This was a slap in the face for Cecil, not only because he expected to be taken into Her Majesty's confidence but he suspected that his name had been there: 'I doubt not but I was and am in her Ladyship's contemplation the person on whom all the figures of that letter did principally play.'

If he was right then the queen was using him as a vehicle to convey to Penelope that the confidentiality of her letter had not been broken. In her first letter Penelope had warned the queen that her brother's enemies would next turn against the queen herself. She had clearly convinced Elizabeth of her sincerity and given sufficient evidence for her beliefs as to make the queen treat them seriously. If Penelope had indeed denounced Cecil it was to remain a secret between the queen and herself and Cecil would never be sure.

Penelope had been 'under command' at St Bartholomews, Lord Rich's London home, although she had evidently escaped for a time to Barn Elms to see her sister-in-law Frances.[24] Now she was free. She used her freedom to return to Leighs Priory to attend to her husband who had fallen seriously ill. Lord Rich was reported to be 'extreme sick and in danger' and Penelope stayed with her husband and nursed him through his illness.[25] She had as her companion the Countess of Southampton and they were later joined by the earl her husband, as reported in a letter of the 30th September 1600: 'My Lord of Southampton is returned out of the Low Countries and is with his Lady at Lord Rich's in Essex'.[26]

The queen postponed any decision about Essex himself until the end of August and then finally released him from house arrest. He could go anywhere, except to the court. He went first to the country to rest and then returned to Essex House but was still barred from the court. In addition to everything else he was deeply concerned about his now disastrous financial position. In particular, he was relying on the queen's renewing the lease of the sweet wines due to expire in September 1600. As so often, Elizabeth vacillated and it was not until the end of October that Essex knew where he stood. The queen refused to renew his grant. When he wrote to her in mid-November to congratulate her on the 42nd anniversary of her accession, his letter went unanswered.

His position, as he saw it, was untenable and led on by some of his friends in particular his secretary Henry Cuffe he began gathering together his comrades and all the disaffected who saw him as their great salvation.

Penelope had returned to London from Leighs after nursing her husband back to health and threw herself into the task of assisting her brother. Her role was to round up supporters for his cause and in this connection she visited as many of her brother's friends as possible to canvass their support. Later they were all to be tracked down and summoned to account. Afterwards Essex was to accuse her of a much more serious involvement and to suggest that he was goaded on by her beyond his own ambitions.

As Essex's plans took shape, news of his intentions was leaked to the government and on 7th February 1601 he was summoned to attend the Privy Council. Fearing imprisonment, he refused to leave his house, saying he was ill.

It was on the afternoon of that day that Shakespeare's play *Richard II* was performed to an enthusiastic audience of Essex's followers. Some of them had visited the players of the Lord Chamberlain's company earlier in the week and persuaded them to restage this old play. The actors were reluctant to revive the play but were tempted by a bonus of 40s.0d. over and above the takings. The significance of the choice of play was, of course, that it depicted the deposing of a reigning monarch. The power of a live performance of Shakespeare's drama to stimulate and embolden its audience was clearly not underestimated by Essex's supporters.

That night Essex supped with Lady Rich, the Earl of Southampton, Sir Christopher Blount and his closest friends deciding what should be done. Convinced that he had so many supporters, he decided to carry on with his plan. Later that night Penelope sent a messenger to Sir Henry Bromley, had him roused from his bed and brought to her and told him that her brother's life was in danger and he must act in the city the next day. The following morning, on the fatal day of the 8th February, she drove from Essex House at ten o'clock to call on the Earl of Bedford and, by sheer force of personality, she forced him to come back with her in her coach without the knowledge of his family. Once she had desposited him there and he was out of her sight, Bedford took fright and would not take part in the events that followed. Instead he fled to the court for refuge.

Early that morning Essex's messengers went out summoning his followers and, as the morning went on, three hundred armed men gathered in the courtyard at Essex House. The queen sent four members of the council including the Lord Keeper and the Lord Chief Justice to learn the cause of his discontent. Essex locked up these emissaries who seemed to treat the event lightly. They were eager to turn it into a social occasion, asking that Lady Rich and the Countess of Essex be 'brought down into the chamber where the lords were, the better to pass the time'.[27] To Penelope this would have been fraternising with the enemy. Instead, she used the incident as an opportunity to boost the morale of her brother's supporters. The prisoners were in a room on the upper floor of the house. She strolled out into the courtyard and began bantering with their guards, calling up that 'if they were true gentlemen they would throw her down the head of that old fellow', indicating the Lord Chief Justice Popham, her particular bête noir. The prisoners, who of course heard it all, soon realised they had underestimated her.[28]

Essex continued with his plan to march on London. He hoped to round up supporters as he went, but the Londoners did not join him and the march was abandoned. He returned home thinking he could still negotiate with the queen because of the important hostages he had taken.

Instead, he found that they had been rescued.

There was a brief siege of Essex House. Lady Rich, the Countess of Essex and their attendant ladies were still in the house and, amid the volleying of guns and flowing of blood, the waiting women 'filled the place with their shrieks and cries'. The fact that the ladies were present shows how unprepared Essex was for a seige. There was a suggestion that the women should be allowed to leave but the Earl of Southampton was against this because it meant unbarring the doors, thus making them all vulnerable. Finally, at ten o'clock that evening the rebels surrendered. By three o'clock the following morning, Essex and Southampton, with their chief supporters, were confined in the Tower. Penelope herself was put into the custody of the Keeper of the Privy Purse.

Thereafter events followed rapidly. The Privy Council was convened on the 13th February and by the 17th the indictments were laid. There is a long roll of the names of those involved in the rebellion. At the head of the list appear the following names:

EARL OF ESSEX	EARL OF BEDFORD
EARL OF RUTLAND	EARL OF SUSSEX
EARL OF SOUTHAMPTON	LADY RICH[29]

It is a measure of the seriousness with which Penelope's part in the affair is regarded that she is named as one of the protagonists.

Essex's trial took place on the 19th February. Amongst the peers who tried him and pronounced the sentence of death was his brother-in-law, Lord Rich. Of the five earls whose names appeared with Penelope's both her brother and the Earl of Southampton were condemned to death for treason, the Earls of Bedford and Rutland were heavily fined, even though Bedford, who had been brought to Essex House by Penelope on the morning of the rebellion had then fled to Court for sanctuary. Only the Earl of Sussex escaped sentence, because he was away from home at the time.

Evidence was given that the plot was conceived the night before at supper which the earl had taken with his closest friends.[30] The names of those who attended the supper were given: the Earl of Southampton, Sir Christopher Blount, Sir Charles Danvers, Sir Robert Vernon (brother of Elizabeth, Countess of Southampton) and Lady Rich. Of those named the first three were condemned to death for treason and Sir Robert Vernon was heavily fined.

At his trial, Essex had remained calm when the inevitable sentence of execution was pronounced. Two days after his trial however, he made a private confession to Cecil and others incriminating his associates. Among those he accused was his sister Penelope, linking her with Mountjoy.

Mountjoy, in Ireland, had not been involved in the events of the Essex rebellion, though he had given his qualified approval to the plan to use the army to secure Essex's release. Once he was in command in Ireland he rejected all such ideas. Southampton had arrived in Ireland in the middle of May with a proposal to revive the plan and Mountjoy refused. Later in the summer Sir Charles Danvers came over to seek a letter from Mountjoy to the queen in which he would voice a complaint about the ill-government of the state and again Mountjoy declined to be involved. Once out of reach of Penelope's influence, he exercised his natural prudence and did nothing further in support of the plan.

He had not abandoned Essex and indeed proved his loyalty by his appeals to Sir Robert Cecil on Essex's behalf. He went out of his way to justify the earl's conduct of affairs in Ireland, maintaining that even if Essex had brought with him a far greater army he could not have achieved anything more in the short time of his stay.

Mountjoy had been trying to obtain Elizabeth's permission to return. Four days before the rebellion he wrote to ask leave to come back and report to her, promising 'if she will have it so I will lie in the porch of her doors and not see my wife [as he euphemistically termed Penelope] till my return to her army as Uriah did'.[31]

The report of the rebellion and that Essex was in the Tower did not reach Mountjoy in Ireland until two weeks after the event. Years later his secretary told how the news

much dismayed him and his nearest friends and wrought strange alteration in him . . . In truth his Lordship had good cause to be wary in his words and actions, since by some confessions in England himself was tainted with privity to the Earl's practices, so that howsoever he continued still to importune leave to come over, yet no doubt he meant nothing less but rather (if he had been sent for) was purposed with his said friends to sail into France, they having privately fitted themselves with many necessaries thereunto. For howsoever his Lordship were not dangerously engaged therein yet he was (as he privately professed) fully resolved not to put his neck under the file of the Queen's Attorney's tongue. But his Lordship's former service, and the necessity of his future employment together with good success, so strengthened him, as without great unthankfulness and popular obloquy, he could not have been questioned upon this weak ground.[32]

Even his loyal secretary was not taken into Mountjoy's confidence, so closely did he guard his every move. He was not a man to shrink from duty or danger but it would be characteristic of him to have ready contingency plans for every eventuality.

Cecil's report of the rebellion, 'so miserable an accident', he termed it, pointed the course Mountjoy must take: 'when you consider how near Her Majesty was to destruction and the kingdom to usurpation, the joy of her preservation will extinguish all other good affections which long familiarity and confidence in the innocence of your friends have bred in you towards them.'[33]

He went on to predict with ominous certainty that by the time Mountjoy received the letter Essex, Southampton and the other principals would have lost their heads. Reading this letter Mountjoy could not fail to see that his first step must be to clear himself of implication. In his careful reply to Cecil, Mountjoy recognised that his

long and inward familiarity with the principal actors of this miserable tragedy may give just reason . . . to look upon me in this matter with some jealousy, yet I am confident in my own conscience and in my prince's favour and justice . . . for the present, I dare assure you, the army is free from infection of this conspiracy and doubt not but to contain it firm and obedient to resist or suppress anything that shall grow in this kingdom, if therein there hath been any seeds of this sedition sowed.[34]

Mountjoy's letter is a masterpiece of precision, every word carefully weighed. To get the tone right he answered Cecil in very nearly the same words as Cecil's own, so that he appeared to be in exact accord with the queen and her secretary. He departed from this only to assure them that the army was not seditous, for the present, and he undertook to maintain its loyalty. He had not been asked about the army but volunteered this information. There is the merest hint in those words 'for the present' that would not escape notice. His reference to the possibility of seeds of sedition within the army and his assurance of his ability to keep the army firm are presented as expressions of his loyalty but at the same time indicate a potential source of further danger which he alone has power to control. Yet, so masterly is the letter that there is nothing that could give offence.

He went on to swear his complete loyalty and allegiance to the queen: 'nothing on earth neither an angel from heaven, shall make me deceive the trust she hath reposed in me.' It was no devil but an angel that could possibly cause him to swerve. There is a subtle reference to Penelope here (whom he called his angel) and he is reassuring the queen that he will not allow himself to be swayed even by Penelope.

Mountjoy also wrote to Lord Nottingham, the Lord High Admiral, for advice. Lord Nottingham replied:

> I think Her Majesty would be most glad to look upon your black eyes here so she was sure you would not look with too much respect on other black eyes. But for that if the Admiral were but thirty years old I think he would not differ in opinions from the Lord Mountjoy.[35]

The gallant compliment to the thirty-seven year old Penelope should not close our eyes to the fact that it was the Lord High Admiral who had carried out the task of laying siege to Essex House whilst Penelope was there, threatening to blow it up. Nor does it conceal the real message. Mountjoy is still in favour with the queen (and indeed was indispensable at

Mountjoy is still in favour with the queen (and indeed was indispensable at this point) but his continuing association with Penelope would only serve to discredit him. Nevertheless, Mountjoy's power to protect the woman he called his wife must have been very apparent.

Although Mountjoy had taken no part in the rebellion, when those involved came to make their confessions his name appeared. He had been involved in the earlier plan to use the army to release Essex. It was at his house in Holborn that a number of meetings of the conspirators had taken place. Southampton related his attempt to persuade Mountjoy to return with the army and although Mountjoy had refused, the episode along with all the other references to him was enough to implicate him, had the queen and her advisers been so minded. Instead, Elizabeth suppressed that part of Southampton's story that referred to Mountjoy and was at pains to absolve her Lord Deputy from any complicity.

The queen now wrote a gracious letter to Mountjoy, acknowledging his faithfulness and love. Just as in Mountjoy's letter to Cecil, there is an undercurrent of matters left unspoken. She asked him to assure himself that none of his captains had 'hollow hearts' towards her and promised to pardon those who had been 'seduced and blindly led' by Essex.[36] Nothing is stated explicitly about his own role but nothing needed to be said. Regarding his request for leave to return she asked him to postpone it for the time being, promising to recall him the next winter and then keep him near her. The reason she gave was an imminent threat from the Spanish fleet and indeed the menace of Spain was a constant concern, since the Irish had repeatedly sought help from Catholic Spain. Spanish forces in fact arrived later in the year.

In his letter to Mountjoy Nottingham went on to tell of Essex's behaviour after his trial and of those upon whom he had so needlessly drawn suspicion, his friend Southampton, his stepfather Christopher Blount, his secretary Henry Cuffe. Worst of all Essex had betrayed his sister, incriminating her in the plot and seeking to pass the blame onto her for goading him on.

> And now, said he, I must accuse one who is most nearest to me, my sister, who did continually urge me on with telling me how all my friends and followers thought me a coward and that I had lost all my

valour; and thus that she must be looked to, for she had a proud spirit.[37]

Nottingham then reported how Essex had spoken about the love affair between Penelope and Mountjoy, 'and spared not to say something of her affection to you. Would your lordship have thought this weakness and this unnaturalness in this man?' Nottingham asks.

During this period Penelope herself had been committed to imprisonment in the house of Henry Sackford, Keeper of the Privy Purse. When no food or linen was provided for her, she asked for 'a cook to dress her meat' and for 'linen and other necessaries' and Lord Rich was requested by the Privy Council to supply these.[38] He ignored the request and six days later on 22nd February had to be ordered by the Privy Council to supply these needs, including all the bedding and hangings she required. In the meantime, her brother had been condemned to death.

Penelope herself was examined by the Privy Council and did not reveal the weakness of her brother but 'used herself with that modesty and wisdom as the report being made unto Her Majesty she was presently set at liberty and sent unto my lord her husband'.[39] Her cool way of conducting herself on this occasion deserves our admiration, particularly when we bear in mind that at this moment when death was all around her, she stood alone. Mountjoy was far away in Ireland, Lord Rich had abandoned her and she had had to face the death and betrayal of her much loved brother.

As well as her own self-possession Penelope had to thank for her freedom the absent figure of Mountjoy. If she had been harmed the consequences could have been momentous. The powerful commander would not have repeated Essex's mistake in returning from Ireland with insufficient men. The queen and her advisers were very much aware of Penelope's protector in his unique position of strength on the horizon, pressing to return. If Mountjoy had been prepared, with reservations, to use the army to support her brother, how much more likely was he to do so to defend Penelope herself. There was certainly enough evidence to implicate her, but it was clearly considered expedient to set her free. She alone of all those actively participating in the events of the rebellion was released without any penalty whatsoever.

After her release Penelope wrote to thank Lord Nottingham for his assistance. Nottingham passed her letter on to Mountjoy. It is a poignant letter:

> For my desserts towards him that is gone, it is known that I have been more like a slave than a sister, which proceeded out of my exceeding love rather than his authority . . . so strangely have I been wronged, as may well be an argument to make one despise the world, finding the smoke of envy where affection should be clearest.[40]

Penelope's complete denial of acting in the rebellion other than 'like a slave' to her brother is indeed the only answer she could have given. Anything else would have been her death-warrant. Nevertheless, there must have been some truth in her brother's accusation. Certainly he had nothing to gain by inventing it. Penelope herself may not have been conscious of the full extent of her part in encouraging Essex in his plans. Her 'exceeding love' for her brother may have caused her to push him further than he had ever intended. She had spurred him on when he had vacillated. He might have held back but for her driving him on, believing it to be for his own good. His mother and sisters had always been extremely ambitious for him and Penelope certainly had the forcefulness to propel him along any course of action she believed to be for his ultimate advancement.

To Penelope, energetically rounding up supporters for her brother, it may indeed have seemed that she was merely carrying out his wishes. But the tone of Essex's accusation, that his sister goaded him on by telling him his friends thought him a coward, has an authentic ring, echoing back to their childhood, to the small boy and his dominant elder sister.

Her 'exceeding love' is not to be doubted and his denunciation of her is the bitterest blow. She attributes it to envy. Why should her brother have envied her? Perhaps because he recognised the strength of character which would not break as his own had.

Penelope's letter to Nottingham is notable for its complete lack of self-pity. Instead her anxieties are for Mountjoy and she gets to the heart of her letter when she begs Nottingham's support for her lover (whom she delicately refers to as 'a worthy friend of yours'). Her letter continues:

> Your Lordship's noble disposition forceth me to deliver my griefs unto you, hearing a report that some of those malicious tongues have sought to wrong a worthy friend of yours. I know the most of them did hate him for his zealous following the service of Her Majesty and beseech you to pardon my presuming thus much, though I hope his enemies can have no power to harm him.

Penelope's courage is remarkable★

Essex was executed on 25th February 1601, only six days after the trial. Mountjoy though spared from implication was refused permission to return from Ireland. Sir Christopher Blount, for his part in the rebellion, was executed a few weeks after Essex, leaving Lettice a widow for the third time. The Earl of Southampton's death sentence was commuted to life imprisonment but he was released by King James on his accession to the throne.

In the aftermath Penelope wisely lay low and there is no further news of her for some time after her release. Then on the 28th December 1602 Rowland White (whose letters to Sir Robert Sidney had ceased on his master's return in time to play a part in Essex's arrest) broke a long silence to voice his apprehension over 'a matter of danger'. 'The storm,' he reported, 'continues now and then, but all depends upon my Lady Rich's being or not being amongst you.'[41] Penelope's part was certainly not underestimated. She had been at the eye of the storm and there was still

---

★For a very different reaction to these momentous events we can turn to the diary of Lady Margaret Hoby, Penelope's ex-sister-in-law. For the 8th January 1601 she records meeting Lady Rich at Walsingham House. After she came home she had toothache which continued for four days. Her entry for the 26th January runs into the 8th February. She is ill and remains weak and cannot go out of her chamber. It is the day of the Essex rebellion. She mentions the arraignment of Essex and Southampton on the 19th and their being condemned to death. She thanks God she is better. She has in fear taken to her bed not to emerge until it is all over and she is safe. Such a frightened reaction is natural, but contrasts strongly with Penelope's own courage. (M. Hoby, *Diary*, p.161).

danger.

Her central role as the last protagonist left connected with the conspiracy was recognised for its importance. Though she herself remained untouched, her very presence could be a danger to others. With the ripples of the storm still not spent nearly two years later, evidence of association with her at the time of the rebellion could still be used to prove a connection with it. Penelope's part in the rebellion was the last link in a broken chain.

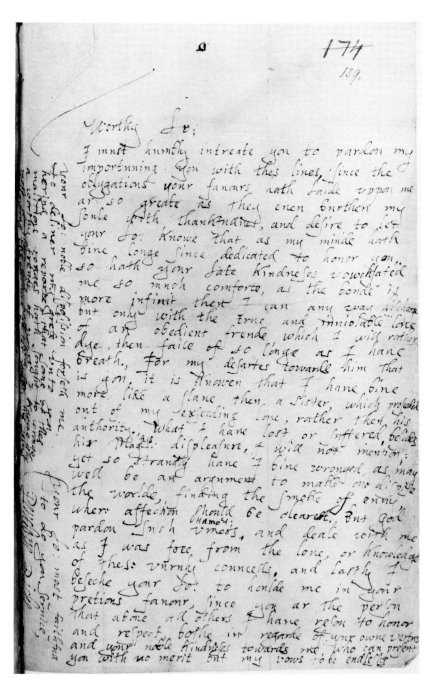

A letter written by Lady Penelope Rich to Lord Nottingham, the Lord High Admiral, in which she excuses her part in the Essex rising. See Page 147.

CHAPTER TWELVE

'No lord in England might compare'

After her brother's death, Penelope was abandoned by her husband. So long as Essex was alive he could be useful to Lord Rich, who would never have risked offending him by publicly rejecting his sister. Now that he was dead, Rich had no further need of Penelope. On her side, any shreds of affection that might have remained could not have survived the part he had played in condemning her brother to death, however much that brother had failed her at the last moment.

These were dark years for Penelope, when she was very much alone and friendless. She had no money of her own and her brother's estate, from which she had previously benefited, had been forfeited to the crown. When she tried to recover her dowry from Lord Rich in order to have something to live on, he refused to return it. Eventually he was compelled to give her an allowance, paid for, of course, out of the income on her dowry. Her future happiness was bound up with Mountjoy's safe return. He had left for Ireland in February 1600 and he and Penelope were to be parted for three and a half years.

Mountjoy was now thirty-seven. He had remained a batchelor, faithful and constant to Penelope, whom he indeed called his wife. He had recently purchased from the Devereux family the great house at Wanstead and there he hoped to lead a peaceful country life with Penelope and their children.[1] A military life was not the one he would have chosen for preference except as a means of advancement.

He had the right personality for leadership. Apart from the more obvious qualities like physical courage and stamina his temperament was particularly suited to the needs of the Irish campaign. He had excellent judgement, being both decisive and judicious, with a quiet confidence in his own decisions. He kept his word in public affairs absolutely and the Irish knew precisely where they stood in their dealings with him, in marked contrast to their experience with Essex. He also had the ability not only to listen attentively to what was being said to him but by carefully watching the speaker to analyse his motives. To many he appeared cold but even his reserve was a contributing factor towards his successful campaigning, for he so closely guarded his secrets that no one knew in advance what his plans would be. He was described as 'a gentle enemy', but he was a man who would pursue his enemies steadily and persistently.[2]

To Tyrone, the Irish rebel leader, he appreared at first an easy target. 'The English commander,' said Tyrone, 'would lose the season of action whilst his breakfast was preparing.'[3] In peacetime Charles liked to breakfast heartily, in war, he limited himself to a dry crust of bread. He looked after his health very carefully, forewarned no doubt by Penelope of her father's and brother's tales of the rigours of the Irish climate. He would wear two or even three pairs of stockings and three waistcoats in winter, with a scarf wound round his neck three times under his ruff. As his secretary commented, 'I never observed any of his age and strength to keep his body so warm.' He was determined to survive.

During the months that followed the rebellion, Mountjoy stepped up the campaign in Ireland. Mountjoy's system for breaking down resistance in Ireland was very different from Essex's. Essex had marshalled his troops in preparation for a major confrontation. Mountjoy's tactics were to march across the country, beating down opposition as he went, destroying crops and leaving behind him small garrisons at strategic points. He starved the Irish into submission and in the resulting famine, they were said to be reduced to eating their own horses for food.

In spite of his successes, he did not always feel Elizabeth was giving him the support he needed. In a letter to her he bitterly likened himself to a scullion. The queen's next letter to him began in her inimitable style: 'Mistress kitchenmaid'. However it went on to assure him of her appreciation of his loyalty and work.[4] Mountjoy longed to return, drawn, it was said 'by the unhallowed ties which bound him to Lord Rich's wife'. On Christmas Eve 1601 he won a resounding victory at Kinsale, not only defeating the Irish but the Spanish forces who had come to their aid, in a battle that established English supremacy in Ireland. Incredibly, it was won with the loss of only six English lives, with Irish losses of more than one thousand. The defeat of the Spanish soldiers at Kinsale completed the work of the Armada in the downfall of Spain and thereafter she was ready to sue for peace. Mountjoy's victory was to prove one of the most far-reaching in its effect of the whole Elizabethan reign.

After the battle a great wave of sickness spread through the English army, many dying from influenza. Mountjoy himself fell seriously ill and for a time it seemed he might not recover. For months he was unable to eat or sleep properly and he suffered severe headaches. Nevertheless he eventually pulled through. Even after the victory the war dragged on and it was not until the following Christmas that the rebellion was finally suppressed and Tyrone surrendered.

Now that he had brought Tyrone down, Mountjoy was magnanimous in victory. He expressed the view that 'the lower he is brought the more it will be for the queen's honour to show mercy.'[5] When Tyrone's sister begged to see her brother he wanted to permit this, saying, 'If I thought the Queen would not be angry I would give the lady leave to come to her brother, for I am loth to make war with women, especially since she is now great with child.'[6]

By March 1603 Tyrone was set to go to England to kneel before the queen and be pardoned.

The queen was now in her seventieth year and her strength was slowly ebbing. She grew weaker and, on the 24th March 1603, she died.

Although Mountjoy was desperately anxious to leave Ireland the new King James wanted him to continue a while longer. At last, on May 29th 1603, Mountjoy sailed for England, bringing Tyrone with him to Wanstead. James showered honours on him, creating him Earl of Devonshire and a privy councillor, giving him grants of lands, appointing him Master of Ordnance and promoting him from Lord Deputy to Lord Lieutenant of Ireland. As the victorious general of the army that had defeated the Irish and Spanish at Kinsale he was given a prominent place in the peace conference of 1604 in which Spain finally conceded defeat to England.

After all the years of misery and separation, now at last Mountjoy began to reap the rewards of his endeavours, settling down to a life of ease and contentment at Wanstead. There he could enjoy all the things that gave him pleasure, hunting and walking in the country, his books, entertaining his close friends, crowned by the fact that Penelope now openly joined him as mistress of Wanstead. As his means increased 'so his table was better served, so that in his latter time no Lord in England might compare with him in that kind of bounty.' He loved the gardens at Wanstead, fishing in its lakes, hunting and hawking in its parks, and he developed a fine library there. The poet Samuel Daniel wrote of him that he did not have

> books as many have
> For ostentation but for use.[7]

He particularly liked reading plays and would make notes in the margins of the books as he read.

For Penelope too the dark times were over for a while at least. Elizabeth had turned against Penelope ever since her letter to the queen in defence of her brother and her support of him during the rebellion. With a new king on the throne Penelope had to reinstate herself and win back a place at court.

The uncertainties that had darkened the latter years of Elizabeth's reign had left their mark and even before her death there was a mood of pessimism and disillusion. However, as long as she was queen, her own moral standards set the tone for the rest of the court.

With King James on the throne the climate of the court changed. Whereas Elizabeth could command respect by the sheer force of her presence, James could not have been more different. Though no fool, he cut a poor figure and was without dignity. Along with his pleasure-loving queen, Anne of Denmark, he plunged into a life of extravagance and luxury. Not that these had been absent during Elizabeth's reign, but then the extravagance had been in celebration of remarkable achievements. Under James the prevailing tone of the court reflected a feverish abandonment to pleasure. It was to be a court of scandal and corruption as well as of magnificent spectacle.

Penelope travelled with other ladies of rank in the spring of 1603 to the border to meet James' queen and escort her to London. At last she was in full favour and her continued support of James dating right back to the late 1580s was not forgotten, During the progress back to court it was observed that 'Now was my Lady Rich grown great with the Queen.' Queen Anne was noticed to behave slightingly to the 'stately old dames' of

Elizabeth's Court and particularly favoured the young women. 'There we saw the Queen's favour to my Lady Hatton and my Lady Cecil; for she showed no favour to the elderly ladies but to my Lady Rich and such like company.'[8] Penelope was then forty.

For a while, Penelope's star was in the ascendancy. She was made a Lady of the Drawing Chamber and was invited to take a leading part in all the court occasions; she dined and supped and went to plays with the royal circle.[9] James conferred on her in her own right 'the place and the rank of the ancientest earl of Essex, called Bourchier.'[10] This gave Penelope precedence over all the baronesses in the Kingdom and of the daughters of all earls except four. The honour lifted the house of Essex out of its disgrace.

For Lord Rich, with none of the abilities to make his mark at such a court, the correct dress for meeting the new king was a matter of deep concern. He agonised with his neighbours and his tailor over the choice between black velvet and black satin, eventually spending twenty pounds on a new outfit for the occasion.[11] He had abandoned Penelope after her brother's rebellion, but continued to concern himself in local affairs, in particular local politics, though not as a candidate himself. For the elections to the new king's first parliament there was a proclamation forbidding canvassing. Nowhere was it disobeyed more than in the County of Essex and Lord Rich was one of the prime offenders. There were two parliamentary seats for Essex and Rich's favoured candidate was his neighbour and long-standing friend, Sir Francis Barrington. Barrington was a fellow-puritan and Rich was determined to see him elected. Another nominee of his was standing for the second seat. However a third candidate appeared on the scene, Sir Edward Denny, supported by the court and in particular by the Earl of Suffolk, Lord Lieutenant of Essex, and so a battle for power commenced.[12]

These two local magnates, Lord Rich and the Earl of Suffolk, each threw the whole weight of his support behind his respective candidate. The earl wrote angrily to his tenants and servants at Saffron Walden and indeed all the townsmen there complaining that they had promised support for Barrington and demanding their 'free consents and voices to my good friend Sir Edward Denny.' Meanwhile, Lord Rich was rounding up support for Barrington, not only soliciting friends, visiting and writing to freeholders of land (who had the franchise), but also arranging refreshments for compliant voters at local inns, supplying the food from his own private stores.

At the same time the Earl of Suffolk as a member of the Privy Council was one of the signatories to a letter addressed to the Sheriff and the rest of the Justices of the Peace for the County of Essex (who included Rich) reprimanding them for disobeying the King's proclamation against canvassing and threatening action for disobedience.

The situation was growing explosive and, in order to keep the peace, the second candidate was persuaded to withdraw, leaving the two rivals to gain election. They drew lots for first place and Denny won.

Apart from highlighting electoral malpractices, the episode shows the extent and limits of Lord Rich's power in Essex and the areas in which he chose to exercise it. His was an intermittent interest in local affairs and it took a parliamentary election to raise the burst of energy he exerted on this occasion. The net result saw him out-manoeuvred, for his second nominee had withdrawn from the election and his favoured candidate had taken second place. At this time also he ceased to be a Justice of the Peace, a position which had occupied him for twenty-one-years, ever since his marriage.

For this first parliament of King James's reign, Charles sat as the Earl of Devonshire. He had first been elected as a Member of Parliament in 1584 and was an experienced parliamentarian.

At about this time the Devereux family found itself threatened with a law suit brought by Sir Robert Dudley, the illegitimate son of the Earl of Leicester and Lady Sheffield to try to establish his legitimacy. In order to succeed he would need to prove that his parents were legally married and this would mean that Leicester's subsequent marriage to Lettice Devereux was invalid. Penelope, always the active member of the family, brought all her influence to bear to assist her mother in refuting the claim. John Coke writing to Fulke Greville on the 31st October 1603 reported: 'My Lady Rich is violent against Sir Robert Dudley; yet I find her much esteemed.'[13]

Sir Robert did not succeed in his claim and, deserting his wife and children, set off abroad to travel, taking with him his mistress Elizabeth Southwell, disguised as a page.

The Earl of Northumberland did not take over the role of protector of the Devereux women. The earl's anti-James views had vanished on

James's accession and he bitterly condemned his dead brother-in-law, Essex. In a letter to King James he wrote:

> His loss is the happiest chance for your Majesty and England that could befall us; for either do I fail in my judgement or he would have been a bloody scourge to our nation . . . he wore the Crown of England in his heart these many years and therefore far from setting it upon your head if it had been in his power.[14]

The Earl of Northumberland's change of heart towards James, once his succession to the throne of England was assured, did not secure him any lasting favour. He was implicated in the Gunpowder Plot of the 5th Novembr 1605. The evidence against him was circumstantial. One of the conspirators was Thomas Percy, a distant relative, whom he had appointed his steward and collector of his northern rents. Percy had been at Syon House, the earl's home on the day before the Plot and Guy Fawkes had come to Syon to look for him. Percy had had some £4,000 from the earl. Northumberland's answer to this was that Percy had been at Syon by mere chance and that the money was rent from his northern estates collected by Percy, out of which he had been cheated. The earl was condemned to pay the huge fine of £30,000 and to imprisonment in the Tower for life, with the Earl of Devonshire one of the commisioners sitting in judgement.

His wife Dorothy pleaded with the Earl of Salisbury, as Sir Robert Cecil had now become, for his release, pestering him so continuously and abusively that he refused to see her. He explained in a letter to Northumberland how he 'forebore to return any one harsh word to the contumelious language she used'.[15] Clearly Dorothy had become even bolder over the years. Nevertheless, she was unsuccessful in her attempt to secure the release of her husband. He remained in the Tower for sixteen years and was only released in 1621, two years after her death.

Meanwhile, the tone of the court was being established. The new queen loved plays and masques and at the beginning of the new reign Penelope took a leading part in these. The most important element in these masques was the sheer spectacle of the presentation, involving elaborate scenery and costumes on which considerable amounts of money were lavished. We have a description of one such occasion: 'The court was a continued maskerado, where she (Lady Rich), the queen and her ladies like so many sea nymphs or Nereids appeared often in various dresses to the ravishment of the beholders'.[16]

On another occasion, the queen and her ladies performed the masque *The Vision of the Twelve Goddesses* by Samuel Daniel. The performance took place on the 8th January 1604 in the Great Hall at Hampton Court, Christmas having been celebrated there that year because of the outbreak of plague in London. The queen herself chose to play Pallas Athene Goddess of Wisdom. Penelope was awarded the coveted role of Venus, Goddess of Love; no mean feat at the age of forty-one and having borne eleven children. All the ladies wore magnificent dresses, loose flowing garments with petticoats of different colours, the materials embroidered satin and cloth of gold and silver. Only the queen wore hers with a difference. According to an eye witness: 'Only Pallas had a trick by herself for her clothes were not so much below the knee that one might see a woman hath both feet and legs which I never knew before'.

The dead Queen Elizabeth's wardrobe was drawn on for costumes. There was great demand for invitations to the performance with the French and Spanish ambassadors competing for seats. The masque was a great success, a magnificent spectacle lavishly presented. Afterwards, according to the custom, the maskers invited members of the audience to join them in the dance with even Charles treading the more sedate 'common measures', though he was excused the livelier galliards and corantoes (the running dances).[17]

For the following year, the queen commisioned Ben Jonson to write a masque with parts for herself and some of her ladies. This was the *Masque of Blackness* presented at court on Twelfth Night 1605 and staged by Inigo Jones who designed not only the elaborate scenery and costumes but mechanical devices, like the great concave shell which conveyed the queen and her ladies across an artificial sea. They played the daughters of Niger (darkening their skins for the performance) and were grouped in pairs, each with its symbol. Penelope played Ocyte and her symbol was a pair of naked feet in a river. The costumes were lavish 'the colours azure and silver but returned on the top with a scroll and antique dressing of feathers and jewels interlaced with ropes of pearl'. One critic thought the dresses 'too light and courtesan-like for such great ones'.

Afterwards there was a great banquet: 'The night's work was concluded with a banquet in the great chamber, which was so furiously assaulted that down went table and tresses before one bit was touched.'[18]

By 1606 when Penelope and Charles were no longer at court the atmosphere had degenerated still further into decadence. Sir John Harington described the reception for the Danish king, Queen Anne's brother, in 1606:

I have been well nigh overwhelmed with carousel and sports of all kinds. The sports began each day in such manner and such sort as well nigh persuaded me of Mohammad's Paradise. We had women and indeed wine too of such plenty as would have astonished each sober beholder. Our feasts were magnificent and the two royal guests did most lovingly embrace each other at table. I think the Dane hath strangely wrought on our good English nobles, for those whom I never could get to taste good liquor now follow the fashion and wallow in beastly delights. The ladies abandon their sobriety and are seen to roll about in intoxication.

He went on to describe the great feast and how after dinner there was a presentation of Solomon his temple and the coming of the Queen of Sheba. The lady playing the Queen of Sheba 'forgetting the steps arising to the canopy overset her caskets into his Danish Majesty's lap and fell at his feet, though I rather think it was in his face ... His Majesty then got up and would dance with the Queen of Sheba; but he fell down and humbled himself before her and was carried to an inner chamber and laid on a bed of state.'

Harington concluded that 'the gunpowder fright is got out of all our heads and we are going on hereabouts as if the devil was contriving every man should blow up himself by wild riot excess and devastation of time and temperance. The great ladies do go well masked and indeed it be the only show of their modesty, to conceal their countenance.'[19]

For a retiring man like the new Earl of Devonshire this court was not the place to spend the rest of his days. Even in the time of Elizabeth the court life had been for him only a means of advancement, not a preferred way of living. He had accomplished all he had set out to do. His achievements in Ireland had brought him recognition in every form, honours, lands, money. Now more than ever he wanted to settle down at Wanstead to all the pleasures that great house could offer. He and Penelope took immense delight in their home, in having 'a house richly furnished and delectable rooms of retreat', in its gardens, in building up the great library and browsing amongst the books, in entertaining their close friends.[20] Their happiness was marred only by the wish to be lawfully married and be able to pass on to their son the earldom and great fortune.

Charles began to brood over the problem to such an extent that it became noticeable to those who knew him well. His secretary Fynes Moryson described how in the last period of his life his cheerfulness left him: 'only some two years before his death upon discontentment, his face grew thin, his ruddy colour failed, growing somewhat swarthy and his countenance sad and dejected.'[21]

His secretary attributed the change to unhappiness in love but discreetly omitted the circumstances, although they were well known to him. He had observed Mountjoy's shy behaviour with women, noting that he was 'not prone to bold discourses with ladies', except when the subject turned to his military action in Ireland, a subject 'extraordinarily pleasing' to him. Moryson had lived in close proximity to Mountjoy for three years and found him reserved, 'a close container of his secrets', and particularly minded that he was 'sometimes too much reserved to his dearest minions', in which category he himself was placed.[22] No doubt he was disappointed not to be taken into his master's confidence more, both in political and more personal matters. In fact, Mountjoy was unlikely to confide the secrets of his heart to anyone except Penelope and certainly not to his secretary, however loyal.

After their return from Ireland Moryson had gone to live at Wanstead and so was well aware of Penelope's role in Mountjoy's life. The fact that he never mentions her in relation to his master is indicative of something beyond mere discretion, amounting to disapproval. This accounts for a comment he made on his master as a lover, finding him 'faithful and constant, if not transported with self-love more than the object and therein obstinate'.[23] The overall impression we have of Mountjoy is certainly one of shyness and reserve but of a self-contained person rather than a man 'transported with self-love'. The accusations of self-love and obstinacy suggest that his secretary saw it as pride and wilfulness in Mountjoy to persist in his love for another man's wife. No doubt Moryson would have been more approving if Mountjoy had at this stage abandoned Penelope and married someone else. His name had never seriously been linked with that of any other woman. The two marriage proposals rumoured about him, one with the Earl of Ormonde's daughter, the other with Lady Arabella Stuart, were mere gossip of which nothing came. When Queen Elizabeth had chosen the epithet 'faithful' to apply to Mountjoy she had, as she usually managed to do, hit upon his essential quality.

Penelope and Charles had their position at court assured but this was not enough. Their situation, though publicly brilliant, was unsatisfactory to them. In 1605 they took what appeared to be their chance to set the seal of respectability upon their relationship when Lord Rich commenced divorce proceedings against Penelope. Far from achieving what they hoped their attempt was to bring disaster to them both.

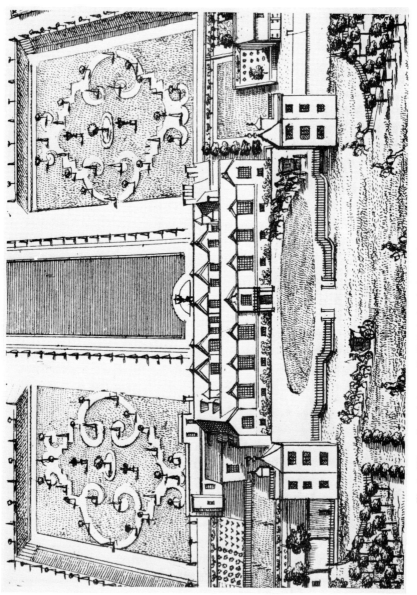

Wanstead House. Successively owned by Sir Richard Rich, the Earl of Leicester, and Robert Earl of Essex, before it became the home of Lord Mountjoy, Earl of Devonshire and Lady Penelope Rich.

CHAPTER THIRTEEN

Divorce and Remarriage: 'Who knit that knot?'

For years Lord Rich had turned a blind eye to his wife's infidelity. He could not have liked being that peculiarly Elizabethan figure of fun, the cuckold, but he endured the situation for the sake of the benefits to be gained from Penelope's influence and connections. In addition it required a certain amount of courage for a husband to divorce a wife since he had to admit publicly that he was a cuckold and would be ordered to pay maintenance to his wife for her to continue living with her lover.

Lord Rich could not expect to receive favours from his wife's lover as he had from her brother and with the lovers now openly living together and very much in the public eye he had nothing to gain by perpetuating the facade of his marriage. Penelope and Charles welcomed the idea of a divorce since they believed it would enable them to regularize their own position.

Penelope co-operated with Lord Rich to enable him to obtain a divorce. To avoid dragging the illustrious name of the Earl of Devonshire through the courts, with characteristic courage she made a confession of adultery with a stranger. The hearing before the Bishop of London's Consistory Court took a whole week and judgement was given on the 14th November 1605. The judges found that the marriage had been solemnized legally and in public, had continued for about twenty-two years and that Penelope had both confessed to and given 'legitimate proofs' of her adultery 'for the years and months and in the places stated in this indictment and especially in the City of London or its suburbs'. The judges pronounced sentence of divorce (in Latin), warning the couple they must not remarry:

We strongly forbid that either of them (while the other is alive) should contract a marriage or other union with anyone else or should presume to rush into another marriage in any way whatever or think it will be allowed or that permission will be given to them as a result of our judgement and this sentence, but we order that they should live chastely and celibately in the future.[1]

An informal contemporary account of the Rich divorce runs:

My Lord Rich and my Lady Rich were divorced upon Friday was sennight before the High Commissioners, when my Lord Archbishop chid my Lord Rich very much and gave my Lady great commendation, telling what an honourable house she was of, and how hardly my Lord had used her, and in the end very honourably (or rather graciously) bade my Lord Rich go among his Puritans; thanks be to God, his grace could not touch my Lady with that heresy, for hers is *error venialis*. This matter hath done her some little good anyway.[2]

How amazing! To be named as an adulteress at the start of the proceedings and to end up being commended by the judges. It is yet another instance of Penelope's extraordinary ability to win people over from initial hostility to her side. Once again, her judges had fallen under the spell of her personality and turned into her enthusiastic supporters. As well as from the judges there was clearly general sympathy for Penelope at this point.

Although such a divorce merely entitled the couple to live apart it had been the accepted practice up to the end of Elizabeth's reign to recognise a divorced couple's right to remarry. King James, however, was concerned with tightening up the marriage laws. In spite of the decadence at court and its sexual laxity James was in public at least highly defensive of conventional morality. In the first year of his reign he re-enacted the canons of 1597 with their strict laws relating to divorce, including the requirements of a bond to be given by the divorced couple that they would live chastely and not marry in each other's lifetime. Then in 1604 came a statute making bigamy a felony punishable by death, though the penalty did not apply if there had been a divorce by the ecclesiastical court.

The timing of the Rich divorce was unfortunate. Had it taken place a few years earlier the ability to remarry would still have applied. As it was Penelope and Charles were to be the earliest victims of the new strict implementation of the divorce laws. The divorce certainly included the sternest of warnings against remarriage but it is possible that they believed that the prohibition would merely involve them in the payment of a penalty and not invalidate their marriage. They took the risk and a month later, contrary to the divorce terms, Penelope and Charles were illegally married. On the 26th December 1605 the wedding ceremony was performed by Mountjoy's chaplain William Laud at Wanstead.

King James was deeply offended with the couple for breaking the new marriage laws, even though he had condoned their behaviour as lovers. A contemporary historian Robert Johnson, writing in Latin, described the King's reaction:

> The king, believing the unfavourable reports unwillingly, when he learnt that Devonshire had bound himself in marriage with another man's wife contrary to justice and divine law, that he had broken a holy and legal contract, the promises, vows and bonds of marriage, angry and incensed with him, although he condemned the crime, nevertheless on account of Devonshire's outstanding courage and loyalty, daily allowed his anger to cool. Firstly in a private rebuke, then in a public one he tried to lead him back from the error of his ways to the path of virtue. But Devonshire had already gone too far to be restrained by words and he resisted the King's efforts. The King then reproved him harshly but without anger. The reproof sank more deeply into his noble mind.[3]

Mountjoy sought to justify the marriage. He wrote a long and learned defence of his marriage to the king in which he brought all his learning to bear. His deep knowledge of divinity is evident in the work but it does not make easy reading. Basing his arguments on the scriptures by a series of sophisticated arguments he was able to prove to his satisfaction, if not the king's, that he and Penelope were free to marry each other.[4] More accessible was the personal letter he also wrote to the king, in which he simply yet eloquently pleaded all the wrongs Penelope had suffered and all Lord Rich's offences to her. Nevertheless he was evasive in one respect at least. He continued to maintain that Penelope was forced to confess her adultery with a stranger in order to give Lord Rich his divorce and so obtain her freedom, ignoring the fact that he and Penelope had been committing adultery for many years. This is his account:

> A lady of great birth and virtue, being in the power of her friends, was by them married against her will unto one against whom she did protest at the very solemnity and ever after; between whom from the first day there ensued continual discord, although the same fears that forced her to marry constrained her to live with him. Instead of a comforter he did study in all things to torment her; and by fear did practise to deceive her of her dowry, and though he forbore to offer her any open wrong, restrained with the awe of her brother's powerfulness, yet, as he had not long in time before in the chiefest duty of a husband, used her as his wife, so presently after his death [ie: her brother's death] he did put her to a stipend and abandoned her without pretence of any cause but his own desire to live without her. And after he had not for the space of twelve years enjoyed her, he did by persuasion and threatenings move her to confess a fault with a nameless stranger, without the which such a divorce as he desired could not by the laws in practice proceed.[5]

His chaplain William Laud also tried to explain away his conduct in performing an unlawful marriage. Laud's biographer, Peter Heylyn, maintained that the future Archbishop had found that there had been an earlier secret engagement between the couple, asserting that

> he found by the averment of the parties that some assurances of marriage had passed between them, before she was espoused to Rich; which, though they could not amount to a pre-contract in Foro Iudicii [in a court of law] . . . yet might satisfy himself in the truth thereof in Foro Conscientiae [in a court of conscience].[6]

The explanation of an early secret engagement between Charles and Penelope is not credible. If there had been any truth in the assertion, it would, without doubt, have been heavily relied on by Mountjoy when he came to write his own justification of the marriage to the king. In that *Defence of his Marriage*, Mountjoy mentions every possible argument available as an excuse, but never once refers to any such pre-marriage arrangement between himself and Penelope. Undoubtedly he would have done so if anything like this had existed.

The story was taken up and elaborated on by Sir Alexander Croke in his History of the Croke Family.

> With all his merit, the Earl of Devonshire was engaged in one unfortunate affair which reflects much disgrace upon his memory. Before the year 1588 in the life of Lord Mountjoy, his brother, he paid his addresses to the Lady Penelope, the daughter of Walter Devereux, Earl of Essex, a lady of great wit and beauty. The attachment was mutual and they were privately engaged to be married to each other. But the lady's friends, considering that he was at that time a younger brother, with little fortune, disapproved of the match and disposed of her to Robert, Lord Rich.[7]

It is clear that Croke in his version was seeking reasons why, if there was such an early secret engagement between Penelope and Charles, it was broken off, and found the explanation in his poverty, as a younger son.

Croke seems uncertain of the dates, referring only to 'before the year 1588'. In fact Penelope was in the strict care of her Puritan guardians in the north until she came to court in January 1581, and by March 1581 the match between her and Lord Rich was being arranged. Moreover Charles himself did not come to court until 1583 and could not have met Penelope until then at the earliest, after her marriage to Rich and after the affair with Philip Sidney. It is clear therefore that the whole story is a myth that has been perpetuated. It may have been invented by Charles and Penelope to persuade Laud to marry them, or by Heylyn to vindicate the archbishop, or by Laud himself in order to clear his name. Laud believed that for his part in performing the marriage ceremony his career had been set back by many years and indeed eleven years later James remembered Laud's part in the marriage, when he was seeking a nomination, saying: 'But was there not a certain Lady that forsook her husband, and married a Lord that was her paramour? Who knit that knot? Shall I make a man a prelate, one of the angels of my Church, who hath a flagrant crime upon him?'[8] Certainly Laud regarded the whole episode as the cross he had to bear and he kept the anniversary as a day of penance. The customary feast of St Stephen became for him a day of fasting and repentance. He composed a special prayer for the pardon of his offence in marrying the couple:

> Neither let this marriage prove a divorcing of my soul from Thy grace and favour; for much more happy had I been if, being mindful of this day, I had suffered martyrdom, as did Saint Stephen the first of martyrs, denying that which either my less faithful friends or less godly friends had pressed upon me.[9]

Forty years later, as Archbishop of Canterbury, Laud did become a martyr at the hands of the Puritans when he was beheaded at the Tower as a traitor.

Some people recognised the good intentions behind the marriage, that it was the earl's only way of putting right the injury to Penelope and their children. The king, however, turned against them, particularly Penelope. 'You have won a fair woman with a black soul,' he told Charles. James had a deep-rooted fear of powerful women and it must have been a relief to him to be able to cast her out. The Earl continued to carry out his official duties though the couple did not appear at court. The extent of their disgrace has been doubted but it was certainly claimed in the subsequent Court of Star Chamber case, the most embittered of all the legal battles concerning the earl's estate, that in the king's eyes he was dishonoured by the marriage. In any case it was to be for only a very short period.

All the contemporary commentators about the marriage wrote from the wisdom of hindsight, in the knowledge that the earl lived for only three months afterwards, and they seemed to have viewed this as divine retribution. A great deal was to be made in the Court of Star Chamber of the earl's supposed grief at the consequences of his marriage. It was to be alleged that ever since his marriage he had been discontented with his life with Penelope, had deeply regretted marrying her, that this was the cause of his fatal illness and so had shortened his life as well as dishonouring him with the king. Contemporary comment may well have been influenced by these allegations even though eventually they were to prove completely unfounded.

Charles and Penelope had been in London, returning together to Wanstead sometime in March 1606. Shortly afterwards Charles decided he needed to go back to London. He left Wanstead on the 25th March and set off in his coach, leaving Penelope and their children behind. He had apparently been well when he left home but whilst visiting Cheapside on that same day he had begun to feel ill. He went to Savoy House in the Strand and from there sent for his lawyer Joseph Earth. He said that on the next day 'he would have Dr. Turner to come unto him to confer with him about the state of his body, thinking he should have a fever.'[10]

Charles's overwhelming concern at this moment was to put into operation a carefully masterminded plan. Well aware that if he let events take their natural course Penelope and their children might find themselves disinherited, he had gone to immense pains to make sure this did not happen. As early as Christmas of 1603 he had been planning for this eventuality, long before either the divorce or his marriage. He had consulted the most able lawyers and asked them to draw up a scheme whereby he might bypass his common-law heir who, if he did not have a legitimate child, would be a distant cousin. These 'grave and learned men' had drawn up a complicated scheme which included re-acknowleging and re-enrolling documents in court every six months and he had been carrying out this practice ever since. They had advised him to keep by him always a form of will 'ready drawn to lie by him that if occasion of sickness or any such like should happen, the said earl might the more speedily and readily declare such further uses [ie: trusts] of the said manors lands and tenements as he purposed.'

His secretary depicted the scene: 'He called to him his most familiar friends, and, telling them that he had ever by experience and presaging mind been taught to repute a burning fever his fatal enemy, desired them (upon instructions then given them) to make his will.'[11] Charles was in fact suffering from pneumonia and at such a time it was certainly inadvisable for him to have made even the comparatively short journey from Wanstead to London. When on the following day he saw Dr. Turner the medical treatment he was prescribed was 'to take physic and be let blood'. The journey on a cold March day and the blood-letting could not have helped his condition.

On the day after his departure Penelope and their eldest son Mountjoy followed him to London to join him at Savoy House.

Charles was to spend the next few days, the last week of his life, putting his affairs in order with the sole object of seeing that Penelope and their children should inherit his fortune. He completed his will and other documents only the day before his death, and indeed the document that needed enrolling in Court was registered only just in time, on the morning of the day he died.

What the world now thought of its recent hero was given in this heartless account of his illness from John Chamberlain: 'the Earl of Devonshire is sick of a burning fever and in some danger for he was on the mending hand and is fallen in a relapse: the world thinks if he should go now it had been better for him he had gone a year or two sooner'[12]

Charles died on the following day, the 3rd April 1606, at Savoy House at the age of forty-three.

There were a number of people with the earl during his last days, particularly on the day before his death when his lawyers, the eight witnesses to his will, friends and attendants were there, including his trusted friend Sir William Godolphin, the Earl of Southampton and Lord Danvers. However, the descriptions of his death do not come directly from any of those actually present. The historian Robert Johnston in his Latin history described it in this way: 'He drew his last breath in the embrace of his dearest wife, who kissed his face and hands, amidst praise and tears. Dressed in mourning, her head shrouded in a veil, night and day she lay on the ground in the corner of her bedroom.'[13]

John Gerard the Jesuit priest, unable to claim a convert, managed both to moralise over the manner of Charles' death and to melodramatize it. He believed that the Earl was 'working his own destruction . . . His love of this lady held him a helpless captive . . . Incapable of shaking himself free from his infatuation he died of a broken heart. With his last breath he invoked, not God, but his goddess, his "angel", as he called her.'[14] Charles' secretary was also one of those who attributed his early death to unhappy love, in this terse account: 'In the last period of his life, after the Irish wars, grief of unsuccessful love brought him to his last end.'[15]

One of the allegations made in the court case was that Charles' last words had been not about Penelope but the king, spoken in delirium as he imagined himself received back into favour: 'Make ready my best coach and coach horses for the King hath sent for me to the Court.'

The witnesses in the case, however, denied that the earl had been delirious or had spoken such words, but had remained calm to the end. As the whole object of the court action was to overthrow the will by discrediting Penelope and by showing Charles as not in his right mind when he made it, this account has to be rejected.

The earl's courtesy and self-possession did not leave him, even during the tedious legalities he had to attend to on the last full day of his life, as this small incident shows. Sir Mathew Carew, one of the Masters of the Chancery Court, came to Savoy House to acknowledge a deed the earl had just signed and reported how earl though 'very sick as his countenance then showed' said he was 'so sorry that he had put him to such pains.'

John Chamberlain's account was prosaic and merciless. Two days after the death he wrote:

> The Earl of Devonshire left this life on Thursday night last, soon and early for his years but late enough for himself, and happy had he been if he had gone two or three years since, before the world was weary of him, or that he had left that scandal behind him. He was not long sick, past eight or ten days, and died of a burning fever and putrefaction of his lungs, a defect he never complained of. He hath left his lady (for so she is now generally held to be) £1,500 a year and most of his moveables and of five children (that she fathered upon him at the parting from her former husband) I do not hear that he hath provided for more than three, leaving to the eldest son (as I hear) between £3,000 and £4,000 a year, to another younger £800 a year and to a daughter £6,000 in money.[16]

Chamberlain's story was inaccurate in a number of respects and in particular he was responsible for spreading the completely unfounded rumour that the earl had acknowledged only three of his five children. Both his wife and each of his children were lovingly provided for by name in his will.

On the same day Sam Calvert wrote to Ralph Winwood in similarly moralising terms: 'My Lord of Devonshire is dead, and most say he is happy, for the world began to change the titles of honour into notes of infamy, for his last most dishonourable and both unlawful and ungodly match. His body is this day carried to Wanstead to be buried.'[17]

Not everyone took such a sanctimonious stance. The poets at least tried to take a larger view of the man who had so recently been England's hero. Mountjoy as a lover of literature had been a generous patron of writers for many years. The first of a whole line of dedications to him had come from Thomas Nashe in 1589 when he dedicated his *Anatomy of Absurdity* to the then Sir Charles Blount. Nashe had chosen Charles as the natural successor to Philip Sidney for the role of ideal courtier: 'England never saw anything more singular than Sir Philip Sidney . . . but nothing so generally applauded in every man's comparisons as your worship's most absolute perfections'.[18]

Of all the poets, the one who knew him best was Samuel Daniel, whom Charles had befriended and supported financially. Daniel wrote a long elegy in which he was concerned to present his patron as he really was. It is a lengthy narrative poem, describing in great detail both Mountjoy's character and many of the important events of his life and it accords in its particulars with the prose descriptions of Mountjoy's secretary Fynes Moryson. It even follows Moryson in not mentioning Penelope at all, though indicating some scandal.

Daniel has promised to show his patron with all his weaknesess, but he is hard-pressed to find any. He noted his 'due reservedess' but this turns out to be more a virtue than otherwise. The only major fault, he concludes, is that:

He was a man
And built of flesh and blood and did live here.[19]

Daniel, aware of the scandalmongers, hopes that some people at least will be as generous to Mountjoy as he deserves:

> As dogs bark at those they do not know
> So they at such they do not understand.
> The worthier sort, who know we do not live
> With perfect men, will never be unkind.

Fynes Moryson had described how Mountjoy had died peacefully: 'I never saw a brave spirit part more mildly from the old mansion than his did.'
Daniel admired the way Mountjoy met his death for he believed that:

> This action of our death especially
> Shows all a man.

Mountjoy's fine end seemed to him to set the seal on his life. Whilst Daniel carefully avoided mentioning Penelope, the future playwright John Ford on the other hand dedicated his elegy *Fame's Memorial* to her, as Countess of Devonshire, addressing her in the most glowing terms. It was his first literary venture (he described his muse as 'unfeathered') and, inspired by her story, he showered praises on a lady he admitted never having met.

The Earl of Devonshire was honoured with a state funeral in Westminster Abbey in recognition of his great services to his country.[20] It was during the preparations for the funeral that the first signs of the serious consequences of the scandal for Penelope, now that she was unprotected, began to appear. John Chamberlain had reported that she was generally recognised as the earl's lawful wife. The matter was now referred to the court heralds in connection with the funeral arrangements and they decided not to recognise her as the Countess of Devonshire. At the funeral the Earl's coat of arms was set up 'in single' without his wife's. Penelope was thus publicly humiliated. Much deeper cuts and more wounding abuses were to follow.

THE WEST VIEW OF LEEZ–PRIORY, IN THE COUNTY OF ESSEX.

Leighs Priory. Lord and Lady Rich's Essex home.

CHAPTER FOURTEEN

Stella in Camera Stellata

The Earl of Devonshire had died a very rich man with vast holdings of land, much of it acquired through his own endeavours. These included the manor of Wanstead in Essex, Fotheringay Castle in Northamptonshire, the manors of Canford in Dorset and Beer Ferris in Devon as well as other properties and estates in those counties and in Somerset, Worcester, Leicester, Cornwall and Southampton. His secretary Fynes Moryson was critical of this accumulation of wealth, calling it 'greedy gathering'. To his way of thinking there was something ungentlemanly in acquiring material possessions along with honour and glory.

Having amassed his fortune Charles in his usual prudent way had started planning early to ensure that it passed on his death to Penelope and their children. Only a few months after his return from Ireland and well before the divorce and his marriage he had begun planning to create a trust over all his estates and on the 10th February 1604 he had completed a deed of indenture which passed all his lands to trustees to hold on his behalf.[1] The trustees were his loyal friend Sir William Godolphin who had been with him in Ireland and his chief legal adviser Joseph Earth.

The purpose of creating a trust was to enable him to dispose of his lands as he wished and to keep his plans secret. It was a principle of English land law that any transfer of land should be made openly, to prevent secret ownership. Transfers were made not merely by written documents but by the parties openly going onto the land and in the presence of witnesses effecting a symbolic hand-over of a piece of earth. To meet the objections of those who did not want their dealings made public methods of circumventing the principle were evolved. Out of this grew the concept of trusts. If the land was transferred to trustees they were the legal owners though they would hold the land not for their own use and benefit but on behalf of beneficiaries.

Charles was well aware in 1604 that as he had no wife and no legitimate children, if he let matters take their course, on his death all his estate would pass to a distant cousin as his common law heir. At this stage he clearly had high hopes of marrying and having a legitimate family. When the 1604 deed was prepared anything seemed possible. In it he provided not only for his future wife's jointure or marriage portion but for up to seven legitimate sons, as well as for a son born posthumously.

Shortly afterwards he created a separate trust over certain properties he owned in Southampton, including the manor of Lyndhurst and since then he had followed his lawyers advice in re-acknowledging and re-enrolling this document in the Court of Chancery every six months. He also kept by him the notes of the trusts on which his lands were held so as to be ready in any emergency to make further declarations of trust.

When Charles fell ill in March 1606 he was aware of the need to bring matters up to date. The deed of 1604 had been based on the possibility of having lawful children and a lawful wife. Even if there had been no doubts about the validity of the marriage his five children had not been born in wedlock and could not have been legitimated on marriage. He had also acquired additional lands since the deed was made and needed to include these. His last energies were expended in making the arrangements.

In the will which was drawn up and signed the day before his death Charles faced up to the painful realities of the situation. His children were referred to by their Christian names, Mountjoy, St. John, Charles, Penelope and Isabella, without surname and described as being the son or daughter of Lady Penelope. She herself was referred to as the daughter of Walter late Earl of Essex and though not formally named as Countess of Devonshire was affectionately called 'my very dear and loving wife'. She was given an interest for her life in all his lands and estates and after her death they were to go to each of the five children and their heirs successively, starting with the eldest boy, Mountjoy. The will also provided for an unborn child. Charles must have entertained hopes that if Penelope was pregnant with a son at the time of his death this child at least, conceived after their marriage, might be declared legitimate. For this reason the child if a boy was under the terms of the will to succeed next after Mountjoy the eldest son. If however the child was a girl she would take her normal place. Each of the children was given an annual allowance and his daughters were to have substantial dowries, the eldest Penelope to have £5,000 at the age of eighteen whilst Isabella and any posthumous daughter were to have £3,000 each.[2]

At the same time as the will Charles also completed a deed of bargain and sale. This was a device for creating further trusts over his lands, enabling the ownership to pass immediately to the beneficiaries and so bypass his comon law heir. The transfer was made in private without the need for any open act of transfer on site, though the document itself had to be enrolled, that is registered and this was in fact done on the morning of the day he died. He appointed five illustrious trustees including the Earls of Salisbury, Southampton and Suffolk.

The first intimations of trouble ahead came only a fortnight after Charles's death from a regular source of gossip at court. Sir Dudley Carleton writing to John Chamberlain noted the vulnerability of Penelope's situation: 'Her estate is much threatened with the King's account, but it is thought she will find good friends, for she is visited daily by the greatest who profess much love to her for her Earl's sake'.[3]

The earl had not yet been buried and it was in this same letter that Carleton mentioned the dispute among the heralds as to whether she was the lawful widow and so entitled to have her coat of arms set up with the earl's at the funeral. Two weeks later the herald's decision had been given against her.

The king's involvement lay in the wardship rights during the heir's minority. However the crown's interest in the estate was only one aspect of the attention now focused upon the earl's vast holdings. Several distant relatives of Charles now came forward to stake their claims. As their relationship to him was somewhat remote there was to be some difficulty in establishing which of them had the best title. Their hopes of succeeding to his lands lay not only in disputing the marriage with Penelope and the legitimacy of the children, but in attacking the validity of the will and other documents. Charles had planned ahead with meticulous care for every eventuality but it is doubtful whether even he could have envisaged the ferocity and bitterness of the attacks and the wide range of fronts on which they would be pursued, including bringing criminal charges against Penelope and the lawyers.

A series of legal battles now began, starting in the Probate Courts. Whilst the executors (the lawyers Joseph Earth and John Wakeman) were seeking to prove the will in the Prerogative Court of Canterbury, Henry Baker one of Charles's 'cousins' disputed its validity in the Court of

Arches. There the eight witnesses to the will gave evidence on oath that it was properly made and that the earl was 'of good and perfect memory' at the time of its making.[4]

The will was again upheld by the Prerogative Court of Canterbury on the 22nd November 1606 though there was an appeal against this decision heard in the Consistory Court at St Paul's Cathedral on the 7th May 1607.[5] There Sir Richard Baker grandfather of Henry Baker contested the will on behalf of the common law heir who had not yet been established. Another of the rival claimants Sir Richard Champernowne, clearly not prepared to rely on such a representative, intervened in these proceedings on his own behalf and was ordered to pay the costs. Again the will was declared valid.

At the same time as they disputed the will Sir Richard Champernowne and Henry Baker were contending in the Court of Wards to decide which of them was the common law heir. That court appointed a jury to hear the case, ordered the executors not to fell the woods or similarly damage the estates and then adjourned the proceedings for a whole year pending the outcome of the other cases.[6]

As well as attacking the will Sir Richard Champernowne also tried to overturn the deed of indenture of 1604. He brought an action in the Court of King's Bench against Sir William Godolphin claiming that he was cousin and heir to the Earl of Devonshire and seeking to reverse the deed on the grounds that it was made in error. Sir Francis Bacon, representing the defendant Sir William Godolphin, answered the allegation with the firm insistence: 'in nullo est erratum,' there was no mistake.[7]

Sir Richard Champernowne was undeterred by these unpromising beginnings and indeed he was to prove an indefatigable litigant. Having failed in these actions he now decided to press criminal charges in the Court of Star Chamber against Penelope and the three lawyers involved. They were accused of forging the will and other documents and using fraud in their making, extremely serious charges carrying penalties of anything short of death, including imprisonment for life, the pillory, slitting of the nostrils and forfeiture of all lands and goods. Both the Earl of Devonshire and the Earl of Essex had formerly sat in judgement in this court. Ten years previously Penelope's brother had been one of the judges in a similar case of forgery of a will, when the accused had been sentenced to imprisonment for life and ordered to have both his ears cut off. Nor was the Court of Star Chamber known to favour women. In one case a woman plaintiff was whipped for being 'clamorous and impudent' and afterwards women were not permitted to bring cases themselves.[8]

The Star Chamber proceedings got under way in the early part of 1607. Sir Richard Champernowne filed a bill of complaint to which Penelope and her co-defendants put in answers on oath. Then began the cumbersome procedure of taking evidence by interrogatories and depositions in which the witnesses were directed to answer lengthy and intricate written questions by sworn statements. Although Star Chamber had not yet reached the degree of notoriety it was to attain in Charles I's time it was already known for its inquisitional character in the sheer weight and complexity of its questioning of witnesses. In fact this was one aspect that was later curtailed when Sir Francis Bacon became Lord Keeper and limited its examination to fifteen articles each containing only two questions. At this time there was no such limit and formidable lists of quesions were prepared to try and trap the defendants and their witnesses. The speciality of the court's interrogation seems to have been in loaded questions based on false premises.

The attack was launched from every angle with a view to bombarding the defendants from all sides. The first broadside was aimed at Penelope to question whether there had ever been a marriage and try to show that there was no possible reason for the earl to have left her anything. The unfortunate William Laud, one of the witnesses to the will as well as the chaplain who performed the ceremony, must have quaked as he saw his career prospects receding still further. Witnesses were asked multiple questions like this one, which starts off simply enough and then builds up into a crescendo of abuse:

> Did the said earl esteem the said lady to be the earl's lawful wife, or did he call her so at any time, and was there any intermarriage between them to your knowledge, and how long since were they married and by whom were they married and . . . if there were any such marriage did not or do you not know that the said Lady Rich could not be the said earl's lawful wife but an Harlot, Adulteress, Concubine and Whore, but of purpose devised to colour their adultery and to countenance their panders?[9]

The ground of attack shifted somewhat to ask these questions:

> Did not the earl much grieve and lament for his marriage with the said lady and was not that or some conceit thereupon and upon unlawfulness thereof the cause or occasion of his sickness and death as you know or think, herein declare the whole truth, what cause the earl had to give his lands or any part thereof unto her or her children . . . Did you not know that the same marriage was most unlawful and that the said lady could not either for herself or children obtain any lands or goods of the said earl but by devices and deceits?

Changing the line of attack yet again it was suggested that far from using 'devices and deceits' she had openly begged the earl to remember her and her children in his will:

> Did not the Lady Rich, at your being there, or at the reading of the said deed use some words to importune the said earl to remember her and her children, or what other words did she then use?

It was alleged that the marriage, if it had ever taken place, caused not only the earl's sickness and death but his dishonour:

> Do you not know believe or have heard that the said late Earl of Devonshire for near three months before his death and until his death was discontented and displeased with his own course of cohabitation with the said Lady Rich and did not he find and perceive that the same had dishonoured him with the King's Majesty and with others and do not you know the same to be true and how do you know the same to be true?

The earl was depicted as having tried to escape from Penelope, as though his last journey from Wanstead had been in flight from a discarded mistress who continued to pursue him to the end:

Did not the said earl the next day following being the 25th day of March last past come from Wanstead in his coach to the Savoy House from the said Lady Rich and being come to the said house did he not there and then say he was not well and that he would the next day following take physic and be let blood or words to the like effect and might not the said earl have better taken physic at Wanstead and more quietly and in a better air than at the Savoy, but that he was weary of the said lady her company?

It was alleged that unable to get away from her he had shown hostility to her and their son when they arrived at Savoy House, turning his back on them and refusing to speak:

Did not the said earl seem much discontented and mislike of the said Lady Rich and her son Mountjoy's coming to him from Wanstead to the Savoy in the time of his sickness, how did the earl express his dislike, what countenance did he show her and her son or either of them as seeming ill willing to see or speak with them . . . did he not turn his face from them as seemingly ill willing to see or speak with them?

The lawyers were accused of inciting the earl to marry Lady Rich either for their own ends or acting under her power. They were asked:

Was not the said will and other deeds drawn and made by the direction of the Lady Rich and of her counsel or of your own head, and what benefit cause or reward or promise of reward have you or any other for the following or soliciting thereof and by whom to be paid . . . Did not your counsel advise persuade or entice the said earl to convey his lands to the said Lady Rich and to her children or to marry her and did you not know that she was then a married woman and could not marry any other, living the Lord Rich?

Penelope was said to have played upon the earl's sensibilities by pretending to be pregnant at the time he made his will:

> Did not the said Lady Rich at her coming to the said earl at that time to London or ar any other time make a show as if she had been with child, did not she or some other tell the said earl that she was with child when was it that she did so tell him or give out that she was then with child . . . was it not done of purpose to have the earl pity her and convey his land to her or her children?

Another main ground of attack sought to invalidate the will and other documents by showing them to have been forged. There were suggestions that the documents had been tampered with, some passages erased and other words substituted. Witnesses were asked:

> What was therein added or stroken out or interlined, when and by whom and who were present to the interlining erasing or altering thereof, and whose handwriting is the said interlining, altering or changing put into the said writing . . . and by whose advice, act or procurement was the same deed antedated?

Numerous questions were asked as to how many sheets of paper had been used for each document, the type of paper used, whether there were any copies or counterparts of the documents and what had happened to them. The interrogation then focused upon what seemed to be a promising area for investigation. There had been a number of blanks left in the will and this caused considerable interest. The lawyers were accused of putting what they liked into the will:

> Was not the said will devised by you or by your appointment and did not you put into the said will many things, uses, estates and persons,

more than was by the said earl advised or commanded (therein declare the whole truth?)

Yet another charge attempted to cast doubts upon the earl's soundness of mind at the time he made the will. Questions were asked suggesting that he was 'not of good and perfect memory'. There were trick questions like this one: 'Was the earl of perfect memory at the making of the said will and how do you know he was of perfect memory?' Very difficult to get that one right. He was alleged to have deteriorated rapidly, becoming 'crazed, feeble, incoherent, senseless, impaired in his memory and judgment'. At the vital moment of the reading of the will in preparation for signing it he was said to have collapsed:

Did not the said earl to your knowledge or as you have heard and do believe on a sudden, before the finishing of the said will and at the very instant time of the reading thereof, fail of his speech and memory and so continue until about two of the clock or nearabouts in the afternoon of the third day of April last past and did not you and other your accomplices then give a new assault to the said earl for his assent to . . . the said will; and the said earl upon your and others' importunities often urging him thereunto saying but yea, did he not presently or within short time after, and within how short a time after say (or use words to the same or like effect) make ready my best coach and coach horses for the king hath sent for me to the court, and were not these the last words the said earl spake?

Too weak even to write his own name, someone, it was said, had to hold his hand and guide it to help him sign. 'Who held his hand?' the witnesses were asked accusingly.

All this and a great deal more of the same kind was hurled at Penelope and her co-defendants in the attempt to convict them on the charges of forgery and fraud. Every possible damaging imputation was made to show her in the worst possible light.

In fact the scurrilous attack brought up remarkably little. All the witnesses maintained that the earl had been quite composed when he made his will although very ill. He had been sitting on a chair with a little table in front of him for his papers. Penelope, far from begging the earl to remember her in his will or helping him sign his name, had not even been in the room at the time. She was not far away though and they could see her in a gallery above, walking and talking to friends. No one had bribed them or influenced them in any way. No one had brought any pressure to bear on the earl to persuade him to make his will, all the documents had been properly made, understood by the earl and were in accordance with his wishes. All the matters which had given rise to the closest cross-questioning had a perfectly reasonable explanation.

The friend who had been closest to Charles was Sir William Godolphin. He gave evidence on oath that the earl had voluntarily made his will, that Lady Rich did not importune him to leave his property to her and had not pretended to be with child. He denied all suggestions that Charles had been unfit to make a will, or that he had uttered 'any incoherent speeches importing that his memory and judgement was crazed, feeble or impaired.'

Explanations were given for the blanks in the will. These were for legacies to his servants and the poor and for the amounts of his daughters' dowries, which he wanted to think over carefully before completing. He had been tired and wished to rest, but the following day he had finalised the amounts and they had been properly filled in on the morning of the day of his death.

Out of all the many witnesses for the plaintiff only one, a yeoman William Toomes, had a word to say against the Lady Penelope. This man declared it his belief that the 'Earl's marriage with the said Lady was the taking of the said Earl's life.' 'The Earl' he said, 'spake four of five idle words the day before he died, but what those words were he doth not remember.' This was hardly proof of anything, let alone evidence of forgery or fraud. All in all he was not a very credible witness. He went on to give his opinion that 'the said earl did persuade himself that the said Lady was with child at the time of her said coming to the said earl' and to observe slyly that he had not 'heard that the lady was brought to bed of a child since the death of the said earl.' This witness's statements however were flatly contradicted by a number of other witnesses, all of them closer to the earl and of more reliable standing.

It does not make any particular sense for Penelope to have invented a pregnancy since she and their children were all well provided for and if the child did not exist it could not inherit. A far more likely explanation is that Charles in his customary prudent way had provided for every eventuality, including the possibility that she might be pregnant at the time of his death. This would be entirely consistent with the similar provision he had made in the deed of 1604 and indeed it was something he had set great store by, since only a child born after the marriage stood any chance of succeeding to his title.

The three lawyer defendants came to make their answers. It was clear from their accounts that Charles had anticipated the likelihood of the will's being disputed and had done everything in his power to see that it should succeed. He had eleven independent witnesses apart from the lawyers present at the signing of the will (eight of whom had signed it) and afterwards the Earl of Southampton had sealed it up in a sheet of clean paper with his own seal and then handed it to Lord Danvers for safekeeping, so that there was no possibility of tampering with it. Charles's foresight had proved to be all too necessary.

John Wakeman described how carefully Charles had kept secret his intentions of giving everything to Penelope and their children. Even the clerk who had written the fair copy of the will was not allowed to see the part relating to the trusts 'to the Lady and her children' but Wakeman himself had written this portion: 'because it was the pleasure of the said Earl that that part of the said will should be very secretly carried.'

Joseph Earth, the chief legal adviser, denied that he had 'inveigled the said late Earl of Devonshire to disinherit the blood and kindred of the said earl.' Everything he had done had been 'with the express pleasure' and

by the only proper instructions of the said earl, thought of by himself long before his sickness whereof he died and carefully consulted upon by his counsel learned . . . The said late earl long before and at his death had a special care by all lawful means to prevent that none of his inheritance should descend to his heir general of whom the said earl made little account.

Far from not wanting to see the Lady Penelope

after he fell sick or at any other time, as in the said bill is untruly alleged . . . he at the special request of the said earl did fetch the said lady to him in his sickness, whose coming to the said earl was very acceptable and welcome . . . and that the said earl, as well before his sickness whereof he died as in all the time of his said sickness was very tender and careful of the said lady and of her children and his greatest care was for their advancement and preferment.

When Penelope came to answer, she did so with dignity and self-possession, denying all the charges and refuting the defamatory allegations absolutely, but not deigning to reply in kind. The whole action was trumped up: 'contrived and prosecuted of malice, for vexation and not upon any just cause or ground of suit, the same being stuffed with slanderous imputations.' Her second answer was given three weeks after the first, on the 19th May 1607. Again she insisted she had been: 'very maliciously slandered . . . with procurement of forgery . . . and other misdemeanours much tending to her defamation reproach and dishonour of her innocency.' By then the case was going in her favour and she pointed out that

the plaintiff doth not prosecute letters or process against her according to a late order in that behalf made in this honourable Court, being as this defendant thinketh in fear to make any further prosecution therein.

Accordingly she

doth appear gratis to the said bill by such name as it hath pleased the said complainant to name or term her in the same bill of complaint, without taking any exception of misnomer for avoiding of all delays and for the more speedy bringing of all the offences and misdemeanours in and by the said bill most falsely and slanderously laid against her, to a speedy hearing in this honourable court.

She had been named in the action as Penelope Lady Rich and called Lady Rich throughout, a name she no longer accepted as hers. In the first answer she had made to the court at the end of April she had described herself as the Lady Penelope Countess of Devonshire. Now three weeks later she was prepared to forego the dignity of the title Countess of Devonshire so long as she was not called Lady Rich. She had become simply the Lady Penelope and this was what she called herself in her second answer. She had no surname.

A court case of this size could drag on for a considerable time as this one looked all set to do. However as far as Penelope's part in it went, it ceased at this point, after her answer of the 19th May 1607. Within weeks of giving this answer she was dead.

The decisions of the Court of Star Chamber are missing but the trial is referred to in two other actions, one in the Court of Wards the other in the Court of Chancery, and it is apparent from the latter that the charges failed.

On the 5th November 1607 the proceedings in the Court of Wards, adjourned for a year, were due to be heard. The Earl of Southampton wrote to the Earl of Salisbury on the 25th October asking that the case be postponed for a further week and was anxious that Salisbury himself should be present.[10] The Earl of Salisbury, as Sir Robert Cecil had become, was Master of the Court of Wards but was also interested in the case as one of the trustees, just as Southampton was.

There are two reports of the case, one by a lawyer John Hawarde, the other much more detailed, prepared for the Earl of Salisbury, at Hatfield.[11] The executors argued that the first thing was to inquire what lands there were for if there were none there was nothing for the common law heir to inherit. They were reasonably confident by now that most if not all the earl's lands had been successfully disposed of, away from the common law heir. The two rival claimants Sir Richard Champernowne and Henry Baker merely wanted the court to decide which of them was the rightful heir, so that the winner might then claim the estate. The executors won their point and John Hawarde's report sets out the pedigrees of the two rivals, each claiming through a female line. The Hatfield report refers to the Star Chamber trial where Sir Richard Champernowne had charged the defendants with forgery of the deeds and describes how in that court 'the defendants answered in December last,

and then did precisely justify the making and executing of the said deeds.'
They had been re-examined in Star Chamber in April and so there was no
need to repeat the exercise in the Court of Wards. The executors wanted to
take part in the Court of Wards case so that they could explain what had
happened to the lands, but Champernowne had said that if they did he
would lose his right to cross-examine them in Star Chamber. The
executors were able to show that this had already taken place and so again
won their point. They were allowed to take part in the Court of Wards
hearing, with the whole question of the lands being investigated not
merely the rival claims to be heir.

The Hatfield report refers to the trusts which Charles had established
over his lands. In dealing with the deed of February 1604 it sets out the
trust contained in that deed as, to the earl for life and then 'after his decease
to his 1.2.3.4.5.6. and 7 sons and of their several heirs male of their bodies
lawfully begotten successively one after another.' Of course Charles did
not have seven sons. It was a legal fiction, dating back to the time before
his marriage when he had so optimistically provided for the future.

As for the rivalry to be Charles' common law heir, Henry Baker was
declared the victor.[12] It remained to establish exactly what he had won.
Charles had achieved his intentions firstly because his lands had been
successfully passed on to trustees before his death and secondly because
Penelope and the children had been specifically referred to by name as the
beneficiaries, and so did not depend upon the lawfulness of their
relationships. The main estates, including Wanstead, Fotheringay Castle,
Beer Ferris and Canford Manor passed to Mountjoy Blount on his
mother's death. The only exception was the manor at Lyndhurst and other
lands in Southampton which Charles had placed upon a different trust to
the rest, for himself and then to his heirs for ever. Henry Baker, aged
twenty years and one month when Charles died, succeeded to these lands
as the earl's common law heir.

Even after all this litigation Sir Richard Champernowne was not
content to accept the situation. Five years later unable to believe that the
prize had eluded him, he was still bringing court actions, this time in the
Court of Chancery.[13] The defendants in this case were all the Blount
children, Mountjoy, St John, Charles, Penelope junior and her new
husband Gervase Clifton, and Isabella, as well as the long-suffering Sir
William Godolphin and the second of the two executors, John Wakeman.

There were by now two notable names missing, Joseph Earth, Charles' chief legal adviser and Penelope herself.[14] Champernowne was still claiming the earl's estate, going over the same ground as before, but also alleging a plot contrived by Lady Rich and 'her servant John Wakeman.' Together they had schemed 'to work upon the weakness of the said earl' and get his money. Wakeman had sought 'to gratify the said lady' and 'to insinuate himself into her favour' and 'to bring profit to himself devised this plot'.

The defendants denied everything as before, claiming that it had all been thoroughly investigated and that there was no new evidence 'to ground this suit upon than such as he hath formerly presented in other Courts'. The defendants had made full answers in Star Chamber and Champernowne had 'made no colour of proof against' any of them. So far had Champernowne's imagination worked that he had invented the story that John Wakeman was Lady Rich's servant. Wakeman had been a legal adviser to the Earl of Devonshire, had attended upon him in that capacity and been paid for his services by the earl. The plot was a complete fabrication. By now it had been established beyond doubt that Charles had not only always intended that Penelope and his children should inherit his worldly goods but had succeeded. Only the children however were to enjoy any of the benefits.[15]

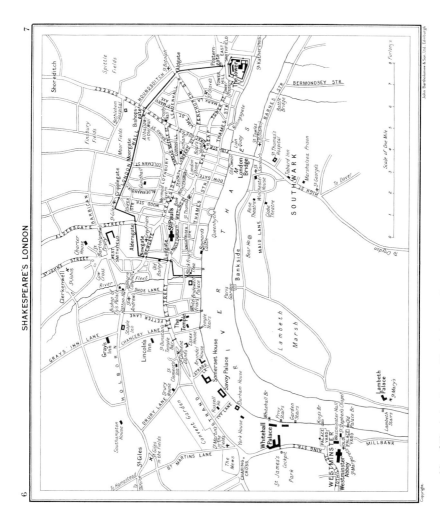

Map of Elizabethan London. Note the important houses, Essex House amongst them, lying along the North bank of the Thames.

CHAPTER FIFTEEN

'Neither Wife Widow nor Maid'

Penelope had been crushed by Charles' death but not defeated. Afterwards she had spent some time with her mother at Drayton Bassett and then returned to her home at Wanstead. There in September 1606 five months after the death she received a welcome visit from her former sister-in-law Frances and her new husband the Earl of Clanricarde.

Life went on for her after Charles's death and in the intervening months she regained something of her former composure. We can see her indomitable spirit rise again in a letter, written to the Earl of Salisbury from Wanstead in September 1606, which carries great charm. Part of this lies in her ability to throw herself into the concerns of others whether it is worrying about the children, paying a graceful compliment about the horsemanship of Salisbury's son, noting the rejuvenating effect on her mother of the youthful company, or the unaffected way she addressed her correspondent. Here is some of the letter:

> While I was at Drayton with my mother, the young hunters came very well pleased, until your servant came with your commission to guide my Lord of Cranborne [Salisbury's son] to my Lady of Derby, which, discontented for fear of parting three days, made them all lose their suppers and they became extremely melancholy till it was concluded that their train should stay at Drayton and they go together with two servants apiece. I fear nothing but their riding so desperately, but your son is a perfect horseman and can neither be outridden nor matched any way. My mother, I think, will grow young with their company; so, longing to hear of your safe and perfect health.
>
> P. Devonshire.[1]

As the court cases got under way she left Wanstead and came to

London to fight the legal battle which was threatening not only to ruin her financially but to destroy her character. She had never worried unduly about reputation but the accusations now levelled at her were quite different to the half-admiring witticisms of the old days, which had usually been at Lord Rich's expense. Throughout all the years of her adultery her standing in society had never really suffered because of it. Ironically, now that she was alone she found herself publicly reviled for past conduct which until her second marriage had been accepted. The world had changed, not she.

Being branded as a harlot was only a small part of the stigma now attached to her name. She was painted as a mercenary schemer, interested only in getting her hands on the Devonshire fortune and using every underhand means to achieve this, bribery and corruption, fraud, forgery and deceit. These were seriously damaging charges and although she answered them with courage it must have been an extremely worrying experience to face alone without the support of a male protector.

She had suffered in the past from severe colds, even in the summer. One such attack left her so weak that she was unable to write, as the Countess of Southampton explained to her husband: 'My Lady Rich that writ to you but very lately, desires you now to excuse her not writing, being so ill of a cold as she cannot now endure to write a word.'[2]

In the midsummer of 1607, the year after Charles' death, and only a few weeks after she had given her answers in the Court of Star Chamber Penelope fell ill of a fever. No further details are known about the nature of her illness. The Earl of Devonshire had died of fever, the description given in his case indicating pneumonia. Whether Penelope also contracted pneumonia after one of her colds or whether it was another kind of fever is impossible to say.

Penelope died on the 7th July 1607 in her forty-fourth year.[3] The reports about her death were brief. Thomas Coke writing to his brother John Coke on the 21st July gave this laconic account: 'The Lady Rich fell sick, sent for Doctor Layfield, disclaimed her last marriage, sent to her first husband to ask forgiveness, and died penitently'.[4]

The Coke family were well acquainted with Lady Rich since John Coke was the intimate friend of her cousin Fulke Greville, with whom he lived after Greville moved out of Essex House and he had been Greville's source of information about her in the past. His brother's report of

Penelope's death-bed disclaimer of her second marriage and request for forgiveness from Lord Rich is uncorroborated but if correct would not necessarily be spontaneous since it would be the duty of the clergy who attended her to extract such repentance.

There is another account of her death written in Latin by the comtemporary historian Robert Johnston, though only published fifty years later. He had described the scene after Mountjoy's death when Penelope utterly dejected lay in a corner of the bedroom for a night and a day in mourning. He related how Penelope 'weighed down by sorrow and grief did not survive him long' and went on to give his account of her story in which he made no mention of a death-bed repentance. His version showed her as more concerned with what would become of her children. According to Johnston it was generally believed to be Penelope's dying wish that her Blount children should not be brought up by Lord Rich. If she had in fact asked Lord Rich for forgiveness this plea would not accord with any show of confidence in him as a step-father. This is his account:

Penelope, sister of Essex, outstanding in beauty, gifted in every quality of mind and body except for chastity, died in the same state of care and meditation as her husband the Earl of Devon. From her youth she was very brave, exceeding virtuous and outstandingly kind. And she would have remained so, had she not contracted an unfortunate union with another man; had she not violated the sacred and proper law of matrimony and caused havoc in a most noble family; and had she not kept the children conceived in this union with another man in her own family because of their physical resemblance in face and figure. This kind of shamelessness cannot be tolerated publicly or privately so that contact with evil may not creep in further and be spread by example, as it is totally opposed to the way of ecclesiastical law. Many people believed that Penelope on her death-bed commended to her first husband his daughter and sons and entrusted her second family to someone else.[5]

There were also reports that she had become converted to Catholicism on her death bed put about by the Jesuit priest Father Gerard who once before had alleged that he had tried to convert her and almost succeeded.

In his autobiography Gerard alleged that shortly before her death Penelope's thoughts were (for the second time by his account) turning towards Catholicism. He had received a letter to this effect from a girl who had gone to Belgium to become a nun and had once been in Lady Rich's service. This last part at least is substantiated. There was indeed such a girl, a Mistress Deacon, who had previously attended on Lady Rich and then in January 1606 entered a Brussels Convent.[6] Father Gerard described how he had been about to go and see Lady Rich when he heard she had died of fever but 'happily she had been reconciled to the Church on her death-bed by one of our Fathers.'[7] This last part of the story is a little glib. The name of the priest who had made the conversion is not given nor any details which might serve to authenticate it.

Gerard's account is suspect for another reason. Thomas Coke reported that she sent for Dr Layfield on her death-bed. Dr Layfield was the rector of St Clement Danes Church in the Strand and the fact that she sent for a Protestant chaplain on her death suggests that she did indeed remain true to that religion.

With no men left in the Devereux family to protect her name it was a field day for the scandal mongers. Here is one reported epitaph:

Here lieth Penelope or my Lady Rich
Or my Lady of Devonshire, I know not which.
She shuffled, she cut, she dealt, she played,
She died neither wife widow nor maid.
One stone contains her: this death can do,
Which in her life was not content with two.

Amusing, even true, but there is something haunting in an age of great consciousness about status to end up with no place, 'neither wife widow nor maid.'

More biting still was this:

The devil men say is dead in Devonshire late.
Of late did Devonshire live in Rich estate

Till Rich with toys did Devonshire bewitch
That Devonshire died and left the devil Rich.[8]

Where Penelope was buried has remained unknown till now. The
scurrilous epitaphs reflected the true situation, that because of the scandal
she had become a source of the deepest embarrassment to her relatives.
Lord Rich had long since disowned her and certainly there was no place for
her in the Rich family tomb at Felstead in Essex. Nor could she be interred
with her second husband the Earl of Devonshire for he had been buried in
state at Westminster Abbey with his coat of arms set up 'in single' without
his wife's.

In the Court of Star Chamber trial, only weeks before her death she
had agreed not to use the title of Countess of Devonshire but refused to be
called Lady Rich. Instead she called herself simply by the name of the Lady
Penelope, without surname.

As she did not belong either to the Rich or to the Blount families she
had inevitably reverted to her family of birth, the Devereux, and it is under
this name that the mystery of her burial is to be solved.

She had died in Westminster and she had sent for Dr Layfield on her
death-bed. Starting from these two facts, I searched for her first in the
records of St Clement Danes Church in the Strand, without success. I then
turned to the records of All Hallows Barking by the Tower, where her
grandfather and three of her brother Robert's children were buried. As
well as being a Devereux family burial place it was close to Walsingham
House in Seething Lane, the home of her former sister-in-law Frances.
Penelope had entertained Frances and her third husband the Earl of
Clanricarde at Wanstead in the early autumn of 1606 and so they had
remained close to the end.

An entry in the unpublished records of this the oldest of the parish
churches in the City of London for the 7th October 1607 reads: 'A Lady
Devereux'.[9] The description could be of no one else.

The fact that the burial took place exactly three months after her death
was by no means exceptional. Sir Philip Sidney's funeral had not taken
place until four months after his death, the delay being occasioned not by
the time it took to ship his body home from the Netherlands (a matter of
two and a half weeks) but because of problems with his estate. There was

insufficient to pay his creditors and his debts were eventually discharged by his father-in-law Sir Francis Walsingham who also paid for the lavish funeral. When Sir Francis himself died shortly afterwards he was buried at night to save the expense of a public funeral. Again, Penelope's ex-guardian the Earl of Huntingdon was only buried four months after his death because of a dispute as to who should pay for the funeral.

The dispute about the Earl of Devonshire's will was still raging at the time of Penelope's death. The fact that his estate had not yet been settled is the obvious reason for the delay in the funeral and for its simplicity. The scandal accounts for the virtual anonymity of the grave.[10]

CHAPTER SIXTEEN

'The Star of Britain'

Penelope left behind her at her death nine children, her two eldest daughters by Lord Rich, Lettice and Essex, and her two sons by him, Robert and Henry; and by Lord Mountjoy her daughters Penelope and Isabella and three sons, Mountjoy, St John and Charles.

Lord Rich went on to remarry, this time for money. In a letter of 21st December 1616, John Chamberlain wrote: 'The Lord Rich, after much wooing and several attempts in diverse places, hath at last lighted on the lady Sampoll [St. Paul], a rich widow of Lincolnshire.'[1]

She was cleverer with money than he was for on the 11th October 1617, Chamberlain was writing:

> Lord Rich is said to be in great perplexity, or rather crazed in brain, to see himself overreached by his new wife, who hath so conveyed her estate that he has little or nothing the better by her and, if she outlive him, like to carry away a great part of his.[2]

By the following year he had bought himself an expensive new title, paying £10,000 to become Earl of Warwick. King James had instituted the practice of selling such honours in the hopes of replenishing his dwindling revenue and there had been a steep rise in the going rate. Again, we have the acid John Chamberlain's comments. In a letter of 8th August 1618 he wrote:

> Sir Robert Rich hath been forced to make a posting journey to court where he hath prevailed so far as to procure his father to be created Earl of Warwick but these dignities cannot defend them from the pens

of malicious poets and libellists who gave them new additions, and in plain terms laid them in another sort as the first [Robert Sidney, Earl of Leicester] to be vinosos, the second [William Compton, Earl of Northampton] crazed, the third [Robert Rich, Earl of Warwick] cornucopia.[3]

The legend of the cuckold lived on.

Lord Rich himself died about eight months after receiving the title and it passed to their eldest son Robert. Dorothy, Countess of Northumberland, died in 1619, two years before her husband's release from the tower. Lettice survived them all. When her brother, aged eighty-six, was on his death-bed it was said that 'his sister, my Lady of Leicester being six years elder can yet walk a mile in a morning'.[4] She lived until the ripe old age of ninety-four and died on Christmas Day 1634.

Penelope's eldest son Robert was to become a prominent Puritan leader. Although both Robert and Henry's upbringing had been very much under their father's control so that his was the formative influence on them, Penelope had been useful when it came to finding Robert a wife. She helped him towards a marriage with Frances, daughter of Sir William Hatton. There was rivalry for this lady's hand, with Judge Gawdy also wanting her for his grandson: 'but the Lady Rich prevented him and winning her goodwill contracted her secretly to her son'.[5]

Robert followed in the puritan tradition of his father, shunning the life of the court which, as Earl of Warwick, he might have enjoyed. In the early part of his career he went as an adventurer to the West Indies and helped to settle colonies there. Later he became Lord High Admiral of England.

Henry Rich the second son, followed the path of his mother and his uncle the Earl of Essex to the court, becoming a favoured courtier. He received many honours including, like his uncle the Earl of Essex, the Chancellorship of the University of Cambridge and he was created first Earl of Holland. Holland House in Kensington, with its fine park, was his London home. He also followed the unfortunate end of his uncle, for he too was beheaded only months before his sovereign, for his part in an intrigue to restore Charles I to a position of authority.

The parentage of these two men was the subject for caustic comment from the Earl of Clarendon in his *History of the Rebellion:*

> The Earl of Holland was a younger son of a noble house and very
> fruitful bed, which divided numerous issues between two great
> fathers; the eldest, many sons and daughters to the Lord Rich; the
> younger, of both sexes to Mountjoy Earl of Devonshire, who had
> been more than once married to the mother. The reputation of his
> family gave him no great advantage in the world.[6]

To Clarendon she was not a person but a 'very fruitful bed', to be
moralised about and contemputously dismissed:

> It shall suffice now to say that there was a very froward fate attended
> all or most of the posterity of that bed from whence he and his brother
> of Warwick had their original; though he, and some others amongst
> them, had many very good parts and excellent endowments.[7]

She who at eighteen had refused to be treatd as a mere chattel and had
proceeded to shape her own life into a liberated individualistic identity,
had reverted to being referred to in this anonymous way. The reluctance
to name her was part of the moral fervour generated against her following
her remarriage. After her death, family respectability was the paramount
consideration. Her sons Robert and Henry would have been old enough at
that time to have had a say in the burial arrangements but they too had
found her an embarrasment. Robert, with his strong Puritan leanings,
would have been ashamed of her morals and Henry, the aspiring courtier,
would not have wished to remind King James of his disgraced mother.

Mountjoy Blount, the eldest son of Penelope and Charles, only ten
when his mother died, had been unable to succeed to the title of Earl of
Devonshire on his father's death but he had inherited the bulk of his
father's estate including the house at Wanstead. There, in September 1607,
two months after Penelope's death but before her funeral had taken place,
King James had stayed on his return from a progress. It has been said that

Wanstead was forfeited to the crown on the Earl of Devonshire's death but this is not the case. The house and its lands passed to Mountjoy Blount but as he was a minor he could not hold land, so until he came of age the benefits passed to the crown. King James stayed there from time to time and enjoyed hunting in its parks. It has also been said that when Mountjoy Blount came of age he was prevailed upon to part with his parents' home in return for a title. John Chamberlain, writing to Dudley Carleton in December 1617, reported: 'Young Blount, Rich or Mountjoy, heir to the Earl of Devonshire, is shortly to be made a Baron for the which he parts with the house and lands at Wanstead but whether to the King or Earl of Buckingham I know not.'[8]

Mountjoy Blount's own version of what happened was very different. According to his account he had allowed his own affairs to be neglected during the years he had been away on military service abroad. It was not until many years later that he discovered that he had been cheated. He found 'the means left to him by his father to be wasted as to the one half. And in particular the Manor of Wanstead . . . to be conveyed away during his minority without one penny recompense to him for it or any other advantage'.[9] By then Charles I was on the throne and he petitioned the king 'that as a subject he may have the benefit of the laws and that the present owner be left to his just defence in law or equity.'

Mountjoy Blount was created Lord Mountjoy in the Irish peerage in 1618. He did not obtain an English peerage until 1627 and the following year was created Earl of Newport. He too was a prominent figure at court, siding with the royalists in the Civil War.

After Lord Rich's death the half-brothers kept on friendly terms. When in 1625 Mountjoy Blount needed leave from his duties in order to get married his elder half-brother the Earl of Warwick appealed to the queen on his behalf, in terms after his father's own heart, pleading that 'wives worth 125 or 130 thousand pounds were not to be had every day'.[10]

Even the moralists had to concede that Penelope Rich had many virtues. Pete Heylyn, Laud's biographer, called her 'a Lady in whom lodged all attractive graces of beauty, wit and sweetness of behaviour, which might render her the absolute mistress of all eyes and hearts.'[11]

The historian Robert Johnston described her as 'outstanding in beauty, gifted in every quality of mind and body except for chastity'.[12] Penelope had lived according to her own code of morality, in defiance of the growing surge of Puritanism. On her death she vanished into obscurity, a victim of the new ethos, because her whole life was an affirmation of all that Puritanism sought to crush. In fact the attempt to obliterate her memory did not succeed, although it has taken several centuries to restore her to her proper place.

So far as her cultural legacy goes first and foremost she has been immortalised as Philip Sidney's Stella. The power of Stella's presence is strongly evident in Sidney's sonnets. Stella is no disembodied figure but is presented as a physical reality. We know the colour of her hair and eyes; her talents, her temper, her moods and attitudes are recorded in a variety of aspects.

The extent of Penelope Rich's influence on Philip Sidney is not capable of precise definition but it is interesting to note that he did not promise to immortalise her by his poetry as Shakespeare and Spenser later promised the recipients of their sonnets. On the contrary , in Sonnet 90, given in the Appendix, he swears the opposite. In this sonnet he asks his mistress to believe that he does not seek fame by his poetry, since his ambition is to win her praise alone:

> Thine eyes my pride, thy lips my history:
> If thou praise not, all other praise is shame.

He insists:

> In truth I swear, I wish not there should be
> Graved in my epitaph a Poet's name.

She is the reader for whom he writes as well as the inspiration of his poetry; without her it would not have been written.

Because she had been Sidney's inspiration she became the inspirer of those who sought to follow him. Some of these were merely the exercises of hacks, jumping onto her band wagon and hoping to ride on it to success. Unlike Sidney, they were writing to please a patron. But some at least of these writers appear to have been genuinely inspired by her or her story. Henry Constable wrote more than twenty sonnets to her as well as two sonnets on the birth and death of her daughter and the sonnet on Nicholas Hilliard's miniature of her. Numerous books were dedicated to her. Bartholomew Young, dedicating his translation of *Diana,* referred to her 'magnificent mind wherein all virtues have their proper seat.' The dedications also included John Florio's translation of Montaignes *Essays* in 1603. In the preface he acclaimed her as 'truely-richest Lady Rich, in riches of fortune not deficient, but of body incomparably richer, of mind most rich.'[13]

It contains a sonnet written by 'Il Candido' (the pseudonym of Matthew Gwinne) in which he addressed Lady Rich as

> perfection's heir, joy's light,
> Love's life, life's gem, virtue's court, heaven's delight,
> Nature's chief work, fairest book his muses' sprite,
> Heaven on earth, peerless Phoenix, Phoebe bright,

He is quoting from at least seven of the *Astrophil and Stella* sonnets, addressing Penelope Rich as the inspirer of Philip Sidney. 'Inspire you can'. he tells her. He is not, he says, trying to compete with Sidney, but merely quoting his verse, though he would like to 'fly higher'. He and the translator offer her these tributes.

John Davies of Hereford addressed a sonnet to her praising her excellence and referring to the delight taken in punning on the felicitous name:

> To descant on thy name as many do.

John Ford dedicated his poem *Fame's Memorial* to her, his elegy on the death of Mountjoy. In it he described Penelope as Mountjoy's

> heart's delight, who was that glorious star
> Which beautified the value of our land.

He showered her with praises as

Wit's ornament, earth's love, love's paradise
A saint divine, a beauty fairly wise.

Better perhaps, because it is more individualised, is this description:

So this heart-stealing goddess charmed their ears
To hear her fluent wit, they blush at theirs.

Other tributes were Richard Barnfield's *Affectionate Shepherd*, ten sonnets by Alexander Craig and works by Gervase Markham. The tradition continued with her children and John Donne wrote verse letters to her two daughter Lettice and Essex.

Thomas Campion went further than most in openly naming her two great conquests in love, Sidney and Mountjoy. In one of his Latin poems he called her 'Stella Brittana', the Star of Britain, and gave her pride of place amongst a host of beautiful women, ancient and modern. He celebrated her in lines that translate as follows:

Still not satisfied with these the god goes on: he burns to hasten higher; far off a great glow appears before his eyes and summons him and promises greater stars. The Star of Britain sparkles from the green myrtle grove, Penelope, whose face will one day set on fire the passions of Astrophil and who with her sweet voice will enchant the conqueror of the Irish. Morpheus stops, captured by the charm of so much beauty, and he marvels that so many passions sprang from one body, all of which he stores in his heart's memory.[14]

This highly romanticised picture was how the Elizabethan poets liked to depict Penelope. However, the dark events of the last two years of her life were more the subject matter for Jacobean tragedy which followed. Her inspiration can be traced in John Webster's *The White Devil,* written five years after her death. There are many resemblances between Vittoria Corombona, his White Devil, and Penelope Rich, 'the fair woman with a black soul'. Each was sold off to a rich but foolish husband; each took a powerful nobleman lover and then lost her position at court; each went on trial accused of being a whore, facing her accusers alone and with dignity. The similarities are too strong to be coincidental.[15]

Musicians and artists, as well as poets, paid her their respects. In the field of music, John Dowland dedicated one of his galliards to her, *Lady Rich Her Galliard,* and another to her brother, *The Earl of Essex's Galliard.* The galliards were the liveliest of the Elizabethan dances, as compared with the stately pavan. William Byrd addressed her in his *Songs of Sundry Natures* and he set the sixth song of *Astrophil and Stella* to music. The eighth song of that sequence was set to music by the French composer Charles Tessier who also dedicated to her in Italian his *Le premier livre de chanson et airs de court.* She was painted by Nicholas Hilliard, who expressed his attachment to her by naming his daughter after her.

These are, nevertheless, peripheral matters when set beside the major events of her life. Penelope had the unique distinction of having been chosen by two of the greatest men of her day. She did not have scores of lovers, but she did have two, both remarkable men on whom she had a vital and lasting influence.

Sidney had been no mere youth but a mature man when he fell in love with her and it was her image that dominated the best of his lyrical poetry. No admirer of that poetry can regret the experience that inspired it. Mountjoy had devoted himself to her for many years and she was the only woman in his life. They remained faithful to each other for sixteen years until death parted them, and their long relationship was as firmly rooted as any marriage. These events in themselves are an indication of her powers.

Her influence in the political sphere cannot be ignored. She played a part in smoothing King James's path to the English throne. Essex's accusation of her following his trial, in which he blamed her for goading him into the rebellion, was not without justification. She had considerable influence over her brother and played an active part in the events surrounding the rebellion. She showed considerable courage, not least in the way she faced her accusers with their immense powers over life and death. In the last analysis they dared not harm her.

Penelope flouted the conventions of her day and this again took enormous courage. She succeeded in coming to terms with a disastrous first marriage and made it work to both partners' advantage. To combine successfully the roles of wife and mother, mistress and court lady at the court of the moralistic Elizabeth required both practical abilities and fine judgement. She survived the ordeals of her own political interrogation, her brother's condemnation of her, the sorrows of his disgrace and execution. She went on to survive her own disgrace following her marriage to Mountjoy and his death so soon after. She deserves our admiration for the strength of character which enabled her to control her own life, refusing to conform to the accepted code, to be manipulated or suppressed.

Her great qualities were her courage and resilience, her vitality and life-enhancing gifts. Her faults were of a piece with these qualities. If she loved pleasure, this was part of her capacity for enjoyment and sociability, of her large and passionate nature. If she enjoyed admiration, she had after all been repeatedly praised for her wit, her beauty and charms, and at least she did not suffer from false modesty. She might well have defended herself in the words of Vittoria Corombona, John Webster's White Devil, on trial as a whore:

Sum up my faults I pray, and you shall find
That beauty and gay clothes, a merry heart
And a good stomach to a feast, are all,
All the poor crimes that you can charge me with.

Her courage revealed itself in so many acts and incidents of her life. It gave her the ability to lead the life she wanted, which not many women of her day, including the aristocratic ones, were able to do. Indeed, when one considers her life one wonders how she was able to get away with so much. She must have had enormous personality to be able to ride rough-shod over the conventions and morality of her time. We should not be surprised to find that she was a source of inspiration to others.

In an age of female subservience, the bold, confident, exuberant

Elizabethan spirit was almost exclusively manifested in the great men of the day. Exceptionally, this same irrepressible vitality blazed through the life of Penelope Rich. By living her life as the confident equal of the great men of her day, Penelope Rich extended the frontiers of possibility.

Appendix

Some Sonnets of Sidney

2

Not at first sight, nor with a dribbed shot
Love gave the wound, which while I breathe will bleed:
But known worth did in mine of time proceed,
Till by degrees it had full conquest got.
I saw and liked, I liked but loved not,
I loved, but straight did not what Love decreed:
At length to Love's decrees, I forc'd, agreed.
Yet with repining at so partial lot.
Now even that footstep of lost liberty
Is gone, and now like slave-born Muscovite,
I call it praise to suffer tyranny;
And now employ the remnant of my wit,
To make myself believe, that all is well,
While with a feeling skill I paint my hell.

24

Rich fools there be, whose base and filthy heart
Lies hatching still the goods wherein they flow:
And damning their own selves to Tantal's smart,
Wealth breeding want, more blist, more wretched grow.
Yet to those fools heav'n such wit doth impart,
As what their hands do hold, their heads do know,
And knowing, love, and loving lay apart,
As sacred things, far from all danger's show.
But that rich fool, who by blind Fortune's lot,
The richest gem of love and life enjoys,
And can with foul abuse such beauties blot;

Let him deprive of sweet but unfelt joys,
(Exil'd for aye from those high treasures, which
He knows not) grow in only folly rich.

30

Whether the Turkish new-moon minded be
To fill his horns this year on Christian coast;
How Poles' right king means, without leave of host,
To warm with ill-made fire cold Moscovy,
If French can yet three parts in one agree,
What now the Dutch in their full diets boast,
How Holland hearts, now so good towns be lost,
Trust in the shade of pleasing Orange tree.
How Ulster likes of that same golden bit,
Wherewith my father once made it half tame,
If in the Scottish court be welt'ring yet.
These questions busy wits to me do frame;
I cumb'red with good manners, answer do,
But know not how, for still I think of you.

35

What may words say, or what may words not say,
Where truth itself must speak like flattery?
Within what bounds can one his liking stay,
Where nature doth with infinite agree?
What Nestor's counsel can my flames allay,
Since Reason's self doth blow the coal in me?
And ah what hope, that hope should once see day,
Where Cupid is sworn page to Chastity?
Honour is honour'd, that thou doest possess
Him as thy slave, and now long needy Fame
Doth even grow rich, naming my Stella's name.
Wit learns in these perfection to express,
Not thou by praise, but praise in thee is rais'd:
It is a praise to praise, when thou art prais'd.

37

My mouth doth water, and my breast doth swell,
My tongue doth itch, my thoughts in labour be:
Listen then lordings with good ear to me,
For of my life I must a riddle tell.
Toward Aurora's court a nymph doth dwell,
Rich in all beauties which man's eye can see:
Beauties so far from reach of words that we
Abase her praise, saying she doth excel:
Rich in the treasure of deserv'd renown,
Rich in the riches of a royal heart,
Rich in those gifts which give th'eternal crown;
Who though most rich in these and every part,
Which make the patents of true worldly bliss,
Hath no misfortune, but that Rich she is.

90

Stella think not that I by verse seek fame,
Who seek, who hope, who love, who live but thee;
Thine eyes my pride, thy lips my history:
If thou praise not, all other praise is shame,
Nor so ambitious am I, as to frame
A nest for my young praise in laurel tree:
In truth I swear, I wish not there should be
Graved in mine epitaph a poet's name:
Ne if I would, could I just title make,
That any laud to me thereof should grow,
Without my plumes from other's wings I take.
For nothing from my wit or will doth flow.
Since all my words thy beauty doth indite,
And love doth hold my hand, and makes me write.

Notes   ˙

References are to the Works of Reference that follow the notes. Books and articles are referred to by authors' surname with abbreviated title where more than one work of an author has been cited.

The following abbreviations have been used:

APC	:	*Acts of Privy Council*
BL	:	British Library
CC	:	County Council
CSP	:	*Calendar of State Papers*
DNB	:	*Dictionary of National Biography*
ERO	:	Essex Record Office
HMC	:	*Historical Manuscripts Commission*
PRO	:	Public Record Office
SP	:	State Papers

Chapter 1 : The Wedding
1. BL Lansdowne Ms 885. f.86
2. Bagot p 33
3. BL Lansdowne Ms 31. f.105
4. Tension VII, 296

Chapter 2 : 'The fineness of her wit'
1. Harrison, *Letters of Queen Elizabeth* , p.19
2. Devereux I, 8. Day and month of birth not given. Chartley baptism records did not begin until 1574.
3. Chamberlin, *Sayings of Queen Elizabeth*, p.v -vi
4. Chamberlin, *Sayings of Queen Elizabeth*, p.267
5. Bartholomew Young, Dedication of his translation of *Diana of de Montemayor*, 1598.
6. *HMC* Salisbury III, 435
7. *Harleian Miscellany* IX : Sonnet four of the first seven sonnets.
8. R. Ascham quoted by O.L. Dick in his introduction to J. Aubrey's *Brief Lives.*

9. BL Lansdowne Ms 17. f.47
10. SP Ireland May 2nd 1572
11. Quoted by Wallace p.22
12. Collins I, 64
13. Feuillerat, III, 126
14. BL Additional Ms 34591.503, quoted by Wallace, p.115
15. Bryskett quoted by Buxton in *Philip Sidney* p.45
16. Languet quoted by Buxton p.45
17. Poem by Thomas Drant quoted by Buxton p.79

Chapter 3 : 'The delights of the English Egypt'
1. *CSP* Ireland 1574–85 LIII, 84
2. *Life of Sir Thomas Smith* (1698) quoted by Tenison III, 27
3. Collins I, 69
4. Collins I, 168
5. Broughton p.4
6. Broughton p.6
7. Murdin pp 300–301
8. Collins I, 301
9. BL Lansdowne Ms 22. f. 200, quoted by Devereux, I, 165–6
10. Printed in *The Carmarthen Antiquary* II part X, 184–201 and in *Gwyneddon 3* pp 255-7 (Cardiff, 1931) Translation by Andrew Hawke

Chapter 4 : 'More dishonour than can be repaired'
1. Collins I, 147
2. *Correspondence of Sidney and Languet* p.144
3. Collins I, 140-142
4. PRO Prerogative Court of Canterbury 34 Carew. Will dated 14th June 1576.
5. BL Lansdowne Ms 24. f.26
6. Longleat Devereux Ms; *HMC* Bath V, 249
7. BL Lansdowne Ms 24. f.208
8. BL Lansdowne Ms 162. f.132
9. Quoted by F Chamberlin *Elizabeth and Leycester* p. 94
10. Collins I, 88

11. Quoted by Tenison III, 159
12. Longleat Devereux Ms; *HMC* Bath V, 205-6

Chapter 5 : 'The rich Lord Rich'
 1. Nichols *Elizabeth,* II, 301
 2. *Shakespeare's England,* I, 93
 3. Harington I, 233-4
 4. Harington I, 235
 5. Harington I, 361
 6. ERO- Felstead Parish Church Burial Records 'The Right Worshipful Mr. Ritchford Rich son and heir unto the Right Honourable Sir Robert Rich Knight, Lord Rich, was buried the 31st May 1580'.
 7. Warwickshire CC Aylesford papers
 8. Records of Admission to Gray's Inn : 2nd February 1592, Robert Lord Rich.
 9. *APC* XIII, (1581-2), 297
10. ERO Quoted by Emmison, *Disorder* p.67
11. Strype, *Aylmer* p.54 : Davids p. 69
12. The mistake originates from Strype p.83; corrected by Craze
13. Collinson pp 343 - 4
14. *HMC* Salisbury XIII, 199
15. Strype, *Aylmer* p.83
16. BL Lansdowne Ms 31.f 105
17. BL Lansdowne Ms 33.f 20
18. Longleat Devereux Ms. f.55b
19. Folger Library, Bagot Papers La 248
20. Camden, *Remaines* p.174 quoted in Sidney, *Poems,* Ed. Ringler p. 441
21. Murdin p.364
22. BL Lansdowne Ms 885. f 86
23. *HMC* Rutand I, 128
24. Nichols *Elizabeth,* II. 248

Chapter 6 : 'He did study in all things to torment her'
 1. BL Lansdowne Ms 885. f 86
 2. Devereux I, 152

3. M. Hoby, *Diary* p 239
4. *CSP* Domestic Elizabeth 1581-90 CL, 85, quoted in Sidney, *Poems* p. 443
5. Longleat Devereux Ms quoted by Tenison V, 70
6. Greville pp 129-30
7. Robertson pp 296-7
8. Lant quoted by Wallace p. 395
9. *Arcadia* Book II Chapter 21 p.353

Chapter 7 : 'The idle housewife'

1. Baptism record at Greater London Record Office, Records of St Mary's Church, Stratford, Bow. On 6th September 1590 Lady Rich was 'churched' after this birth : see *Throckmorton Diary* quoted by A. L. Rowse, *Sir Walter Raleigh*.
2. Montaigne, *Essays* translated by John Florio (London 1910) II. Rawson transposed the dedication from Vol. I and the mistake has been followed by other writers.
3. BL Lansdowne Ms 57.f.51 : letter written 10th September 1588
4. Lambeth Palace, Bacon Ms 658. 198
5. Hulton Ms quoted by Devereux I, 446-7
6. Memo relating to Essex's extravagances and the decision to move him: Longleat Devereux Papers, V. f.55b.
7. Memo Longleat Devereux Papers, V. f.63b.
8. Quoted by Tenison VI, 143
9. Bodleian Tanner Ms 78.12, quoted by Tenison.
10. Thomas Dudley to Earl of Leicester : *Leicester Correspondence,* ed. Bruce, p.47 quoted by Tenison VI, 75
11. *CSP* Spanish III 1550-1586, 477
12. *PRO SP* 121. 161. 22 Calendared in *CSP* Domestic 1581-90, CLXI, 22
13. Marriage Licences issued by the Bishop of London 1520-1610, *Harleian Society Publications* XXV, 120
14. Strype, *Aylmer* pp 197 and 326
15. BL Lansdowne Ms 39.f.171
16. BL Lansdowne Ms 39.f.181
17. Tenison first made the identification, IX, 508

18. Folger Library, Bagot Papers L a 459
19. A J Perrett in *Transactions of the Worcestershire Archaeological Society* (1942) pp 10-18; F M Jones pp 186-7
20. In *An Apology of the Earl of Essex* written 1598, printed 1603, to Anthony Bacon
21. Earl of Essex to Sir Robert Cecil quoted by Devereux I, 233
22. *Fortescue papers,* ed. Gardiner, Camden Society 1871 pp xvi-xvii, quoted by Tenison VIII, 442.

Chapter 8 : 'Love the reward of love'
1. Moryson II, 265
2. Naunton p.92
3. Moryson II, 263-4
4. Naunton p.90
5. Naunton p.81
6. Naunton p.92
7. *Notes and Queries* 7th Series VIII, 110
8. Printed by P J Blok in *Correspondence inedité de Robert Dudley,* quoted in Constable *Poems* Ed Grundy, p. 28.
9. Hatfield Cecil Papers XVIII: 50 nicknames written in Lord Burghley's hand.
10. *HMC* Salisbury III, 435

Chapter 9 : 'This rich praise, that you alone are you'
1. Baptism records at Westminster City Council Archives, Records of St. Clement Danes Church.
2. Bartholomew Young, Dedication of his translation of Diana of de Montemayor.
3. Longleat Devereux Papers; *HMC* Bath V, 262
4. Warwickshire CC Aylesford Papers (on microfilm, originals at Packington)
5. *HMC* De L'Isle and Dudley II, 152
6. *HMC* De L'Isle and Dudley II, 268; Collins II, 43
7. Baptism record at Westminster City Council Archives.
8. The two letters have been printed as *Essex to Stella*, ed A. Freeman.
9. *HMC* De L'Isle and Dudley II, 236; Collins II, 18

10. Longleat, Devereux papers; *HMC* Bath V, 261
11. Warwickshire CC Aylesford papers
12. Printed in *'The Secret Correspondence of Sir Robert Cecil with James VI'* ed D. Dalrymple (1776) p.29, quoted by Harrison, *Advice* p.21.
13. PRO SP 14.11.9 Calendared in *CSP* Domestic 1603-10, p.183. The essay is printed in full in Yates pp 206-211.

Chapter 10 : 'My Lady Rich's desires are obeyed as commandments'
 1. Warwickshire CC Aylesford papers
 2. Bagot papers L a 224
 3. Bagot papers L a 911
 4. Bagot papers L a 272, quoted by Falls p.65
 5. *HMC* Salisbury XV 175; Hatfield, Cecil Papers CI.16
 6. *HMC* Salisbury XV, 179; Hatfield, Cecil Papers CI.25 Both this letter and the one noted above (note 5) mistakenly endorsed '1603'. See Akrigg p.87 for correction of dating.
 7. ERO. The hiding place was rediscovered in 1931.
 8. Gerard pp 33-5 Gerard's account is undated (in Chapter headed Winter 1591 Spring 1594) Falls p 64 suggests the episode took place 'about 1592' but ERO sources show March 1594 to have been occasion of Gerard's stay at Broadoaks.
 9. *CSP* Venetian 1610-1613 XII, 368
10. Originals of these letters now moved from Penshurst to Kent Archives. These extracts are taken from *HMC* De L'Isle and Dudley II, 163 onwards and Collins I, 348 onwards.
11. Warwickshire CC Aylesford papers
12. M.C. Bradbrook, *John Webster* (London, 1980) sees this letter as having some sinister significance, with Essex meeting his sister in the fields in order to exchange secret information. I see no evidence for this. For my comments on this book see *English*, XXXI 188-90 (Oxford, 1982).
13. Hatfield, Cecil papers LV.55
14. Lambeth Palace, Bacon Ms. 657. 46.61
15. Lambeth Palace, Bacon Ms 1.68; Ungerer I, 232-3
16. Translation at Lambeth palace, Bacon Ms 653. 74,144-5
17. This family correspondence is at Packington, on microfilm at Warwickshire CC. The letters are from this collection, unless

otherwise stated.

18. Lacey p.23
19. Collins II, 91; *HMC* De L'Isle and Dudley II, 322
20. Collins II 92-3; *HMC* De L'Isle and Dudley II, 328

Chapter 11 : 'The storm continues'

1. The precise figure is £29,993.4s 6d. Longleat Devereux papers; Bath V 257
2. Collins II, 90
3. Hatfield, Cecil Papers XCIX. 167
4. Hatfield, Cecil Papers CI. 25
5. Collins II, 127-129
6. Hatfield, Cecil Papers CCVI.95 Calendared as 'before 1599'. Mr Donnall is William Downhall, in Essex's service and later fined for his part in the Essex Rising.
7. Collins II, 132
8. Collins II, 149
9. Naunton p.93
10. Collins II, 153
11. *CSP* Domestic CCLXXIII 1598-1601, 365
12. Collins II, 154
13. There are many copies of this letter, seven in the British Library alone. Only one copy has a date: BL Stowe 150.f.140, dated 1st January 1600 (1599, old style). I have accepted the dating as correct, although the letter has usually been taken to have been written later. (Each of the copies has small variations in wording.)
14. *HMC* De L'Isle and Dudley II, 435
15. P.S. to Letter quoted by Rawson p.228
16. *CSP* Domestic Elizabeth 1598-1601 p.392
17. Chamberlain I, 86
18. These letters of Rowland White printed in Collins II, 171 onwards; *HMC* De L' Isle and Dudley II, 442 ff.
19. *CSP* Domestic 1598-1601 p.414
20. Chamberlain I, 96
21. Moryson II, 314
22. *CSP* Ireland 1600 p.346
23. Sir Robert Cecil's letter is a scrawled draft, written by another hand

but amended by himself. It is only dated '1600', but from its contents appears to answer Lord Buckhurst's letter of the 13th August, 1600. From its length and the amount of work which has gone into its drafting, Cecil clearly regarded it as important. Original at Hatfield, Cecil Papers CLXXXI.62

24. Collins II, 212
25. Collins II, 215
26. Quoted by Akrigg, p.107
27. *CSP* Domestic 1598-1601 p.548
28. Letter Henry Garnet to Claudius Aquaria, 11th March 1601 Arch. S. J. Rome Anglia II. 172, quoted in Caraman *Henry Garnet* (1964).
29. *CSP* Domestic (1598-1601) p.546: *HMC* Salisbury XI, 44
30. From Examination of Edward Bushell: *CSP* Domestic 1601: 'Conceives that first occasion of Essex taking the course he did was on Saturday night . . . the persons who supped with him were . . . [as named in text]
31. *CSP* Ireland 1600-01 p.174
32. Moryson II, 354-5
33. *CSP* Domestic 1598-1601 p.547
34. CSP Ireland 1600-01 p.198
35. Goodman pp 15-16
36. Moryson II, 356
37. Goodman p.17
38. *APC* XXXI 1600-01, 167, 176-177
39. Goodman p.17
40. Goodman p.19; Bodleian, Tanner Ms 114. f.139
41. *HMC* De L'Isle and Dudley II, 618; Collins II, 262

Chapter 12 : 'No Lord in England might compare'
1. Purchased 15th March 1599.
2. Moryson II, 266
3. Rawson p.221
4. *CSP* Carew 1589-1600 p.481
5. Moryson II, 213-4
6. Moryson II, 262
7. From 'A Funeral Poem'.
8. A Clifford, *Diary*, p.9

9. Nichols, *James* I, p.31
10. *CSP* Domestic 1603-1610 p.32 (17th August 1603)
11. *History of the Barrington Family* p.14 (see note 12)
12. ERO; BL, Egerton Ms 2644, 120, 128; *Transactions of Essex Archaeological Society* VII n.s. (1884) – *History of the Barrington Family*, p.14 onwards; C Thompson in *Essex Journal*, Spring 1979.
13. *HMC* XII Report Appendix I, Cowper, 23, I.45 (Coke Mss).
14. From *Correspondence of King James VI of Scotland with Sir Robert Cecil and others*, ed. Bruce (1861) p.67, quoted by Harrison, *Advice* p.25.
15. E.B. de Fonblanque II, 293, quoted by Harrison pp 35-36.
16. Quoted by Rawson p.269.
17. Carleton to Chamberlain, Letters p 55-6
18. Nichols *James*, I, 473
19. Harington, quoted in *The Pelican Guide to English Literature II*, 354
20. Moryson II, 264
21. Moryson II, 261
22. Moryson II, 266
23. Moryson II, 267

Chapter 13 : Divorce and Remarriage: 'Who knit that knot?'
1. BL Additional Ms 38170.f.82-84
2. BL Egerton Ms 2804. f.203 Letter from Philip Gawdy to his brother 26th November 1605; *HMC* 7th Report, Barrington Mss Appendix p.527
3. Johnston p.420
4. BL Stowe Ms; University of London Library Ms 20 ff. 84-107
5. BL Lansdowne Ms 885.f.86
6. Heylyn pp 52-53
7. Croke II Book III, 239
8. *Life of Dr Williams, Bishop of Lincoln*, quoted by Rawson p.287.
9. Le Bas pp 11-12
10. PRO STAC 8. 108.10 Subsequent quotes from Star Chamber case are under this reference (Dr Turner was the husband of Anne Turner, later executed for her part in the Overbury murder).
11. Moryson II, 337
12. Chamberlain I, 222
13. Johnston p.420: Rawson p.291, mistranslated the Latin words 'pannis

pullis, vitisque obsita 'as 'refusing alike bread meat and wine ' and this
has been followed by later writers.
14. Gerard p.35
15. Moryson II, 267
16. Chamberlain I, 226
17. *HMC* Buccleuch 45, I, 63
18. Quoted by Buxton, *Philip Sidney,* p.214
19. Daniel's 'A Funeral Elegy'
20. All that remains at Westminster Abbey is a record 'for a rail in the
    Church at the funeral of the Earl of Devonshire'; Westminster Abbey
    Muniments, 41089.

Chapter 14 : Stella in Camera Stellata
1. This Deed of Indenture was a 'Fine'. Fines and recoveries were a
   complex method of dealing with land transfers, involving fictitious
   actions in the Court and were used as devices for barring entails and for
   transferring the lands of a married woman. A copy of this Deed is at
   PRO C 142.306.146, included in the Earl of Devonshire's Inquisition
   post mortem. An 'Inquisition post mortem' was held, for the benefit
   of the Crown, upon the death of a landowner to ascertain what lands
   he owned, who his heir was and the heir's age, in order to ensure that
   the Crown's feudal rights were protected. A writ was taken out by the
   Crown in the Court of Chancery and the information about the estate
   filed there, whilst the Court of Wards investigated such matters as the
   heir's age and any rival claims and was the Court in which the heir
   must 'sue out livery of seisin', i.e. show he was entitled to possession.
2. PRO Probate 11.108.51 Stafford
3. Carleton to Chamberlain Letters, p.77
4. PRO Probate 11.108.51 Stafford
5. The Will was originally proved on 3rd June 1606 but was re-examined;
   sentence at PRO Probate 11.109.322.
6. Hatfield, Cecil papers, CXXIII. 156
7. Croke's *Reports* 2 Jac. p.160
8. The Court of Star Chamber could hear both civil and criminal cases,
   its criminal jurisdiction extending over seven types of offence:
   perjury, forgery, riot, maintenance, fraud, libels, conspiracy. Only

the pleadings and depositions are known to exist, whilst the decree and order books are missing. In a Report of a Committee of the House of Lords in 1719 it was stated that 'the last notice of them that could be got was that they were in a house in St. Bartholomew's Close London': quoted by W.P. Baildon in his edition of John Haywarde, *Les Reportes del Cases in Camera Stellata*. This book does not however contain a report of the Star Chamber proceedings since the report (p.341) begins 'In Curia Wardorum' i.e. it relates to the Court of Wards proceedings.

9. All quotations from Star Chamber case at PRO STAC 8.108.10.
10. Hatfield Cecil papers CXCIV.14
11. Hatfield Cecil papers CXXIII.156
12. PRO Inquisition post mortem Ch.306.146
13. PRO C. 2. 19. 56
14. Joseph Earth died in 1609. Dudley Carleton, never one to miss a witticism, wrote on the 4th October 1609 'Joseph Earth went into his mother earth at Wanstead two days before the King came last thither'. Carleton to Chamberlain Letters, p.113.
15. Unable to admit defeat, Sir Richard Champernowne as a last resort appealed to the King. In 1614 he petitioned King James requesting him to intervene and complaining that his Chancery action had only just come on for hearing although it had been started nine years previously. He was vainly trying to secure a speedy conclusion, but two years later the case was still going on. Huntington Library Mss EL 5975 and 5977.

Chapter 15 : *'Neither Wife Widow nor Maid'*
1. Hatfield, Cecil papers CXCIII.15
2. *HMC* Salisbury XV, 113
3. PRO Ch.306.146 Recorded in Earl of Devonshire's Inquisition post mortem that Lady Penelope Rich died on 7th July 1607 in Westminster.
4. *HMC* XII Report Appendix i. Cowper I, 63
5. Johnston p.443
6. *CSP* Flanders VIII, p.274
7. Gerard p.36
8. Quoted in Sidney, *Poems* (ed Ringler) p.559; Hudson quotes a further

'epitaph'.

9. Parish Register of All Hallows Barking by the Tower entered as 'A là Devorax'

10. Hudson's explanation for the failure to refer to Penelope, amounting even to a conspiracy of silence, is that her adultery offended Puritanism. The cult of Sidney as a Christian and Protestant hero necessitated the suppression of any scandal, hence the silence about his relationship with her. Her adultery with Mountjoy received similar treatment in view of the unfavourable light it would shed on the Earl of Warwick, another leading Puritan, if his mother was revealed as an adulteress.

Chapter 16 : 'The Star of Britain'

1. Chamberlain II, 44
2. Chamberlain II, 101
3. Chamberlain II, 162-3
4. Quoted by G.E.C. *Peerage* VII, 552
5. Chamberlain I, 204
6. Clarendon I, 137
7. Clarendon VI, 405
8. Chamberlain II, 122
9. *CSP* Domestic 1611-18 p.504; PRO SP 16.181.77
10. *CSP* Domestic 1625-1626 p.52
11. Heylyn p.52
12. Johnston p.443
13. Dedication to Vol II (see Note 2, Chapter 7)
14. *The Works of Thomas Campion* ed W.R. Davis (London 1969). Author's translation.
15. The author has made this the subject of a separate article.

Works of Reference

A. MANUSCRIPTS
All Hallows by the Tower: Parish Records
Bodleian Library

British Library:	Additional	MSS
	Egerton	MSS
	Landsdowne	MSS
	Royal	MSS
	Stowe	MSS

Essex Record Office, Essex County Council
Exeter College Library
Folger Shakespeare Library
Greater London Record Office
Guildhall Library
Hatfield House: Cecil Papers
Henry E. Huntington Library
Lambeth Palace Library: Bacon correspondence
Longleat: Devereux Papers Volume V
Public Record Office
Warwickshire County Council: Aylesford papers
Westminster City Council Archives: St Clement Danes Parish Register

B. PRINTED CALENDARS AND COLLECTIONS
Acts of the Privy Council
Calendar of State papers, Domestic
Calendar of State papers, Foreign
Calendar of State papers, Irish
Camden Society Publications
A. Collins, ed: *Letters and Memorials of State: Sidney Papers (London, 1746)*
Essex Archaelogical Society: *The History of the Barrington Family (1884)*
Essex Record Office Publications
Harleian Miscellany
Harleian Society Publications
Historical Manuscripts Commission: Reports on Collections (generally)

Historical Manuscripts Commission: Bath V. MSS

Historical Manuscripts Commission: De L'Isle and Dudley MSS

Historical Manuscripts Commision: Salisbury (Cecil) MSS

Law Society's Library: *Croke Reports*

W. Murdin (Ed): *A Collection of State Papers: Lord Burghley* (London, 1759)

C. BOOKS AND ARTICLES: PRIMARY SOURCES

G.P.V. Akrigg, *Shakespeare and the Earl of Southampton (London 1968)*

J. Buxton, *Sir Philip Sidney and the English Renaissance (London, 1966)*

Dudley Carleton to John Chamberlain, Jacobean Letters (1603-1624), ed. M. Lee (New Brunswick, 1972)

J Chamberlain, *Letters* (2 volumes) *Memoirs of American Philosophical Society* XII ed. N.E. McClure (Philadelphia, 1939)

W.B. Devereux, *Lives and Letters of the Devereux* (2 vols, London, 1853)

F.G. Emmison, *Elizabethan Life: Disorder* (Chelmsford, 1970)

C. Falls, *Mountjoy: Elizabethan General* (London, 1955)

J. Gerard, *Autobiography of an Elizabethan* translated by P. Caraman (London, 1957)

R. Gittings, *Shakespeare's Rival* (London, 1960)

G. Goodman, *The Court of King James I* (2 Vols. London, 1839)

J. Harington, *Nugae Antiquae* 2 Vols. (London, 1804)

G.B. Harrison, *Henry Percy: Advice to his son* (London 1930)

Lady M. Hoby, *Diary, 1599-1605* Edited by D.M. Meads (London, 1930)

H.H. Hudson 'Penelope Devereux as Sidney's Stella', *Huntingdon Library Bulletin* VII (1935), 89-129

F. Moryson, *An Itinerary* 4 Vols. (Glasgow, 1907)

R. Naunton, *Fragmenta Regalia,* Harleian Miscellany II (London, 1744)

M.S. Rawson, *Penelope Rich and her Circle* (London, 1911)

Sir Philip Sidney, *Poems,* ed. W.A. Ringler Jr. (Oxford, 1962)

L. Stone, *The Family, Sex and Marriage in England* 1500-1800 (London, 1979)

J. Strype, *Life of Bishop Aylmer* (Oxford, 1821)

E.M. Tenison, *Elizabethan England* I - XII A (Warwick, 1933-1961)

M.W. Wallace, *Philip Sidney* (Cambridge, 1915)

F. Yates, *A Study of Love's Labour's Lost* (Cambridge, 1936)

D. BOOKS AND ARTICLES: SECONDARY WORKS

J.P. Anglin, 'The Court of the Archdeacon of Essex, (1571-1609)' (University of California PhD Thesis 1965, copy at ERO)

J. Aubrey, *Brief Lives,* ed. O. L. Dick, (London,1976)

E. Auerbach, *Nicholas Hilliard* (London, 1961),

W. Bagot, *Memorials of the Bagot Family* (Blithfield, 1824)

R. Bagwell, *Ireland under the Tudors,* (5 vols, London, 1890)

W.P. Baildon, *Court of Star Chamber* (Les Reportes del Cases in Camera Stellata) (London, 1894)

Banks' Dormant and Extinct Baronage

J.L. Beatty, *Warwick and Holland* (Colorado, 1965)

H.E. Bell, *An Introduction to the History and Records of the Court of Wards and Liveries* (Cambridge, 1953)

T. Birch, *Memoirs of the Reign of Queen Elizabeth I,* 2 Vols, (London, 1754)

T. Birch, *The Court and Times of James I,* 2 Vols (London, 1848)

M.C. Bradbrook, *John Webster: Citizen and Dramatist* (London, 1980)

R.S. Bridges and others, *Shakespeare's England,* (2 Vols, Oxford, 1916)

R. Broughton, *Devereux Papers, Camden Miscellany* XIII (London, 1924)

Burke's Extinct Peerage

J. Buxton, *Elizabethan Taste,* (London, 1964)

W. Camden, *Annals of King James I,* (2 Vols London,1706)

D. Carleton, *Memorials of Affairs of State in the Reigns of Queen Elizabeth and King James I* (3 Vols, London, 1725)

B. Castiglione, *The Courtier,* Trans. G. Bull (London, 1967)

F. Chamberlin, *The Sayings of Queen Elizabeth* (London, 1923)

F. Chamberlin, *Elizabeth and Leycester* (New York, 1939)

Earl of Clarendon, *The History of the Rebellion* (London, 1717)

Diary of Lady A. Clifford, Ed, V. Sackville-West (London, 1923)

P. Collinson, *The Elizabethan Puritan Movement* (London, 1967)

D. Connell, *Sir Philip Sidney: The Maker's Mind* (Oxford, 1977)

H. Constable, *Poems* ed. J. Grundy (Liverpool, 1960)

L.S. Costello, *Memoirs of Eminent English Women* (4 Vols, London, 1844)

M.R. Craze, *A History of Felsted School* (Ipswich, 1955)

F.H. Cripps-Day, *History of the Tournament,* (London, 1918)

A. Croke, Genealogical History of the Croke Family (2 Vols, Oxford, 1823)

S. Daniel, *A Funeral Poem* (London, 1606)

A Book of Masques: The Vision of the Twelve Goddesses, by S. Daniel, ed. J. Rees (London, 1967)

T.W. Davids, *Annals of Evangelical Non-Conformity in Essex* (London, 1863)

Dictionary of National Biography

R. Devereux, *Letters: Essex to Stella,* ed. A. Freeman (Boston, 1971)

D. Du Maurier, *Golden Lads* (London, 1975)

F. G. Emmison, *Elizabethan Life : Morals and the Church Courts* (Chelmsford, 1973)

C. Falls, 'Penelope Rich and the Poets', *Essays by Divers Hands, Royal Society of Literature,* XXVIII (Oxford, 1956)

J. Ford, *Fame's Memorial* (London, 1606)

J. Ford, *The Broken Heart,* ed. D.K. Anderson (London, 1968)

P. Gawdy, *Letters of Philip Gawdy* (London, 1906)

G.E.C. Complete Peerage

F. Greville, *Life of Sir Philip Sidney* (Oxford 1907)

W. Hands, *Fines and Recoveries* (London, 1825)

A.C. Hamilton, *Sir Philip Sidney: a Study of his Life and Works,* (Cambridge, 1977)

G.B. Harrison, *The Life and Death of Robert Devereux, Earl of Essex,* (London, 1937)

G.B. Harrison, *The Letters of Queen Elizabeth* (London, 1935)

P. Heylyn, *Cyprianus Anglicus,* (London, 1671)

C. Hill, *The Century of Revolution 1603-1714,* (London, 1974)

T. Hoby, *The Courtier, Trans.* of Castiglione, *Tudor Translations,* XXIII, (London, 1900)

G.E. Howard, *A History of Matrimonial Institutions* (3 Vols, Chicago, 1904)

R. Howell, *Sir Philip Sidney the Shepherd Knight* (London, 1968)

J. Hurstfield. *The Queen's Wards* (London, 1973)

R. Johnston, *Historia Rerum Britannicarum* (Amsterdam, 1655)

F.M. Jones, *Mountjoy: The Last Elizabethan Deputy* (London, 1958)

W.J. Jones, *The Elizabethan Court of Chancery* (Oxford, 1967)

C.L. Kingsford, 'Essex House, formerly Leicester House and Exeter Inn', in *Antiquaries Journal, Archaeologia,* LXXIII), 1-54 (Oxford, 1923)

R. Lacey, *Robert Earl of Essex: An Elizabethan Icarus,* (London, 1971)

T. Lant, *The Funeral of Sir Philip Sidney* (London, 1588)

C.W. Le Bas, *The Life of Archbishop Laud, The Theological Library,* XIII

(London, 1832)

G. Marañon, *Antonio Pérez,* Trans. C.D. Ley (London, 1954)

T. Milles, *Catalogue of Honour* (London, 1610)

W.D. Montagu, *Court and Society from Elizabeth to Anne* (2 Vols, London, 1864)

K. Muir, 'Sir Philip Sidney', British Council Phamphlet (London, 1960)

J.E. Neale, *Queen Elizabeth* (London, 1934)

J. Nichols, *Progresses of Queen Elizabeth* (3 Vols, London, 1823)

J. Nichols, *Progresses of King James* (4 Vols, London, 1828)

J.G. Nichols, *The Poetry of Sir Philip Sidney* (Liverpool, 1974)

W. Notestein, 'The English Woman 1580-1650,*Studies in Social History,* ed. J.H. Plumb, XXII (London, 1955)

J.H. Oldham, *A History of Shrewsbury School* (Oxford, 1952)

B. Osborne, *Justices of the Peace 1361-1848* (Shaftesbury, 1960)

F. Osborne, *Secret History of the Court of King James* (2 Vols Edinburgh, 1811)

F. Pollock and F.W. Maitland, *The History of the English Law* (Cambridge, 1968)

J.M. Purcell, 'A Cup for my Lady Penelope', *Modern Language Notes,* XLV (1930), 310

P. Quenell, *Shakespeare: The Poet and his Background* (London, 1963)

G. Reynolds, *Nicholas Hilliard and Isaac Oliver* (London, 1971)

J. Robertson, 'Sir Philip Sidney and Lady Penelope Rich' *Review of English Studies,* XV (1964), 296-7

A. L. Rowse, *The England of Elizabeth* (4 Vols, London, 1950-1971)

A. L. Rowse, *William Shakespeare : A Biography* (London, 1963)

J. Sargeaunt, *History of Felsted School* (Chelmsford, 1889)

S. Schoenbaum, *Shakespeare's Lives* (Oxford, 1970)

W. Shakespeare, *Love's Labour's Lost,* ed. J.D. Wilson, (Cambridge, 1962)

W. Shakespeare, *Sonnets,* ed. J.D. Wilson (Cambridge, 1969)

Correspondence of Philip Sidney, ed. S. A. Pears, (London, 1845)

P. Sidney, *Arcadia* (London, 1977)

Complete Works of Sir Philip Sidney, ed. A. Feuillerat, (4 Vols, 1912-26)

E. Sitwell, *The Queens and the Hive* (London, 1971)

J. Stow, *Annales of England* (London, 1605)

Stow's Survey of London, Ed. C. L. Kingsford (2 Vols, Oxford, 1908)

L. Strachey, *Elizabeth and Essex* (London, 1928)

R. Strong, *The English Icon : Elizabethan and Jacobean Portraiture* (London, 1969)

R. Strong, *Nicholas Hilliard,* (London, 1975)

J. Strype, *Ecclesiastical Memorials,* (6 Vols, Oxford, 1822)

Tanner Letters, Ed. C. McNeill (Dublin, 1943)

C. Thompson, 'The 3rd Lord Rich and the Essex Election of 1605', *Essex Journal,* 1979

Thoroton's Antiquities of Nottinghamshire, Ed. J. Throsby, (Nottingham, 1790)

E.M.W. Tillyard, *The Elizabethan World Picture* (London, 1972)

G.M. Trevelyan, *Illustrated English Social History:* II (London, 1960)

G. Ungerer, *A Spaniard in Elizabethan England: The Correspondence of Antonio Pérez's Exile* (2 Vols, London, 1974–6)

J. Webster, *Three Plays*, ed. D.C. Gunby (London, 1972)

N. J. Williams, *Elizabeth: Queen of England* (London, 1967)

J.D. Wilson, *Life in Shakespeare's England,* (London 1968)

V.A. Wilson, *Queen Elizabeth's Maids of Honour* (London, 1922)

Index